Poverty amidst prosperity

England was the wealthiest nation in the world in the nineteenth century, but urban poverty remained widespread and deep. Many observers sought to explain this awful paradox. In their investigations they asked whether the poor were to blame for their position because of their feckless lifestyles, or were they pushed into it by an unfair economic system?

This new study addresses the issues raised by middle-class outsiders, but in a fresh approach it focuses on the urban poor themselves and explains their way of life from within. Using working-class autobiographies and other evidence from working-class people themselves, Carl Chinn shows how people reacted to poverty and brings to the fore their coping strategies. He asserts that the urban poor were not passive victims of their circumstances but that they fought against poverty with the support of neighbours and kin, and that they formed thriving villages in a dreadful environment.

This book provides the ideal introduction for students seeking to understand poverty from 'below' as well as 'above'. Its wide range of evidence, clear analysis and strong argument stress the importance of communities and give a voice to those whom traditional history has marginalised.

NEW FRONTIERS IN HISTORY

series editors

Mark Greengrass
Department of History, Sheffield University

John Stevenson
Worcester College, Oxford

This important series reflects the substantial expansion that has occurred in the scope of history syllabuses. As new subject areas have emerged and syllabuses have come to focus more upon methods of historical enquiry and knowledge of source materials, a growing need has arisen for correspondingly broad-ranging textbooks.

New Frontiers in History provides up-to-date overviews of key topics in British, European and world history, together with accompanying source material and appendices. Authors focus upon subjects where revisionist work is being undertaken, providing a fresh viewpoint welcomed by students and sixth-formers. The series also explores established topics which have attracted much conflicting analysis and require a synthesis of the state of the debate.

Published titles

C. J. Bartlett   Defence and diplomacy: Britain and the Great Powers, 1815–1914

Jeremy Black   The politics of Britain, 1688–1800

David Brooks   The age of upheaval: Edwardian politics, 1899–1914

Conan Fischer   The rise of the Nazis

Keith Laybourn   The General Strike of 1926

Panikos Panayi   Immigration, ethnicity and racism in Britain, 1815–1945

Daniel Szechi   The Jacobites: Britain and Europe, 1688–1788

John Whittam   Fascist Italy

Carl Chinn   Poverty amidst prosperity: the urban poor in England, 1834–1914

Forthcoming titles

Paul Bookbinder   The Weimar Republic

Joanna Bourke   Production and reproduction: working women in Britain, 1860–1960

Michael Braddick   The nerves of state: taxation and the financing of the English state, 1558–1714

Ciaran Brady   The unplanned conquest: social changes and political conflict in sixteenth-century Ireland

David Carlton   Churchill and the Soviets

Barry Coward   The Cromwellian Protectorate

Neville Kirk   The rise of Labour, 1850–1920

Tony Kushner   The Holocaust and its aftermath

Alan O'Day   Irish Home Rule

Poverty amidst prosperity
The urban poor in England, 1834–1914

Carl Chinn

Manchester University Press
Manchester and New York
Distributed exclusively in the USA and Canada by St Martin's Press

Copyright © Carl Chinn 1995

Published by Manchester University Press
Oxford Road, Manchester M13 9NR, UK
and Room 400, 175 Fifth Avenue, New York, NY 10010, USA

Distributed exclusively in the USA and Canada by St Martin's Press, Inc.,
175 Fifth Avenue, New York, NY 10010, USA

British Library Cataloguing-in-Publication Data
A catalogue record for this book is available from the British Library

Library of Congress Cataloging-in-Publication Data
Chinn, Carl.
  Poverty amidst prosperity: the urban poor in England, 1834–1914 /
Carl Chinn.
     p.   cm. – (New frontiers in history)
  Includes bibliographical references and index.
  ISBN 0-7190-3989-4 (hbk). – ISBN 0-7190-3990-8 (pbk).
    1. Urban poor–England–History–19th century. 2. Urban poor–England–
History–20th century. 3. Working class–England–History–19th century.
4. Working class–England–History–20th century. I. Title. II. Series.
HV4546.A3C55   1995
305.5'69'0941–dc20

ISBN   0 7190 3989 4 *hardback*
       0 7190 3990 8 *paperback*

First published 1995
99 98 97 96 95   10 9 8 7 6 5 4 3 2 1

Printed in Great Britain by Bell and Bain Ltd, Glasgow

Contents

Preface and acknowledgements   vii

Introduction: what is poverty?   1

1   The extent of poverty   8
Two nations
The investigation of urban poverty
Poverty and class
Poverty lines

2   The causes of poverty   38
Poverty: personal failings or economic forces?
Poverty and the unskilled
Poverty and the skilled
Poverty and people with disabilities
Poverty and age
Poverty and gender
Poverty and ethnicity

3   The environment of poverty   76
Poverty and housing
Poverty and health

4   Reactions to poverty   102
Poverty: punishment and philanthropy
Poverty: physical inefficiency and social reform
Poverty and the residuum

Contents

5 Living in poverty   126
      The abyss
      Neighbourhoods

    Conclusion   152

    Selected documents   155

    Bibliographical essay   175

    Index   177

To all those millions who have fought their poverty with dignity
and respect for others.

Preface

My Great-Grandad Chinn never earned more than 20s a week before 1914. An unskilled man, his wages as a blacksmith's striker were so low that his wife had to work or else their family could not have survived. Great-Granny Chinn took in washing for the wealthy, but even with her earnings poverty was ever present. On a number of occasions they had 'to do a moonlight flit' – leave their home at night – because they were in arrears with their rent. They needed more income and so my Grandad Chinn was taken out of school when he was eleven. His mom gave him the money to buy a pair of long trousers, the symbol of manhood, and told him to go and find a job. He did, and soon after so did his younger brother. The family's circumstances began to improve, especially after Great-Granny Chinn started up as a wardrobe dealer. She would go round Moseley and get old clothes from middle-class people – although she had to knock at the back door and negotiate with a servant. Twice a week she would rent a pitch at Birmingham's rag market, where she would lay her wares on the floor. She had 'the gift of the gab' and she could make a few bob.

In the First World War my Grandad Chinn was wounded, and after he was discharged from the Army he went to work in a factory. Soon after, he started up his own small business. It didn't take off and so he became a street bookie. This was an illegal occupation, but Grandad took his bets where he grew up in Studley Street, Sparkbrook, and he had the protection of the local people. He did very well as a bookmaker, and when my Dad was a baby the family moved from a tiny three-roomed back-to-back into a house with a parlour and which fronted on to the street. By the late 1930s they were able to rent somewhere bigger nearby, but Dad and his brothers and sisters still felt they belonged to Studley Street. This had a bad reputation as the toughest place in the area, but like so many poorer neighbourhoods it was the site of a strong community. Even though it was regarded as 'a rough old hole', its people were proud of 'The Manor' as they named it ironically. In part this was because they were connected to each other by intermarriage and through two main kinship networks. One of these was that of the Chinns, Stokes, Beedons and Wheldons; another was that of the Masons, Coates, Careys and Prestons. In the 1960s Studley Street was cleared and its people were moved out, but even now many of them meet regularly for reunions arranged by myself and Joycie Coates.

My Mom's family also come from a hard street whose people had a deep sense of belonging. My Great-Granny and Great-Grandad Wood settled in Whitehouse Street, Aston, about 1914 and Granny (we always called them Granny and Grandad) became well loved as the woman who laid out the dead, brought babies into the world and knew remedies. One of her favourites was a cure for chilblains. She advised people to urinate into a chamber pot and soak their feet in it. Granny had many other remedies, which she had learned as a child in Worcester and which had been passed on for generations. Grandad was from Tewkesbury and became a stoker at 'The Met' railway carriage works, but during the 1920s he was out of work for a long period. He should have gone on the means test but he hated the thought of this because it was degrading and demeaning. Granny had to take in washing and go out charring and my Nan remembers pinching coke off the barges so that the family could have a fire. She was the oldest daughter of their twelve children and with her big brother, Billy, she helped to rear her younger brothers and sisters. My Aunt Win remembers that when my Nan was fourteen and went to work she bought the little ones Christmas presents. They were the first they had been given. Aunt says that Nan and Uncle Bill never had much of a life when they were young because of their responsibilities. Even now Nan bears the scars of her childhood poverty. Her feet are a mess because she had to wear badly fitting charity boots given out by the *Birmingham Evening Mail*.

When she was twenty Nan married my Grandad Perry. He came from another poor part of Birmingham, but he was unfortunate because he didn't have the support of family or kin. Grandad's mom died when he was young and his dad was very cruel. He would lock his children in the attic and not give them enough food. In 1922, when Grandad was fourteen, he was thrown out of his home and he had to go and sleep in a lodging house. One of his mates told his parents and they fetched my Grandad to live with them. He was always grateful to Mr and Mrs Field for their kindness.

After his marriage, Grandad lived in my Nan's street so my Mom grew up as part of a big extended family. Apart from her younger sister she had Granny and Grandad Wood and their bachelor son Bobby, Uncle Alf and Aunt Win, who lived with my Nan, Uncle Bill and his five children, Aunt May and her son, and Aunt Nance and her fourteen children. Most of the adults drank in the little corner pub, The Albion, and went to the Irish dance in Whitehouse Street. They were respected, but they were also a family you didn't cross. If you had a row with one, then you had the lot of them to deal with – and it was the same with the Chinns on the other side of the city.

By the later 1940s Nan and Grandad were doing quite well. They were both at work in factories but they continued to live in a decaying back-to-back up a courtyard which had communal facilities. As Mom told me, there's not much fun in sharing a lavatory with another family, or in having to do your washing in a 'brew'us' used by six others. Nor is it romantic when you sleep in an attic without lighting and have to burn the bugs off the ceiling with a candle before you get into bed. Poverty is not a bed of roses, nor is living in a slum house. But what made life tolerable was the sense of togetherness, the games in the street, the sing-songs in the pub, the granny who was always there for you, and the mom and dad who worked for you and hoped you would get on and have an easier life than they had.

My Mom and Dad did get on and me and my brother had childhoods which were a lot less hard than those of our relatives. We were the first two ever to have a choice about what we did with our lives. But if Mom and Dad got on they never forgot where they came from. They remain loyal to the streets of their upbringing. When we were kids they took us each week to visit our families in the 'old ends'. And when these areas were knocked down they made sure we still kept in touch. They drilled into us the knowledge of the hard work and cleanliness which lay behind the industry-grimed walls of the houses in Aston and Sparkbrook. They stressed the importance of community. They made sure that we appreciated the benefits we had because of the hard graft of all our family. They made us aware that we had a choice that was denied to so many. They made us proud of our own people.

I could not have written this book if my Mom and Dad, Sylv and Buck, had not told me their stories and made me aware of the debt I owe to those who were poor. Nor could it have been accomplished without the memories of my Nan, Lil Perry, and my Aunt Win Martin in particular. I owe much to the constant encouragement of my wife, Kay – who is from the north Dublin council estates, now well known through the writings of Roddy Doyle – and our children Richard, Tara and Catríona; and I thank also 'Our Kid' Darryl, who has always backed me up. Academically, I acknowledge the influence of Dorothy Thompson, whose urgings and advice led me to be a historian; of John Bourne, who has been a good friend as well as a thoughtful colleague; and of Harvey J. Kaye, who is an enthusiastic supporter of my research. I thank also my special-subject students, who have contributed to this book through their questioning and keen interest; the local history and community librarians of Birmingham Library Services, who have been generous with their knowledge; and John Stevenson, Series Editor, and Jane Thorniley-Walker, History Editor of Manchester University Press, who have helped me with their advice and criticism.

The beliefs my family have instilled in me have been reinforced by my work in schools and community libraries and I pay tribute to all those Brummies and others who have shared with me their life stories. Many belong to areas from which outsiders shrink in fear, but through their experiences and actions they show that their neighbourhoods are not frightening but are places in which people are struggling valiantly to live with respect. One of the continuing indictments of English society is the way in which so many people are condemned not for their characters but for their address. A terrible injustice is done to them. England remains a divided nation and will stay so until outsiders begin to recognise the talents, skills, intelligence, potential and pride of the poor. We need to work with them and not for them. Perhaps then we can begin to defeat poverty.

Introduction: what is poverty?

I am lucky. I have never suffered the problems of poverty. I was unemployed for a long period and received state benefits, but I had a decent house to live in, a supportive family who were able to help me financially, and educational qualifications which gave me the hope of a well paid job. When I was out of work I was often short of money, but I was fortunate not to be affected by bad housing, a polluted environment, ill health, and the prospect of no escape. Poverty is about a lot more than being hard up. It is about having a limited choice. It means the inability to do what you want when you want. It is about exclusion. It means that a person is marginalised by society.

For some politicians and theorists there are no poor people in late-twentieth-century England. Instead there are those who are in need: but does not this acknowledgement beg the question 'in need of what'? If many citizens require a higher income, better housing, sufficient fuel, a good education, and healthy conditions in which to live, are they not poor? Not according to the adherents of the new liberalism. In the opinion of former Conservative minister Sir Keith Joseph, 'a family is poor if it cannot afford to eat'.[1] Such reasoning asserts that poverty is defined by an absolute criterion – an absence of the minimum resources needed for physical survival, like food, clothing and basic shelter. In this simplistic view there can be no poor people in a developed country. Poverty becomes a distant problem, located in the Third World.

This thinking declares that the English poor disappeared with the acceptance of the Beveridge report and the coming of the Welfare State. Brought about by the Labour governments of 1945–51, it transformed the system of social benefits by providing money and services to children and pregnant women and to all those who were ill, injured, infirm, disabled, old, and unemployed. The new structure was in sharp contrast to the hated means test of the 1930s. This had been based on excluding people from assistance wherever possible, a process achieved through assessing not only the savings and possessions of applicants for aid but also the incomes of other members of their family who lived with them. The legacy of the means test was fear and shame, feelings which ensured that its successor would be built on the principles of universality and need.

For all the obvious successes of the Welfare State, the needy did not go away – that goal could have been achieved only through an effective shift of wealth away from the rich. And despite the wishful thinking of the new right, the words 'poverty' and 'poor' have stayed in use. Indeed, both have become more noticeable since the onset of mass unemployment and widespread irregular and low-paid work in the 1980s. The realisation has grown that in this decade there was a significant change in the trend of British society. As Martin Pugh explained, since 1906 governments had effected a steady but modest redistribution of income away from the wealthy towards the poor. This had been achieved by graduated taxation and social welfare. But after 1979 this trend was reversed. In that year 'the top 20 per cent of wage earners had enjoyed 37 per cent of all income after tax, by 1988 they had 44 per cent'. During the same period, the poorest twenty per cent in Britain watched as their share of the national income dropped drastically from 9.5% to 6.9%.[2]

The present debate about poverty has become sharper with the recognition that deep inequalities persist in England, but its roots lie in the 1960s. In that decade full employment began to disappear, and in an atmosphere of social change the poor were 'rediscovered' by investigators like Ken Coates, Richard Silburn, Richard Titmuss, Brian Abel-Smith and Peter Townsend.[3] The acute French observer of English society, François Bédarida, indicated the significance of these men. He asserted that 'they brought to light great "patches of poverty", a whole unseen and unheard world living below the poverty line'. Their research 'showed with blinding clarity that, in

2

the midst of abundance and state welfare, at least 5 million people, about 10 per cent of the population, lacked the means for a reasonable minimal standard of living.'[4]

Absolute poverty might have gone from England, but there were still people who were poor relatively. The basis for this opinion was articulated clearly by Townsend following his detailed survey of living standards in 1968–69. He stated that 'individuals, families and groups in the population can be said to be in poverty when they lack the resources to obtain the types of diet, participate in the activities and have the living conditions and amenities which are customary, or at least widely encouraged or approved, in the societies to which they belong'.[5] This conviction that poverty had to be regarded as a relative phenomenon had influenced commentators before. In 1937, G. D. H. and M. I. Cole concluded that there was no doubt that the lives of the poor were better than in the past, but they added that 'a people is poor whenever it is poorer than it needs to be, in view of the national capacity for the production of wealth. By that standard, Britain today is poorer than China'.[6]

The Coles were contributors to an ongoing discussion about the condition of England in the 1930s. As John Stevenson and Chris Cook pointed out, this meant that the issues of poverty, ill health and bad housing were politicised.[7] They have remained in the political arena, as has the proposition that each person should have a minimum quality of life as measured by the standards of her or his own country. Yet if poverty is to be regarded relatively, the point then arises 'comparative to what criteria?' Critics claim that such a concept is too amorphous to be of use; that it is subjective; and that it lacks the rigour needed for social scientific research. It was the awareness of such questioning which led Townsend to try to bring objectivity to his belief in relative poverty. He identified a line below which those who lived could be regarded as poor.[8] This threshold was determined by two factors: the first was the income of a household; and the second was the extent to which the members of that unit lacked twelve items on a deprivation index.

Although the Conservative government believes that a poverty line cannot be established firmly, welfare organisations and researchers continue to make use of the notion. As a result there are a variety of such minimum levels competing for attention. For example, in 1989, thirty-seven per cent of Birmingham's population could be regarded as poor if the measure taken was those eligible for income support, plus their dependants. If the threshold was raised to include citizens who could claim standard housing benefit and their dependants, then '50% of the city's population lived in or on the margins of poverty'.[9]

There are no generally accepted factors by which the poor can be identified relatively. This is because the values of one person are not those of another, as was exemplified in 1991 when a MORI poll asked 1,800 Britons how they would define the poor. A list was made of thirty-two items which the respondents considered were essential for someone to have if he or she were not to be in poverty. They included a telephone, a television, a 'best outfit' of clothes for special occasions, at least two pairs of all-weather shoes, a roast joint once a week, and an annual holiday away from home. It was reported that a Birmingham businessman declared 'that since he did not eat two meals a day, or indulge in a hobby, and had not taken a holiday for six years, then he must be one of the new poor even though he owned a chain of five shops'.[10]

Those who argue that there is relative poverty in England are confronted continually by the problems of definition and comparison. It is proclaimed that their position is proven useless and false by the consumption patterns of the 'needy', amongst whom there is a greater proportion of families with satellite receivers and video recorders when compared with the middle class. Such arguments stress that if there is poverty in England it is because those who are poor have spent their money unwisely. Consequently they cannot be seen as suffering from primary or absolute poverty. They are to blame for their situation and are living in self-induced secondary poverty, out of which they could rise if they wished. These judgements dismiss the divisions in English society caused by unemployment, low pay and casual work; they forget the increasing gap between rich and poor; they ignore the way in which lifestyles and purchases are influenced by class; they presume that the 'needy' have no right to spend their money on what they wish; and they are blind to the big advantage the affluent have over the poor – much greater choice.

The emphasis on the culpability of the poor for their poverty is disturbing because it increases their marginalisation. It is also dangerous. In their desire to stress the way in which the poor differ from 'normal' society, some commentators have put forward the view that there is a culture of poverty. They propose that there is a self-perpetuating, almost hereditary aspect to the poor. In the United States of America this theory has racial overtones, as it is applied mostly to African-Americans, whilst in England it is redolent of class bias and moralistic assumptions. These prejudices are epitomised by the term the 'underclass'. It is used to describe the supposedly semi-criminal, thriftless, work-shy, volatile and potentially violent population which lives in the country's large council estates and inner cities. The adherents of this view assert that no one is excluded from society by unemployment or poverty. Instead a person is alienated by her or his own refusal to take on a useful social role. The claim is made that such people are encouraged in their negative lifestyles by Britain's overgenerous welfare system.

An American political scientist, Charles Murray, is the main proponent of the theory of the 'underclass'. His writings led to a furore when they were published in the *Sunday Times* in 1992. Despite his apparent 'right-wing' views, Murray received some qualified support from left-leaning commentators. This situation led one critic of Murray's opinions, Kirk Mann, to a scathing condemnation of 'the real welfare beneficiaries'. These were the members of the middle class who received tax relief on their mortgages and who were assisted by a 'special tax status' on pension funds, company cars, school fees and private medical insurance. The fact that the 'middle class get more than the poor' indicated the 'crass hypocrisy of the chattering classes', for 'whilst they divorce, get tax handouts from government, have extra-marital relationships, tuck into their booze, fiddle their expenses and commit frauds, they question the morals of the poor and suggest that workfare might not be such a bad idea'.[11] Mann also showed that the whilst the 'underclass' was a new description, the thinking behind it was well established. It is a point that Murray conceded. He noted that Victorian investigators into poverty had written of 'the dishonest poor', those who had an aversion to regular and continuous work and who wasted their money. These people were reckoned to be more primitive than other English men and women. They were thought to be those who would not or could not join in the march forward by 'civilised society'.[12]

The upper and middle classes of Victorian England were marked out by their confidence. They boasted that the sun never set on their Empire. They proclaimed that they were destined to lead other nations. And they bragged that their civilisation was pre-eminent. Their self-belief was assured because they lived in a country which had become rich through industrialisation. But in the midst of prosperity there was much poverty. Millions of English people did not share in the profits of commercial and industrial success. Deprivation and distress were widespread and obvious. In each town and city, public and civic buildings were surrounded by slums. The poor crowded into these insanitary districts. They rented badly built dwellings which had inadequate facilities. They did the dirtiest, hardest and most dangerous jobs. They ate the worst food. They suffered ill health and early deaths. Poverty blighted their lives.

The poor had no options. Their lives were circumscribed by a lack of money. They had insufficient incomes to rent better houses in more salubrious districts. But many observers ignored this reality. They pronounced that poverty was a chosen condition. They asserted that the poor were those who were thriftless and feckless. And they stated that the muckiness of the slums was caused by dirty people who did not wish to raise themselves out of the mire. The social investigators of the later nineteenth century indicated the falsehood of these scathing generalisations. They showed clearly that most of those who were poor could not be blamed for their predicament. Poverty was the result largely of economic conditions over which individuals and families had no control. This realisation had deep implications. It meant that governments could not ignore the poor. They had to help them.

As M. E. Rose has explained, 'if two themes can be said to mark recent writing on the history of poverty in Britain, they are those of continuity and relativity'.[13] These two themes have revised the opinion that change and progress distinguished English society before 1914, and they have led to a more pessimistic assessment. At the same time, historians have realised that the poor were not statistics devoid of form and feeling. They were people, and they need to be seen from within their own communities as much as from without. This approach has meant that the poor have come to be regarded in a more positive light. They were not passive victims of an unfair society. They acted to help themselves. They worked hard to earn money. They developed strategies to cope with insecure earnings. They strove to keep clean and to maintain moral standards. They supported each other as kin and neighbours. They bonded together to form communities. They fought back against the ravages of poverty.

Notes

1   K. Joseph and J. Sumption, *Equality*, London, 1979, p. 28.

2   M. Pugh, *State and Society. British Political History 1870–1992*, London, 1994, p. 312.

3   K. Coates and R. Silburn, *Poverty: The Forgotten Englishmen*, Harmondsworth, 1973; B. Abel-Smith and P. Townsend, *The Poor and the Poorest*, London, 1965.

4   F. Bédarida, *A Social History of England 1851–1990*, London, 1990 edn, p. 257.

5   P. Townsend, *Poverty in the United Kingdom*, Harmondsworth, 1979.

6   G. D. H. Cole and M. I. Cole, *The Condition of Britain*, first published 1937, New York, 1985 edn, p. 437.

7   J. Stevenson and C. Cook, *The Slump*, London, 1979, p. 52.

8   Townsend, *Poverty in the United Kingdom*, pp. 249–51.

9   Birmingham City Council, *Poverty in Birmingham. A Profile*, Birmingham, 1989, p. 11.

10   D. Ellam, 'Whose poverty line is it anyway, Brussels?', *Birmingham Post*, 4 March 1992.

11   K. Mann, 'Kept behind in class', *Guardian*, 9 December 1992.

12   C. Murray, 'Underclass. The alienated poor are devastating America's cities. Is the same happening here?', *Sunday Times Magazine*, 26 November 1992.

13   M. E. Rose, 'Poverty and self-help: Britain in the nineteenth and twentieth centuries', in A. Digby, C. Feinstein and D. Jenkins (eds), *New Directions in Economic and Social History, Volume II*, Basingstoke, 1992, p. 149.

1

The extent of poverty

Two nations

Change, movement, youth and newness: these features seemed to characterise English society in the 1800s. England, once agricultural and rural, now appeared to be urban and industrial. Observers watched in amazement as sleepy villages and ancient market towns were swamped by the explosive growth of manufacturing cities like Birmingham, Manchester, Salford, Bradford, Leeds and Sheffield. They looked on in wonder as whole regions were blackened with the smoke pouring from factories and works. And they worried about the consequences of the new social system which appeared to have emerged suddenly in these places. Filled with youngsters migrating from the countryside, the industrial towns and cities looked like enemy strongholds in which the rebelliousness of adolescents had triumphed over the deferential attitudes of older people.

Amidst the transformation of England there was much which stayed the same. Even after the marked rural depopulation of the second half of the century, agriculture was a major source of employment and large numbers of people continued to work in domestic service. The old society of orders and paternalism was not pushed out completely by the horizontal divisions of class. Throughout the nation, aristocrats and gentry held on to the high ground of political power and social prestige. Nor was London ousted from its pre-eminent position by the manufacturing regions of the Midlands and north. This failure was matched by the inability of industrialists to wrest dominance within the middle class from those involved in the capital's financial and commercial sectors. And although members of the working class made up eighty per cent of the population, their authority was in inverse proportion to their numerical superiority.[1] All working-class women and many men were disenfranchised. England was ruled by a few.

In spite of these continuities, the face and feel of the country was changing and by the end of the 1800s the most striking alteration was obvious. England was urban. In 1901, London County Council's share of the nation's population was 14.7%, and if Greater London is taken into account then one in five English people lived in the metropolis. Without exaggeration, P. J. Waller described it as 'the largest city in the world, a plural city which encompassed almost every kind of city and was supreme in each'.[2] Elsewhere in England and Wales, citizens were gathering densely in other urban areas. In 1801, London was the only place which had 100,000 or more inhabitants; one hundred years later there were thirty-seven such cities, accounting for 43.7% of the national population.

This amazing urbanisation cannot be divorced from industrialisation, even in places which were not associated readily with the making of things. Liverpool grew because it was the port for the industrial north-west; Blackpool expanded because it was the playground for the region's workers; and London and York were as much centres of production as they were focal points for services. Still, the great manufacturing cities were the most conspicuous of all in the urbanisation of England. They looked and smelled different; their populations were almost exclusively made up of the working and middle classes; they epitomised the new society; and their size and importance seemed to be extending.

As M. J. Daunton noticed, 'the formation of new towns was virtually over by 1870, and continued urban growth came not by the sudden appearance of upstarts so much as by the increasing dominance of the largest of the existing towns'.[3] Birmingham, Manchester, Newcastle and Leeds all moved outwards. Agricultural land was covered in buildings and the great cities became connected to surrounding towns, so much so that in 1879 one contemporary wondered how far their local influence 'will yet extend'.[4] What soon became obvious was that this influence expanded until the great cities had become the centres of conurbations like the West Midlands, south-east Lancashire, Tyneside and Wearside, and West Yorkshire.

If the urbanisation of the manufacturing districts excited the interest of commentators, so did the riches associated with them. Impelled by industrialisation, the national income increased eightfold during the nineteenth century while the population multiplied itself only by four. This meant a rise in the share of wealth for each person: between 1851 and 1881 alone the national product rose from £523 million (£25 per inhabitant) to £1,051 million (£35 per inhabitant). These figures led Bédarida to exclaim that 'the growth of the economy seemed miraculous'. Impressive gains in the national prosperity continued even towards the end of the 1800s when the United States of America, Germany and other European nations began to offer serious competition in trade. By 1913 England's share of the world's industrial production had dropped to fourteen per cent compared with thirty-two per cent in 1870, but its growth rate stayed steady at an annual average of just over two per cent. For Bédarida the strengths of the nation's economy were manifold up to 1914, when 'total British investment overseas reached the fantastic sum of £4,000 million, or about half the domestic stock capital, and one-fifth of all the capital in the world. These investments brought in £200 million a year to their owners, or the equivalent of the whole French national budget! Surely these were signs of flourishing capitalism and prosperous capitalists.'[5]

Burgeoning towns and cities proclaimed the waxing wealth of England. So did the railways, which carried its goods internally, and the great ships, which took them around the world. Affluence was made clear in other ways. Pen nibs replaced goose quills; brass bedsteads ousted those made of wood; and the purchase of a host of 'luxury' items increased significantly – from jewellery to woollen carpets, and from gas lamps to fine china. A general material improvement was shown by the opening of stores to service the consumer – Lipton's, Home and Colonial, Rackhams, Lewis's and many more; by the sales of foodstuffs like tea, sugar, cocoa and chocolate as much as by the buying of cigarettes, matches, soap and Christmas cards; by the development of seaside resorts for holidaymakers; and by the popularity of sporting venues which charged for the entry of spectators. Real and tangible betterment characterised the lives of large numbers of English people, and not only in monetary terms, for as John Benson indicated, along with income, free time also 'grew very significantly'.[6]

It was felt that all classes had benefited from the progress of the nation. Without doubt many aristocrats had. They owned the major sites on which were built houses, works, railways and canals: the Dukes of Sutherland in the Potteries; the Dukes of Devonshire and Buccleuch in Barrow-in-Furness; the Earls of Dudley and of Dartmouth in the Black Country; the Earls of Calthorpe in Birmingham; and the Dukes of Westminster in London. They were winners because of economic change and this success reinforced the wealth and status they derived from their ownership of great country estates. In the 1870s, when a skilled worker earning about £100 a year was considered well off, the Duke of Bedford's annual income was £141,793. Few others could match this enormous sum, but even the gentry – the knights of the shires – received between £1,000 and £10,000 each year.[7]

The fortunes of the upper class remained great, whilst the abundance of the middle class increased along with its numbers. G. R. Porter, a statistician, made this plain in 1847. He stated that the improvement in the wellbeing of the nation was no more apparent than in the homes of the 'middle classes'. These were filled with 'not carpets merely, but many articles of furniture which were formerly in use only among the nobility and gentry', whilst the walls were covered with paintings or engravings.[8] The continuing prosperity of the upper middle class is recalled in autobiographies like that of Mildred Boulton. Her father was the last chairman of the Handsworth Urban District Council before it was swallowed up by Birmingham in 1911, and her childhood home was like those of all the friends and neighbours of the family. They lived in 'large commodious houses, packed with massive furniture, heavy draperies, white lace curtains and enormous pictures in elaborate gold frames, and as for bric-a-brac, the Edwardian drawing room had to be seen to be believed'.[9]

Those who belonged to the lower middle class could not emulate such affluent lifestyles. In particular, many clerks were in low-paid jobs. On a limited income they struggled to be respectable. As a correspondent to the *Birmingham Advertiser* noted as early as 1835, this goal was bound up with outward appearances: 'People are too apt to imagine riches and honours make a man respectable, or some think a coat not threadbare makes a man respectable.'[10] Such a connection remained powerful throughout the period before 1914. By way of their clothes and homes, the lower middle class proclaimed their respectability – even though some of them lived 'at the extreme verge of gentility', like Leonard Bast in E. M. Forster's novel *Howard's End* (1910).[11] Although hovering in their social position, clerks knew that in most cases they enjoyed more security, a higher income and a better standard of living than the members of the working class. Their status was matched by that of many small shopkeepers. Walter Allen made this plain in his autobiographical novel, *All in a Lifetime*, set in Birmingham before the Great War. The author's fictional self was Billy Ashted, the son of a skilled worker. Through attendance at classes at the Mechanics' Institute he made friends with George Thompson, whose parents kept a corner shop. Ashted was impressed by this. When he visited the Thompsons he felt that 'to enter, to go behind the counter into the living-quarters beyond, was to climb a rung in the ladder of status and power'. The tea he shared with his hosts emphasised their difference. It was 'a very much better meal than we ever had at home on Saturday night; cold boiled ham and brisket, with picalilli and pickled onions and cheese and cocoa'.[12]

Confident in their rising numbers and growing wealth, the influence of the middle class was felt in social and political matters. As they perceived it, the linchpin of their success was self-help, independence, hard work and determination. This led to the conviction that anyone could join their ranks if he or she motivated themselves to do so. In the words of John Stuart Mill, English people were 'free to employ their faculties and such favourable chances as offer, to achieve the lot which may appear to them most favourable'.[13] There were some men and women whose lives appeared to support such thinking. One of them was Emma Rayson. Born in 1872 in a poor part of Birmingham, she was the daughter of a railway porter. By the age of twenty she was married to G. Barton, a local solicitor, and in the succeeding years she achieved renown as 'the most famous photographer of her day'.[14]

Rayson's achievements were outstanding and rare, but there were enough self-made men to give credibility to the belief that their example could be copied by any male. Their fictional archetype was Mr Bounderby in Dickens's novel *Hard Times*, set in

12

the Lancashire mill town of Preston. A rich man, 'banker, merchant, manufacturer, and what not', Bounderby was a paragon of doggedness and doughtiness and had come to his position through his own endeavours and initiative. In the process he had gone through a number of metamorphoses – 'vagabond, errand-boy, vagabond, labourer, porter, clerk, chief manager, small partner, Josiah Bounderby of Coketown'.[15] The satire of Dickens indicated the unusualness of such socio-economic climbing, but it did not diminish support for a central tenet of middle-class thought.

There can be little doubt that the upper and middle classes profited from industrialisation, and plenty of observers felt that the working class had gained also. According to the German writer J. G. Kohl, in 1844 their wages were high and sufficient, and although he noticed an immense disproportion between the rich and poor this situation was not caused by economic conditions. Rather it was the result of the extravagant, wasteful and squandering personalities of 'large masses of the people'.[16] His sentiments were shared by a correspondent of the *Quarterly Review* (1860) who affirmed that 'if the condition of the labouring classes in this country be viewed by the light of history, it will be found, that, instead of undergoing a "process of degeneration", the process has been one of solid and steady improvement, and that the chief evils from which working-people suffer are those which only themselves can cure'.[17]

Such rosy views were challenged strongly by those who recognised that large numbers of the working class did not share in the nation's plenty. One of their number was an MP for Shrewsbury, Robert Slaney. In 1840 he noted that the 'opulent and powerful' of England were part of 'the most fortunate class of the most favoured country in Europe'. Self-satisfied and content in their position, it was difficult to convince them 'that there is severe and extensive distress and danger near them'. Like some other commentators, Slaney was certain that the labouring classes had not received their fair share of the vast wealth which their hands had created.[18] This view was reinforced by a writer in *Fraser's Magazine* who sought to understand the prevalence of misery and want. He contended that 'everywhere throughout England a force is at work which bears down the wages of the operative with the profits of the capitalist, until the profits swallow up the wages'.[19]

Contemporaries who disputed the standard of living have been followed by historians. In a protracted debate which has focused on the years before 1850, optimists have marshalled statistical evidence to prove their case whilst pessimists have countered them with the gathering of qualitative material.[20] Through the welter of assertion, denial and counter-assertion it seems that if some working-class people were 'winners' from industrialisation, there were many who were 'losers'. And there continued to be losers throughout the period before 1914. Even if the standard of living of the working class improved in absolute terms, it can be argued that it did not do so in relation to the expanding riches of England. Glaring inequalities persisted and poverty continued unabated in the wealthiest country in the world. As an American, Henry George, put it in 1879, this dreadful paradox was 'the great enigma of the times'.[21] His book *Progress and Poverty* was subtitled *An Inquiry into the Causes of Industrial Depressions and of the Increase of Want with Increase of Wealth. The Remedy*. It gained wide publicity and set off fierce discussions.

George highlighted the contradictions and unfairness of English society. These features continued to strike writers who were concerned with social matters. In 1905, L. G. Chiozza Money wrote *Riches and Poverty*. He was an avowed proponent of a radical redistribution of wealth by means of 'substituting public ownership for private ownership of the means of production'. This standpoint was arrived at because Money believed his researches underlined an unjust economic system. He detailed how the aggregate income of the forty-three million inhabitants of the United Kingdom was approximately £1,710,000,000. Out of this, one and a quarter million rich people took £585 million; those who were comfortable numbered three and three-quarters million and had £245 million; whilst there were thirty-eight million citizens who were poor and who took £880,000,00. Money compared his findings with those of Dudley Baxter forty years previously (Document 1). He did not belittle advances made since then in the lives of the working class. There had been an increase in their wages as much as a rise in the purchasing power of money, whilst the death rate had fallen. Still, Money's conclusion was stark: 'the position of the manual workers, in relation to the general wealth of the country, has not improved'.[22]

Commentators who were not statisticians emphasised this point from a more impressionistic perspective. Thomas Wright, 'the journeyman engineer', was an astute analyst of his own class. In

1873, six years before George's study, he had announced that 'never was the contrast between rich and poor so great, and to the poor so stinging, as it is at the present time'.[23] The same judgement had been made twenty-six years previously. Porter may have written that England had made 'the greatest advances in civilisation that can be found recorded in the annals of mankind',[24] but for many of his fellow citizens the 1840s was a time not of comfort but of hunger. Few observers wrote with more feeling about the inequity of poverty amidst prosperity than did Thomas Carlyle. Although an enemy of democracy, this Scot of working-class stock was dismayed and outraged by the suffering of the English workers and their exclusion from the wealth of the nation. His pamphlet *Past and Present* (1843) is a first-rate example of the passions aroused by an awareness of such injustice (Document 2).

The seriousness of the economic divisions declaimed against by Carlyle was affirmed by Benjamin Disraeli. In his social novel *Sybil* (1845) he stressed that England was rent between the rich and the poor. The gulf between the two was so wide that they were like separate nations 'between whom there is no intercourse and no sympathy; who are as ignorant of each other's habits, thoughts and feelings, as if they were dwellers in different zones or inhabitants of different planets; who are formed by a different breeding, are fed by a different food, are ordered by different manners, and are not governed by the same laws'.[25] As a Tory, Disraeli's simplistic division of English society was reflected by the categories of the bourgeoisie and proletariat put forward by the socialist Friedrich Engels in his 1844 study, *The Condition of the Working Class in England*.[26] Like his political opponent, Engels, a German factory owner, discerned that urbanisation and industrialisation had not benefited everyone; that great poverty existed in England; that there was a dangerous chasm yawning between the working class and the rest of society; and that the political movement of Chartism was a result of the anger and resentment of the working class at not sharing in the gains of national prosperity.

These two men were not the only writers affected deeply by the flux of the turbulent thirties and the hungry forties. As Carlyle explained in 1839, 'the condition and disposition of the Working Classes is a rather ominous matter at present; that something ought to be said'.[27] Much was said and continued to be said. Inspired by a mélange of motives – fear, guilt, political ideology, Christian concern, and humanitarianism – some members of the middle class embarked on the task of bringing the 'condition of England' question to the attention of a wide audience. Like the Fabians in 1884, those with a social conscience asked continually 'why are the many poor?'

The investigation of urban poverty

There had been studies on poverty before the 1800s, but the social investigators of that century differed in a number of respects from their predecessors. First, they were more numerous. Second, they had swollen in size because of the urban and manufacturing revolutions, and it was the great towns and cities on which they focused. There were books which related to the agricultural poor, such as Charles Kingsley's novel *Yeast* (1848) and Sir Henry Rider Haggard's *Rural England* (1902), but the hardships of farm labourers were long-standing and familiar. Interest in rural poverty was overwhelmed by the scale, density and dangerous implications of its urban counterpart. Finally, the socio-economic commentators of the nineteenth century were affected by the realisation that poverty need no longer be the 'natural state' of the majority of English people. In the perceptive words of J. F. C. Harrison, for most of history the whole of society was poor. In these circumstances 'even a more equal distribution of wealth could have improved conditions only to a limited degree'. This situation was changed by industrialisation and 'for the first time material abundance became a realistic possibility'.[28]

Social investigation covered a wide range of styles and forms, but two main approaches are evident. One group of researchers sought to give their readers an impression of poverty and a feel for the lives of the poor – whether for positive or negative reasons. Prominent amongst these were novelists like Arthur Morrison, author of *A Child of the Jago* (1896); journalists such as Henry Mayhew, who wrote *London Labour and the London Poor* (1861–62); and religious writers of the type of the Reverend T. J. Bass, author of *Down East Amongst the Poorest* (1904). These impressionistic observers were balanced by those who preferred to tell the story of poverty through statistics. In this field there were the commentaries of doctors like Hector Gavin, who produced *Unhealthiness of London* (1847); there were the local government reports of Medical Officers of Health, such as Dr John Robertson of Birmingham; there were the findings of bodies like the Manchester Statistical Society (founded 1833); there were the inquiries of national governments, exemplified by the impressive *Report* of the Parliamentary Select Committee on the Health of Towns (1840); and there were the works of early social scientists, such as B. Seebohm Rowntree's *Poverty. A Study of Town Life* (1901). Writers and researchers often straddled the line between the impressionistic and the statistical, and membership of the two groups was not exclusive. Equally, many investigators did not concentrate on poverty specifically, but focused on the environment in which the poor lived, or on social conditions in general.

Studies such as these were carried out in all the major towns and cities of England, but before the 1850s national attention was drawn like a magnet to the cotton district of Lancashire and Cheshire. Here urbanisation, the factory system and the rise of class were at their most obvious, especially in the region's capital. According to Canon Richard Parkinson, compared with Manchester 'there is no town in the world where the distance between the rich and the poor is so great, or the barrier between them so difficult to be crossed'. A plethora of publications poured out about the place called aptly by Asa Briggs 'the shock city of the age'.[29] They included Engels' seminal work which did so much to shape Marxist thinking, but *The Condition of the Working Class in England* owed much to other studies, especially Peter Gaskell's *The Manufacturing Population of England* (1833) and J. P. Kay's *The Physical and Moral Condition of the Working Class Employed in the Cotton Manufactures in Manchester* (1832).

Polemical books were not the only ones written about the town and its people. As T. Thomas has noted, novelists also looked at Manchester as 'a touchstone of the new industrial and moral order'.[30] Their number included Francis Trollope, writer of *The Life and Adventures of Michael Armstrong, the Factory Boy* (1840); Charlotte Tonna, author of *Helen Fleetwood* (1841); and the celebrated Elizabeth Gaskell, whose *Mary Barton. A Tale of Manchester Life* (1848) shook the conscience of the nation with its revelations of poverty. Seven years later Gaskell wrote *North and South*, another story founded on the separation of the classes and the need for communication between them. By then, national interest in the north-west had begun to wane as the focus of upper- and middle-class concern shifted sharply towards London.

Jose Harris has stated with justification that for many years the capital had demanded notice because of its size, the number of its poor, and the fear of their disorder.[31] Even when Manchester was the lode star of most social investigators, London continued to draw attention. In the words of Gertrude Himmelfarb, as it was 'the political, the financial, the commercial, the social and the cultural capital of England, so it was also the "capital of poverty"'.[32] In 1837, for example, James Grant wrote about 'the lords and the commons' in *The Great Metropolis*; and four years later W. Weir brought to notice the slum of St Giles in Charles Knight's six-volume work, *London*. From December 1849, the social problems of the capital gained a greater audience with the revelations of Henry Mayhew in the *Morning Chronicle*.

By this date, the factory towns of Lancashire no longer seemed frightening and strange. Chartism had declined, class conflict appeared to be lessening and the new industrial society was becoming more familiar. But interest in the working class in general was sustained by regular and horrific reports about the deaths caused by the cholera epidemic of 1848. These reinforced arguments that public health was a major problem. Increasingly the connection was made between the ravages of pestilence and poverty. Foremost amongst those who did so were the editor and writers of the *Morning Chronicle*. According to E. P. Thompson, they were affected by 'an acute, temporary, and almost hysteric wave of social conscience', and by a desire for social reconciliation between the working class and the rest of society.

On 18 October 1848 it was announced that the paper would start a series of articles which would present 'a full and detailed description of the moral, intellectual, material and physical condition of the industrial poor throughout England'. Letters on 'Labour and the Poor' were sent in by a number of correspondents. Charles Mackay covered Liverpool and Birmingham, Angus Reach reported on some northern manufacturing districts, including Sheffield, and Shirley Brooks sent in notices about the Midlands and rural areas. None of these achieved the fame of their London-based colleague, Henry Mayhew. Thompson explained that Mayhew's seventy-six letters seized public interest in a way which has scarcely ever been equalled in British journalism'.[33] Later he extended his work and it was published as *London Labour and the London Poor* (1861–62).

With the end of the cholera epidemic and the beginnings of the mid-Victorian boom, concern with the metropolitan working class became less marked. Poverty appeared to be declining. The poor seemed to be a residual problem. They were not, as became apparent in the 1860s. Gareth Stedman Jones has argued that this decade 'represented a watershed in the social history of London'.[34] It began with a harsh winter and a rise in the price of bread. Riots broke out. This scenario was repeated six years later. At the same time there was another outbreak of cholera, and in 1867 the Thames shipbuilding industry collapsed. Many upper- and middle-class people were fearful of disorder. Others were struck by the inequity of English society. These anxieties led to the popularity of journalism about life in the slums. Prominent amongst the writers in this genre were John Hollingshead, author of *Ragged London in 1861*; and James Greenwood, who brought to notice *The Seven Curses of London* (1869). The difficulties of the urban poor elsewhere in England also gained attention. In 1864, Hugh Shimmin brought to his readers *The Courts and Alleys of Liverpool*. Two years later Arthur Ransome and William Royston made a *Report upon the Health of Manchester and Salford*. In the same year James Hole used much evidence from West Yorkshire to write *The Homes of the Working Classes*; and in 1867, in Birmingham, John Palfrey had published *Mission Work Among the Destitute or Scenes in the Abodes of the Poor*. For all their relevance, none of these studies made as much impact as those which centred on London.

In the succeeding years the capital's poor came to dominate the writings of social commentators, but their sight shifted from the slums which lay hard and fast to the homes of the rich in the West End. Like Jennings' Buildings in Kensington, many of these were swept away by redevelopment in the mid-Victorian years.[35] As a result, the focus of fascination became the poverty-stricken areas in the east of the city. This trend became most apparent during the 1880s when growing foreign competition in trade exacerbated a domestic economic depression. The combination of these factors led to the realisation that England was no longer the world's supreme industrial and imperial force, and they induced a loss of confidence in the minds of influential people. In an introspective mood, they began to recognise the failures of capitalism and not its triumphs. The belief in progress crashed on the rocks of pessimism. As E. P. Hennock has recognised, 'between the publication of Andrew Mearns's *The Bitter Cry of Outcast London* in 1883 and that of General William Booth's *In Darkest England and the Way Out* in 1890, educated opinion in England repeatedly found its attention drawn to the existence of great poverty in the midst of plenty'.[36] These and other studies seemed to prove that the heart of the Empire was diseased and weakened. As in the 1830s and 1840s when Manchester was the symbol of the shame and greatness of industrial England, so from the 1880s was London a metaphor for the disgrace and pride of imperial England.

Most obvious of the problems affecting the capital was an apparently dangerous split between the rich and the poor. Within a couple of miles of the City of London and of Westminster – the seats of political, economic and imperial power – was the East End. Poverty was rampant in this huge city within a city. So too were bad housing conditions and overcrowding. Its cramped area was viewed as a foreign country. In it lived colourful street traders and an increasing number of East European Jewish immigrants. But the East End was not just picturesque. It was feared as a place from which the poor would rush out to attack the wealthy. Such worries were exaggerated by the West End riots of 1886 and by the revival of socialism, which raised the spectre of class war. For William J. Fishman, the result was that the East End of London became 'a national institution: a reservoir of constant fantasy, to be drawn upon with profit, by both religious and secular "salesmen"'.[37]

By the end of the 1880s fear of unrest had dwindled. Upper- and middle-class opinion was moved by the plight of the female match workers, who had gone on strike because of dreadful working conditions and low pay; and they were impressed by the well behaved, orderly conduct of the striking dock workers in 1889. But interest in the poor continued to be great. Reformers were preoccupied by their slum dwellings and by their physical appearance. There were deep worries that the urban poor were physically inefficient. It was thought that they were not fit enough to be good workers and soldiers for an imperial nation. This conviction seemed to be sustained by the poor performance of the British Army in the South African war. It was felt that city-bred troops had been proven inferior to the rural-living Boers.

The idea of urban degeneracy was most associated with the East End of London. So was the idea of poverty. But the poor were not absent from other places. Indeed, Mearns' pamphlet and the articles of his contemporary George Sims were not about the East End of London. They related to the district round the Elephant and Castle, south of the River Thames. Separated from the West End by this massive physical and psychological barrier, the poor in the south of the capital were ignored in the popular consciousness. So too were those in the great cities of the Midlands and the north. As the Reverend Bass of Birmingham stressed in 1904, whilst he rejoiced that money and social workers were drawn to 'help the poor of the Great City, we cannot close our eyes to the fact that the pathos of the situation seemed to obscure the East End outside London, the areas of suffering and destitution, overcrowding, and bad housing in the large cities of England'.[38] This contention was supported by others, in particular by Charles E. B. Russell, who wrote *Social Problems of the North* (1913) (Document 3).

Poverty and class

Wherever and whenever social investigators were active, most of them were pushed forward by a need to publicise the extent of poverty. As in the later twentieth century they faced the difficulty of how to identify the poor – although in the turbulent years before 1850 this was not so great a problem. In common with Disraeli, many writers described the rifts in English society in polarised terms. Drawing a sharp contrast between the rich and the poor, all of the working class fell into the latter category. Engels made this clear. In his interpretation the proletariat included most of the lower middle class, who also had been impoverished by the victory of capitalism. Even a liberal writer like William Cooke Taylor could agree that society was gathering into two great camps. In his *Tour in the Manufacturing Districts* (1841) he visited Bolton and revealed that its 'misery is contagious: it has spread from the operative class to the grades of the middle rank more immediately above them; it ascends higher as it extends wider, threatening to involve all in one common mass of pauperism'.[39]

Contrary to Engels' assessment, the lower middle class was not subsumed into the working class. Nor were links broken between

21

the two. They were exemplified by the life of James Hopkinson, born in 1819 in the village of Cropwell Butler, Nottinghamshire. His father described himself as a 'gentleman', although it is likely that he had a workshop for one period, whilst his mother ran a grocer's shop. Despite the seeming middle-class status of the family, James was apprenticed to a cabinet-maker in Nottingham. He continued to make his living in this trade after he had served his time, mostly in self-employment in Liverpool and then in Loughborough, until he died in 1894. At certain stages in his life Hopkinson could have been labelled as working class, at others he could have been called middle class.[40] Many other men and women had similar experiences, as John Burnett has indicated in *Useful Toil*, a collection of autobiographies of working people.[41] Such instances led Harris to propose that before 1914 'the most open and frequently traversed class frontier was that between the upper-working class and the lower-middle class (a frontier whose limits were greatly enlarged by the growth of teaching, clerical, and other tertiary occupations)'.[42]

If the divide between these two classes was less clear cut than might be supposed, then it is also apparent that the working class was not an undifferentiated mass of people. This was recognised early in the century by some writers. In 1834 a contributor to *Fraser's Magazine* discerned that labourers were 'contradisting-uished from mechanics and artisans', two groups whom Robert Slaney excluded from the 'poorer classes' in 1840.[43] Members of the working class themselves recognised similar differences. This is indicated by the memories of George Jacob Holyoake, a well known Chartist leader from Birmingham. His father had been born into the middle class, but after becoming an orphan he became a workman at the Eagle Foundry, where he was to stay for more than forty years. A self-respecting person with 'mechanical ability', he was admired both by his workmates and his employers – to whom he refused to doff his hat. Holyoake's mother, Catherine, was another strong character. She 'had a workshop attached to the house, in which she conducted a business herself, employing several hands,' making horn buttons. Her son George worked with his father and became a whitesmith – an artisan with status both in the factory and in the community – and he lived with his family at 1 Inge Street. By the end of the nineteenth century this neighbour-hood had fallen into 'decay and comfortlessness', but seventy years before 'it was fresh and bright'. Opposite the Holyoakes' home was a clump of trees, nearby was a 'green' on to which backed the flower-filled garden of a relative, and at the end of their street was a small wood in the grounds of a parsonage. Amongst their neighbours was Mrs Massey, who sold bread and tarts 'which lay enticingly in a low, broad, bay window'; an old lady who used to charm away warts and 'other maladies'; a baker and miller; a widow who kept 'the best grocer's shop in those parts'; and an Irishman who ground glass for opticians.[44]

The Holyoakes were not unusual in their circumstances. Other working-class people enjoyed regular and relatively good pay, resided in well built homes in a clean environment and owned possessions which were not essential to survival. This was made plain in an interesting and intuitive commentary, 'Pictures of the People Drawn by One of Themselves', published in the *Birmingham Morning News* (1871). The author described the enviable lot 'of the skilled artisan or foreman, who can command from two to three pounds a week'. Such people lived 'on the skirts of the town, within easy reach of the green fields, in a neat house, containing parlour, sitting room, and kitchen, with two or three bedrooms, and outhouses complete'. Although the author was anonymous, the style and arguments of the articles resemble the contemporaneous writings of Thomas Wright.[45]

Prosperous working-class lifestyles are indicated in autobiographies which relate to the turn of the century. They are epitomised by the memories of Frederick Willis, a hatter. Once his family had been middle class. Now its members lived in Burdock Road, 'designed for all types of the working classes, from labourers to skilled craftsmen and mechanics, with a sprinkling of Civil Servant clerks'. The Willises were conscious that they were 'not of them, and our neighbours had the same feeling about us'. Yet they all rented 'soundly-constructed houses each with six rooms, scullery, a little front garden and a larger one at the back'. The kitchen was also the living room, whilst 'The Parlour' was an 'almost sacred' special place which boasted the family's prize possessions and was used rarely.[46] C. H. Rolph's childhood was not as comfortable as that of Frederick Willis, although his family rented similar houses in Finsbury Park and Fulham, London. His father earned only 28s a week as a police constable, yet Rolph was determined to emphasise that his was 'not a story of poverty'.[47]

If it is inapplicable to argue that every working-class person lived in poverty, who were the poor? Just as this question is problematical in the late 1900s, so was it in the last century. Adam Smith was the arch proponent of laissez faire and his book *Wealth of Nations* (1776) is the guiding text for supporters of today's new right. Still, he agreed that poverty had to be seen in relative terms: 'By necessaries I understand, not only the commodities which are indispensably necessary for the support of life, but whatever the custom of the country renders it indecent for creditable people, even of the lowest orders to be without'.[48] But within one nation there can be a huge disparity between the lives of people in one class and those in another. As a result, it is almost impossible to agree on what are the customary necessaries of the country. Moreover, the expectations of some persons might mean that they call themselves poor when others regard them as affluent.

These difficulties of definition and comparison are exemplified by the memories of Molly Hughes. As a child in the 1870s she lived in a big house in Canonbury, London. Although she wrote that she and her four older brothers had few toys, these included a large box of plain bricks, two dozen soldiers, ninepins, plenty of marbles and 'a large and resplendent horse and cart'. The games of the siblings were carried on in their own playroom. This was wallpapered, hung with pictures and it had 'a large table, a warm carpet, a fire whenever we liked, a large ottoman for storage and to serve as a window-seat'. Their mother 'often permitted herself' the indulgence of a drive in Hyde Park in a hired coach. When money was plentiful, her father liked to take all the family to a cricket match in a wagonette 'and give us all a big lunch, and invite any cricketers home to supper'. Mr Hughes was on the Stock Exchange and his earnings fluctuated. In his daughter's opinion, this ensured that the family 'wavered between great affluence and extreme poverty'. She also avowed that 'a settled income has its attractions possibly, but it can never be the fun of an unsettled one'.[49]

It is instructive to compare this account with that of Will Thorne, founder of the Gas Workers' Union in 1889 and a Labour MP for West Ham for almost forty years. Thorne was born in 1857 in Farm Street, Hockley. He recalled that this Birmingham district did not have 'the free air of a farm during those early far-off days; just the ugly houses and cobbly, neglected streets that were my only playground for a few short, very short, years'. When he was six, Thorne went to work turning a wheel for a rope and twine spinner. His wages were 2s 6d (12½p) a week. For this amount he laboured from six in the morning until six at night, with half an hour allowed him to eat his breakfast, and a further one hour for his dinner. On Saturdays he finished at one o'clock. After this he went to his uncle's barber shop, where he lathered the faces of men who were to be shaved. He did this until eleven o'clock at night, and again on Sunday for six hours from eight o'clock in the morning. From this employment, Thorne earned another 1s. When he was seven, the young Brummie's father died and 'our poverty compelled my mother to take any work she could get'. This was to sew twelve hooks and twelve eyes onto a card for a manufacturer for the price of 1½d per gross of cards. Out of this sum Mrs Thorne paid for her own needles and cotton. Despite the hard work of mother, son and older daughter who also sewed hooks and eyes, the family was 'so poor at the time that my mother had made an application for relief to the Birmingham Board of Guardians for Poor Law'. They were granted four loaves and 4s per week. The bread was 'about as bad as could possibly be' and Thorne had to walk two miles to fetch it from the Poor Law Office. Even with this meagre help, 'those were days of hunger for all of us, especially on a Tuesday, when both bread and money had run out. In fact, Tuesday was nearly always a fast day.'[50]

In absolute terms, the Thorne family was poor and their poverty was made more extreme relative to the prosperity both of Birmingham as a city and of England as a country. For all that Molly Hughes thought that she was poor, her family was not in absolute poverty, and it would be inapplicable to regard them as relatively poor. They may have experienced economic difficulties on occasions, but they continued to live in a large house and to eat well – and most of the time they employed servants. Perhaps their income was not as regular as that of other upper-middle-class people, but compared with millions of members of the lower middle class and the working class, Molly Hughes and her parents were well off – even when they had to cut expenditure. In the nineteenth century as much as in the twentieth, poverty has to be seen 'as a complex mixture of low income, poor quality housing, fuel poverty, low education and employment opportunities and poor health'.[51] By this definition, huge numbers of English people were poor before 1914, a situation which was made clear by the figures gathered by the social investigators of the later 1800s.

Poverty lines

The nineteenth century was the age of statistics. National censuses were inaugurated and refined; the registration of births, deaths and marriages was made compulsory; and societies across the country devoted themselves to the collection of evidence about sickness, mortality and living conditions. Studies and reports abounded and in many of them the poor figured large. But during the 1830s and 1840s especially, few inquiries focused specifically on those in poverty. One that did was an investigation by Joseph Adshead into 'the more indigent population of Manchester'. He found that this group amounted to upwards of 12,000 families, making up approximately one-third of the city's inhabitants.[52] These are suggestive numbers, but it is difficult to compare them with those relevant to other places. For many contemporaries, the general conflation of the poor with the working class meant that the extent of poverty was taken for granted. It did not need to be proven by firm statistics.

During the mid-Victorian years reports continued to be made on sanitation and housing whilst journalists began to bring to their readers 'tales about those living in the slums'. Occasionally, some of these commentators did give some intimation of the numbers who were poor. In 1849, Reach noted in the *Morning Chronicle* that out of Birmingham's population of 230,000, 'at least 30,000 are supposed to be of the poorest class'.[53] This was about thirteen per cent of the inhabitants. Given the correspondent's use of the word 'poorest' it is probable that the poor formed a greater proportion. Certainly they seemed to do so in St Philip's, Clerkenwell. In 1861 the Reverend W. R. Wroth stated that this London parish contained 9,000 people. Of these, he estimated 5,000 were in poverty, with 'the rest far from wealthy'.[54] Both his figures and those of Reach were impressionistic. Neither were founded on a detailed statistical inquiry. Yet allowing for this problem, they made it clear that the numbers of the poor were great. But few of the upper and middle classes were persuaded that this was so. The general prosperity of the mid-Victorian period led to the feeling that those in poverty were a residual group. They were not, as became clear in the 1880s. Six years into that decade, the editor of the *Pall Mall Gazette* commissioned a number of inquiries into the depression in England. These researches led to the declaration that in London 'a quarter at least of the population was always on the verge of distress'. Hennock has proved that in the month in which these articles appeared Charles Booth began his own survey into the poor and the nature of their poverty.[55] Belonging to a Unitarian family from Liverpool, Booth was a businessman who had a lifelong interest in social problems. In 1887 he presented an interim report on his findings to the Royal Statistical Society. Sixteen years later, his work was completed. Published as *Life and Labour of the People in London*, its seventeen volumes were divided into three series, covering poverty, work and religion.

The first volume (1889) was confined to the East End of London. It has been praised by Albert Fried and Richard M. Elman as 'a vast compendium of charts, maps, statistics, harrowing descriptions of families, homes, streets, conditions of work'.[56] Booth's enquiries showed that in this area 35.2% of the population was poor or in want, a proportion which dropped to 30.7% if London as a whole was taken into account.[57] His figures were based largely on information provided by school board visitors about families with school-age children. He also obtained evidence from a variety of other volunteers like teachers, sanitary and factory inspectors, relieving officers of poor law boards, charity workers, members of the clergy, police officers, employers, and trade union and friendly society officers. The material gathered in this way was supplemented by facts from the national census and by observations from his own visits to the East End and from those of his paid assistants. Paul Barker has pointed out that Booth's investment of time and energy was prodigious, whilst he was 'the impressario of a talented team whose members undertook specific assignments'.[58] Amongst them was Beatrice Webb, later a founder of the London School of Economics; Ernest Aves, who became a chairman of the Board of Trade; Clara Collett, who was to be employed as a senior investigator for women's industries at the Board of Trade; and Hubert Llewellyn Smith, who carried out another social survey on London in the 1930s.

Barker asserted that Booth was the 'pioneer of the empirical school of English sociology', whilst Rosemary O' Day claimed that in its day his survey 'represented a great breakthrough'.[59] Its significance is indisputable, but it is important to be aware of Hennock's caution. He highlighted 'the relative lack of sophistication' in Booth's methodology relating to those 'in want'. Even though he cross-checked his evidence, 'in the end it was impressions that he counted and his conclusions are only as reliable as were the impressions in the first place'. There was no door-to-door investigation, and there 'were no figures of income or expenditure generally available by which the impressions could be checked'.[60] Equal care needs to be taken with regard to Booth's separation of the people of London into eight classes headed 'A' to 'H'. Of these, 'A' and 'B' were the very poor and 'C' and 'D' the poor. Booth acknowledged that the distinction between the two groups was 'necessarily arbitrary'. The poor had 'a sufficiently regular though bare income, such as 18s to 21s per week for a moderate family'. Accordingly, the very poor were those who from any cause fell 'much below this standard'. Their means were insufficient for a decent and independent lifestyle according to 'the usual standard of life of this country'.[61] The vagueness of these definitions is obvious: what was a decent independent life according to the standard of living of England and what was 'a moderate family'?

Despite reservations about Booth's methods and his interpretations, his monumental study stimulated great interest and it became the marker for others who researched the numbers of the poor. In 1901, B. Seebohm Rowntree wrote *Poverty. A Study of Town Life*. In it he paid tribute to his precursor's 'classical work'. The son of a wealthy chocolate manufacturer, Rowntree added that his own investigation was an attempt to compare the conclusions from the metropolitan survey with those from a smaller urban unit like York.[62] Rose has stressed, however, that Rowntree 'did far more than merely dot the i's and cross the t's of Booth's survey. Taking Booth's methods as his starting point, he developed and considerably improved his technique.'[63] This was evident in the way Rowntree drew a precise poverty line of an income of 21s 8d a week for a family of a man, woman and three children. It was reached after a detailed assessment of the sum necessary 'to provide the minimum of food, clothing and shelter needful for the maintenance of merely physical efficiency'. In stark terms, Rowntree highlighted for his middle-class readers the implications

28

of living below his poverty line. 'Merely physical efficiency' meant that the members of a family lived on the margins of society, exempt from enjoying the ordinary pleasures which so many people took for granted (Document 4). According to J. H. Veit-Wilson, Rowntree did not believe that anyone 'could live a social life on the primary poverty line', but he knew that his audience thought that it was possible to do so.[64]

Rowntree's second major contribution to social investigation was the distinction he made between two types of poor people. Those in primary poverty had an income which was too low for them to afford even the minimum necessaries he had laid out. Families in secondary poverty had total earnings sufficient for them to live above this level except that some of their money was 'absorbed by other expenditure, either useful or wasteful'. In spite of the inclusion of the word 'useful', Rowntree believed that the major cause of secondary poverty was an unwise pattern of spending money: 'drink, betting, and gambling. Ignorant or careless housekeeping, and other improvident expenditure, the latter often induced by an irregularity of income.' As this last phrase indicated, it was felt that fecklessness could be brought about 'by the adverse conditions under which too many of the working classes live'.

According to Rowntree, in 1899 – the year in which his research was carried out – 27.84% of York's population was in either primary or secondary poverty. His findings were based on a massive house-to-house enquiry of 11,560 families living in 388 streets. Almost every working-class person in the city was covered. This impressive result was achieved with the help of voluntary workers and a full-time investigator. Their schedule included details on rent, type of housing, numbers in a family, occupations, ages, gender, and sometimes wages. Space was allowed for judgemental remarks on the appearance of the people visited. Following the collation of the material, an estimate was made of the income of every working-class family. Its size and the rent it paid were taken into account and then these figures were compared with Rowntree's standard of minimum necessary expenditure. This allowed an estimate to be made for the number in primary poverty. Those in secondary poverty were ascertained in a more impressionistic manner. The total number of the poor was guessed at in two ways. Households were noted where there was 'obvious want and squalor', or else information was obtained from a member of the family or from a neighbour 'to the effect that the father or mother was a heavy drinker; in other cases the pinched faces of the ragged children told their own tale of poverty and privation'. From the overall figure Rowntree subtracted those who were poor through no fault of their own. This left him with 17.93% of the population living in secondary poverty.[65]

In part, it is the impressionistic bias in Rowntree's work which has led to a revision of his reputation as an empiricist who was interested in the gathering of facts objectively. For if Briggs praised him as someone who 'devised effective methods for measuring material poverty', then Karel Williams declared that Rowntree's gauging of the total number of poor was not so much imprecise as reckless. More than this, his primary poverty line was 'arbitary and could be moved up and down according to taste'. Much of Williams' argument is obscured by jargon as much as it is marred by stinging attacks on other historians. Yet it is difficult to disagree with his sentiment that Rowntree's study was littered with value judgements. As he maintained, it manifested 'a supplementary concern with the moral and spiritual life of the working classes'.[66]

The author of *Poverty* was a Quaker and a member of the upper middle class. It is inconceivable that he was unaffected by his background, by his religious beliefs, and by his views against gambling and drinking and in favour of land reform. An awareness of these prejudices need not negate the importance of Rowntree's findings. Whether or not his poverty line could have been drawn higher or lower and irrespective of his divisions between primary and secondary poverty, the crucial point remained that a huge proportion of English people were poor. It was this bolstering of Booth's revelations in relation to a provincial city which caused so much public interest. In the words of C. F. G. Masterman, a journalist and Liberal politician, the problem of poverty was so immense that it was 'surely enough to stagger humanity'.[67]

The researches of Rowntree and Booth became the key comparisons for other investigators. In *Housing Conditions in Manchester and Salford* (1904) T. H. Marr observed that rents in the two Lancashire cities were higher than in York even though there was little difference in wages. Consequently, 'it is obvious that poverty in our district must be more intense'.[68] Marr contented himself with this statement, explaining that an enquiry similar to

Rowntree's would be needed if the numbers of the poor were to be ascertained exactly. Three years later, Florence Bell dedicated her study of Middlesborough to Booth. Like him she recognised a poverty line, as she did the notion that some people were absolutely poor. The wife of a major ironmaster, Bell 'carefully investigated' 900 households. She found that in 125 the people 'never have enough money to spend on food to keep themselves sufficiently nourished, enough to spend on clothes to be able to protect their bodies adequately, enough to spend on their houses, to acquire a moderate degree of comfort'. But her work was 'far from being a scientific study of quantification and classification'. According to Angela John, although it included some statistics and useful details about budgets, 'the overall effect is that of a rather appealing personal response which is nonetheless remarkably illuminating and informative about social conditions'.[69]

Following Marr and Bell, two people did embark on an exhaustive social scientific project with a clear and well set out methodology. They were Arthur Bowley, a leading statistician, and A. R. Burnett-Hurst. Both were sponsored by the Ratan Tata Foundation, which had been formed 'to promote the study and further the knowledge of methods of preventing and relieving poverty and destitution'. Their survey of 1912 and 1913 covered four towns ranging in size from 23,294 inhabitants to 90,064. They were Northampton, dominated by the shoe industry; Stanley, a mining centre; Reading, where the major employer was a biscuit manufacturer; and Warrington, a place where there was a variety of industries. This investigation differed from its predecessors in the use of random sampling, in the detailed analysis both of wages and the composition of working-class households, and in the use of a new minimum standard to maintain physical health. Rowntree's level provided a point of comparison for the poverty line of Bowley and Burnett-Hurst. They agreed that the nature of such a level was abstract and arbitrary but they felt that it remained useful. The expenditure of the vast majority of families may not have conformed to their provisions, but at least they offered an index of the lowest earnings 'necessary to maintain physical health, provided that income is laid out with the sole purpose of maintaining it, and therefore enables one to state the *minimum* number of families whose incomes fall below that standard' (italics here and elsewhere are from the source).

31

The rigorous social scientific approach of the two men indicated that 'in Northampton one person in every eleven, in Warrington just over one person in every seven, in Stanley one person in every sixteen, *in Reading more than one person in every four* of the working classes, was at the time of the enquiry living in "primary poverty"'.[70] These results made clear a number of issues. First, despite significant differences between the four towns each had large numbers of poor people. Second, poverty was not restricted to the great urban centres. Third, whatever the defects in the methodology of Booth and Rowntree their conclusions about the proportion of the poor in the population were not wild or fanciful. Indeed, they may have been understated.

It is important to be aware that there were those who rejected definitions of absolute poverty. By adopting relative criteria they could expand significantly the numbers of those who were poor. The arguments of such people were shown in 1861 in the *Penny Newsman*. They revolved around a discussion about the ability of a working-class family of three to live on 18s a week. It was argued by one letter writer that such a figure allowed only for bare necessaries and could lead to 'pinch and privation'. Another explained that the average number of children in a working-class family was four and it was essential to take notice of this in any standard of living. In the opinion of this working man, a wage of £1 10s a week was needed for the 'comfort' of such a household.[71]

Ten years later a more detailed assertion of relative poverty was made by the unknown writer of 'Pictures of the People'. He laid out what 'a decent Birmingham mechanic can live upon if he wishes to keep a moderately comfortable house over his head'. If he were married with four school-age children, then he and his wife would expect four meals each day. Breakfast would consist of tea or coffee with bread and butter or toast spread with dripping or lard; meat and vegetables would make up dinner at mid-day; the early evening meal of tea would be the same as breakfast; bread, cheese and beer would be supper. The children would miss out on this meal, and for breakfast they would have boiled milk and bread. This diet could be varied by eating fish on one day and by the addition of a pudding on Sunday. It was stressed by the author that 'an ordinary workman does not expect to be continually mortifying his appetite, and if his home dietary is to be any better than that of a prison or a workhouse, it is difficult to conceive a more moderate scale than that laid down'.

Contrarily, Rowntree's standard diet was determined by the calories needed to keep someone in mere physical health. It allowed only bread and cheese for a meagre 'lunch', it did not include 'butcher's meat' and it omitted beer. Each week the specified expenditure on food was 3s for an adult and 2s 3d per child. This contrasted with the 3s 2d for each person which was given in 'Pictures of the People'. The writer of this piece also budgeted for the rent of a three-roomed house; for the purchase of materials for fire, light and washing, as well as for odds and ends like crockery, boot blacking, tapes and cotton; for the buying of clothes and boots; for subscriptions to friendly societies to insure against the sickness and death of each member of the family; and for the payment of the 'children's school pence'. Similarly, Rowntree's figures provided for rent and household sundries such as boots, clothes, fuel and soap – all of which were deemed necessary. Schooling was now free and so this expense could be disregarded in his calculations, but purposely he excluded payments to sick and burial clubs. Nor did he pay attention to 'other legitimate charges' as they were termed by the earlier commentator. These embraced expenses caused by the birth of a new baby; support for a religious group; membership fees for an educational or mental improvement society; charitable donations; paying for amusements, an occasional cheap trip or 'a week's holiday in the summer for health's sake'; and personal indulgences 'such as a pipe and a social glass of beer'. Taking all these into account, the commentator of 1871 pronounced that 'a workman who would provide for a family of four children by his own exertions, and preserve his independence, must earn regularly about 35s. per week'.

This poverty line was high and generous compared with those of later middle-class investigators, but it was realistic and inexcessive in relation to the wealth of England and to the necessaries of life which many of its people believed were essential. If it were adopted, it meant that at least 200,000 of Birmingham's citizens 'at a moderate computation' were 'constantly battling for mere existence'.[72] This was a staggering fifty-eight per cent of its inhabitants, almost double the proportion of the poor given by Booth and Rowntree. Of course, this amount was not reached by social scientific enquiry but it was arrived at by a thoughtful and knowledgeable commentator. Whatever the merits of this writer's conclusions, few members of the middle class were prepared to accept such calculations. Many of them had absolute notions about poverty. Only a few challenged this stance. Rowntree and other social scientific investigators did approach the concept of relative poverty, but as Veit-Wilson maintained, their models were based on their opinions as experts.[73] They showed no inclination to ask the majority of the population for their views. The debate about poverty continued within a framework which was constructed neither by the working class nor by the poor. Still, the evidence gathered by middle-class social investigators did lead to shifts in the balance of that argument. This was most evident in the way upper- and middle-class opinion was affected by revelations about the causes of poverty.

Notes

1   J. Benson, *The Working Class in Britain 1850–1939*, Themes in British Social History, Harlow, 1989, p. 3.

2   P. J. Waller, *Town, City & Nation. England 1850–1914*, Oxford, 1983, p. 24.

3   M. J. Daunton, 'Urban Britain', in T. R. Gourvish and A. O'Day (eds), *Later Victorian Britain 1867–1900*, Basingstoke, 1988, p. 37.

4   R. K. Dent, *Old and New Birmingham. A History of the Town and its People*, Birmingham, 1880, p. 618.

5   F. Bédarida, *A Social History of England 1851–1990*, London, 1990 edn, pp. 8 and 100–1.

6   J. Benson, *The Rise of Consumer Society in Britain, 1880–1980*, Themes in British Social History, London, 1994, p. 11.

7   J. F. C. Harrison, *Late Victorian Britain 1870–1901*, Glasgow, 1990, pp. 29–30.

8   G. R. Porter, *The Progress of the Nation in its Various Social and Economical Relations from the Beginning of the Nineteenth Century*, London, 1847, p. 532.

9   M. Boulton, *As I Remember*, Birmingham, 1993, pp. 15 and 21.

10   *Birmingham Advertiser*, 8 January 1835.

11   L. Bast, *Howard's End*, London, 1910, cited in D. Read, *England 1868–1914. The Age of Urban Democracy*, London, 1979, p. 27

12   W. Allen, *All in a Lifetime*, first published 1959, London, 1986 edn, pp. 69–71.

13 J. S. Mill, *Principles of Political Economy*, first published 1848, cited in H. Perkin, *Origins of Modern English Society*, London, 1985 edn, p. 424.

14 P. James, 'Discovering Mrs G. Barton', *Birmingham Historian*, 10, 1994, pp. 9–13.

15 C. Dickens, *Hard Times*, first published 1854, Harmondsworth, 1969 edn, pp. 58–60.

16 J. G. Kohl, *Journeys Through England and Wales*, London, 1844, pp. 142–3.

17 'Workmen's earnings and savings', *Quarterly Review*, 108, 1860, p. 83.

18 R. Slaney, *Suggestions as to the Improvement of the State of the Poorer Classes in Large Towns*, first published 1840, New York, 1985 edn, p. 2; R. Slaney, *A Plea to Power and Parliament for the Working Classes*, first published 1847, New York, 1985 edn, p. 5.

19 'Labour and the poor', *Fraser's Magazine*, 41, 1850, p. 3.

20 J. Rule, *The Labouring Classes in Early Industrial England 1750–1850*, Harlow, 1986, pp. 27–45.

21 H. George, *Poverty and Progress. An Inquiry into the Causes of Industrial Depressions and of the Increase of Want with Increase of Wealth. The Remedy*, first published 1879, cited in Read, *England 1868–1914*, p. 238.

22 L. G. Chiozza Money, *Riches and Poverty*, first published 1905, London, 1980 edn, frontpiece.

23 T. Wright, *Our New Masters*, first published 1873, New York, 1984 edn, p. 40.

24 Porter, *The Progress of the Nation*, p. 1.

25 B. Disraeli, *Sybil or The Two Nations*, first published 1845, Oxford, 1981 edn, pp. 65–6.

26 F. Engels, *The Condition of the Working Class in England*, first published 1845, Harmondsworth, 1987 edn, pp. 111 and 148–50.

27 T. Carlyle, 'Chartism', first published 1839, in A. Shelston, *Thomas Carlyle: Selected Writings*, London, 1971, p. 151.

28 J. F. C. Harrison, *The English Common People. A Social History from the Norman Conquest to the Present*, London, 1984, p. 397.

29 A. Briggs, *Victorian Cities*, Harmondsworth, 1968, pp. 96 and 114.

30 T. Thomas, 'Representations of the Manchester working class in fiction', in A. J. Kidd and K. W. Roberts (eds), *City, Class and Culture. Studies of Cultural Production and Social Policy in Victorian Manchester*, Manchester, 1985, p. 193.

31 J. Harris, 'Charles Booth's *Life and Labour of the People in London* Conference', Milton Keynes, 15 April 1989.

32 G. Himmelfarb, *The Idea of Poverty. England in the Early Industrial Age*, London, 1984, p. 309.

33 E. P. Thompson, 'Mayhew and the *Morning Chronicle*', in E. P. Thompson and E. Yeo (eds), *The Unknown Mayhew. Selections from the Morning Chronicle 1849–50*, London, 1971, pp. 11 and 22.

34 G. Stedman Jones, *Outcast London. A Study in the Relationship Between the Classes in Victorian Society*, London, 1984 edn, p. 15.

35 J. Davis, 'Jennings' Buildings and the Royal Borough. The construction of the underclass in mid-Victorian England', in D. Feldman and G. Stedman Jones (eds), *Metropolis. London. Histories and Representations since 1800*, London, 1989, pp. 11–39.

36 E. P. Hennock, 'Poverty and social theory in England: the experience of the 1880s', *Social History*, 1, 1976, p. 67.

37 W. J. Fishman, *East End 1888. A Year in a London Borough Among the Labouring Poor*, London, 1988, p. 1.

38 Rev. T. J. Bass, *Down East Amongst the Poorest*, Birmingham, 1904, p. 1.

39 W. Cooke Taylor, *Notes of a Tour in the Manufacturing Districts of Lancashire*, first published 1841, London, 1968 edn, p. 44.

40 J. B. Goodman (ed.), *Victorian Cabinet Maker. The Memoirs of James Hopkinson 1819–1894*, New York, 1968.

41 J. Burnett (ed.), *Useful Toil. Autobiographies of Working People from the 1820s to the 1920s*, London, 1994 edn, pp. 252–3 and 288–95.

42 J. Harris, *Private Lives, Public Spirit: Britain 1870–1914*, The Penguin Social History of Britain, London, 1994, pp. 8–9.

43 'Present conditions of the people. By the author of "Old Bailey Experience". Class I. Labourers in cities and towns', *Fraser's Magazine*, 9, 1834, p. 72; Slaney, *Suggestions as to the Improvement of the State of the Poorer Classes*, p. 4.

44 G. J. Holyoake, *Sixty Years of an Agitator's Life*, London, 1900, pp. 10–11 and 15–16.

45 'Pictures of the people drawn by one of themselves. No. IV – How they live – (continued), *Birmingham Morning News*, 1871, Birmingham Library Services; T. Wright, *Some Habits and Customs of the Working Classes by a Journeyman Engineer*, London, 1867, and *Our New Masters*, London, 1873.

46 F. Willis, *101, Jubilee Road. A Book of London Yesterdays*, London, 1948, pp. 88–107; and *Peace and Dripping Toast*, London, 1950, pp. 18–30.

47 C. H. Rolph, *London Particulars. Memories of an Edwardian Boyhood*, Oxford, 1982, p. 12.

48 A. Smith, *An Inquiry into the Nature and Causes of the Wealth of Nations*, first published 1776, cited in Himmelfarb, *The Idea of Poverty*, pp. 531–2.

49 M. V. Hughes, *A London Child of the 1870s*, first published 1934, Oxford, 1977 edn, pp. 3–13.

50 W. Thorne, *My Life's Battles*, first published 1925, London, 1989 edn, pp. 13–6.

51 Birmingham City Council, *Poverty in Birmingham. A Profile*, Birmingham, 1989, p. 11.

52 J. Adshead, *Distress in Manchester. Evidence (Tabular and Otherwise) of the State of the Labouring Classes in 1840–42*, London, 1842, p. v.

53 C. Reach, 'Birmingham. Parochial and moral statistics. Letter I', *Morning Chronicle*, 7 October, 1850.

54 J. Hollingshead, *Ragged London in 1861*, first published 1861, New York, 1985 edn, p. 258.

55 Hennock, 'Poverty and social theory', *Social History*, p. 71.

56 A. Fried and R. M. Elman (eds), *Charles Booth's London. A Portrait of the Poor at the Turn of the Century Drawn from his Life and Labour of the People in London*, first published 1969, Harmondsworth, 1971 edn, p. 25.

57 C. Booth, *Life and Labour of the People in London, volume 1*, London, 1889, pp. 35 and 62; and *volume 2*, London, 1891, p. 21.

58 P. Barker, 'Charles Booth', in P. Barker (ed.), *Founders of the Welfare State*, London, 1984, p. 42.

59 R. O' Day, 'Retrieved riches. Charles Booth's *Life and Labour of the People in London*', *History Today*, April 1989, p. 30.

60 Hennock, 'Poverty and social theory', *Social History*, p. 74.

61 Booth, *Life and Labour of the People in London, volume 1*, p. 33.

62 B. S. Rowntree, *Poverty. A Study of Town Life*, first published 1901, New York, 1980 edn, pp. vii–viii.

63 M. E. Rose, *The Relief of Poverty 1834–1914*, Studies in Economic and Social History, Basingstoke, 2nd edn, 1986, p. 29.

64 J. H. Veit-Wilson, 'Paradigms of poverty: a rehabilitation of B. S. Rowntree', *Journal of Social Policy*, 15:1, 1986, p. 84.

65 Rowntree, *Poverty*, pp. x, 14 and 144, 117, ix, 14–17 and 115–18.

66 A. Briggs, *Social Thought and Social Action. A Study of the Work of Seebohm Rowntree, 1871–1954*, London, 1961, p. 327; K. Williams, *From Pauperism to Poverty*, London, 1981, pp. 354–5, and 358.

67 C. F. G. Masterman, 'The social abyss', *Contemporary Review*, 81, January 1902, p. 25.

68 T. H. Marr, *Housing Conditions in Manchester and Salford*, Manchester, 1904, p. 24.

69 F. Bell, *At the Works*, first published 1907, London, 1985 edn, A. John (ed.), Introduction, pp. x and 51.

70 A. L. Bowley and A. R. Burnett-Hurst, *Livelihood and Poverty*, first published 1915, New York, 1980 edn, p. 37.

71 Hollingshead, *Ragged London in 1861*, pp. 282–7.

72 'Pictures of the people drawn by one of themselves. No. I. The contents of the portfolio; No. II. – How they live; No. III. – How they live (continued) ', *Birmingham Morning News*; and Rowntree, *Poverty*, pp. 86–110.

73 Veit-Wilson, 'Paradigms of poverty', *Journal of Social Policy*, p. 69.

2

The causes of poverty

Poverty: personal failings or economic forces?

It would be a mistake to believe that only working-class people could suffer hardships. Many clerks lived in fear of unemployment and a fall into the ranks of the 'shabby genteel'. The loss of status of such individuals was proclaimed by a frazzled appearance: boots blackened and with cracks pasted over in an attempt to hide them; coat seams inked; a muffler – a working man's piece of clothing – tucked in under a vest and acting as a shirt, collar and necktie; a hat sponged and ironed to make it look respectable; an ancient umbrella; and a pair of worsted gloves 'through which his fingers will protrude, despite the state of darnation in which his wife has placed them'.[1] A similar fate could befall small manufacturers. They were vulnerable to business failure because of the vagaries of fashion, a lack of capital, and the superior technology of larger firms. And the livelihoods of small shopkeepers were as dependent upon fragile foundations. A national or local slump could lower their incomes, as could the 'cutting' competition from rivals.

Mayhew set down the stories of two tradesmen who became destitute because of these forces and whom he encountered in the London Asylum for the Homeless Poor.[2] Like them, Kezia and Thomas Davis's family were 'victims of circumstances'. They had strong connections 'with fairly well-to-do families' in Birmingham. Kezia was the daughter of 'a fairly prosperous' jeweller and electroplate manufacturer, whilst her father-in-law was 'a brass-fender maker in a small way'. For some reason, his only son, 'never came into his own'. Thomas had been a publican, auctioneer and shopkeeper, but 'poverty, with all its horrors and sufferings eventually hovered over the family'. In the mid-1850s he was stricken with temporary blindness and had to be led around Birmingham by his sons 'to pick up a copper or two'. Soon after, he regained his sight and with his two oldest boys tramped to Sheffield and Liverpool in search of work. Unable to find it, they made a 'long and tiresome walk' back to their home city. One of his sons, William, later became well known as the leader of the Brass Workers' Union.[3]

The recognition of cases like this does not diminish the close tie of poverty with class. Simply, the great majority of the poor were working class. There were other connections. Those who were unskilled were more likely to be poor than artisans. The regularly employed had a better chance of escaping the ravages of poverty than casual and seasonal workers. A higher proportion of children than of adults were poor. Younger people were less susceptible to poverty than were the elderly. Women had a worse chance of becoming poor than did men. People with a disability were more probable to live in poverty than were the able bodied. And members of ethnic minorities were more noticeable amongst the poor than they were amongst those who were affluent. All these people were linked not only by their poverty. The greater number of them were poor because they had no choice to be anything other.

In 1976 an European Community survey showed that forty-three per cent of the respondents from the United Kingdom felt that those who lived in need did so because of 'laziness and lack of willpower'.[4] Even some of those who were poor shared these beliefs, as Townsend indicated three years later. Many of those in poverty 'conclude that it is individually caused, attributed to a mixture of ill-luck, indolence and mismanagement, and it is not a collective condition determined principally by institutionalised forces, particularly government and industry. In this they share the perceptions of the better off.'[5] These attitudes were as prominent before 1914. One of their most strident supporters was Helen Bosanquet, a prolific writer on the poor, a social worker and a leading figure with the Charity Organisation Society. A. M. McBriar has stated that at its elementary level, the doctrine of this

body 'depended upon the Victorian belief in self-help'.[6] As
Bosanquet put it, 'the true reformer knows that he must begin with
the minds, the interests, of the people themselves'.[7] In her opinion,
a lack of money did not cause poverty; rather, it was brought on by
the character weaknesses of the poor. They were marked out by
their absence of energy, responsibility, forethought, and wise
expenditure. These personality defects could be exacerbated by
indiscriminate charity, which allowed the thoughtless to continue
in their wayward lives without pushing them to improve
themselves through individual effort.

Bosanquet's language was more sophisticated than that of most
of the critics of the poor, but at their core her arguments were the
same: poverty was a chosen condition. This view was deeply
entrenched. In 1834 a writer in *Fraser's Magazine* declared that
urban labourers were characterised by their reckless improvidence,
depravity, and profligacy. Many of them earned good pay, 'most of
which is carried to the gin and beershops, or spent in the lowest
public-house tap-rooms'.[8] Two decades later, William Lucas
Sargent, a friendly commentator on the working class, stated that
nothing was more common than to hear denunciations of the
wasteful spending of working people, of the imprudence of their
early marriages, of their lack of frugality, and of their drunkenness.[9]
Prejudices of this kind bolstered the conception that the poor could
escape their situation if they wished. Such thinking took little
account of an economic system which militated against planning
for the future and which inhibited saving. Still, as James Treble has
stated, 'not all poverty was the product of exogenous forces which
the individual was powerless to influence. It could also stem from
personal failings.'[10]

Working-class people themselves were alert to this fact.
Benjamin Rushton was a famous Chartist speaker in West
Yorkshire and on one occasion he preached a political sermon on
the theme, 'The poor ye have always with you'. Rushton pointed
out that there were 'three distinct classes of poor'. There were 'the
halt, the maimed and the blind'; there were those 'who had striven
and worked hard all their lives, but had been made poor by the
wrong-doing and oppression of others who had deprived them of
their God-given rights'; and there were men who made themselves
poor 'by their reckless or careless manner of living'.[11] Jack
Lanigan's father was one of them. In the 1890s he was a skilled

worker and 'one of the best engravers' at Locketts Ltd of Manchester, 'but could he drink'. It is apparent that his drinking habits left only enough money for the rental of an insanitary and decrepit dwelling. In it his sons had to sleep on a hard straw mattress covered only by old coats and sacks. When he died he left no funds for his burial and so 'he was laid to rest in a pauper's grave'. Afterwards his family stayed together because his wife took in washing whilst his young sons laboured as lather boys.[12]

During the same decade, in Bolton, Alice Foley's family also suffered poverty because of a father who was a 'feckless husband'. An intelligent man, he had once worked as a scene-shifter in a theatre. This had led him to learn by rote most of the Shakespearean soliloquies. Sometimes 'with unexpected dignity, he stalked round the house declaiming magnificent passages from the plays'. On other occasions he would 'read aloud to the family the novels of Dickens and George Eliot'. But these happy times were made futile because he 'worked in fits and starts, punctuated by bouts of heavy drinking and gambling' and by disappearances which lasted for weeks. Survival and eventually a better standard of living was achieved through the wash-tub earnings of Mrs Foley and the wages of her oldest daughter, Cissy.[13]

By contrast, Thomas Morgan had to cope with a hard life on his own. He was one of thirteen children, and six of his siblings died at a young age. Of the rest, one sister was sent from 'truant school' to be a servant in Wales, another was adopted by relatives who lived at a distance from London, and 'all the others they all left home before they were twelve year old, somebody took 'em in ... neighbours mostly'. When he was thirteen Thomas himself went to a charity school, but before that he had suffered gross neglect from his coal-heaver father. He was a heavy gambler, and he and his wife 'were known as the two biggest drunkards in Waterloo and Blackfriars'. Unlike her insensitive husband, Mrs Morgan did make some efforts to care for her children. Out of her own earnings she paid for cheap food and the rent of a room – although the family often moved because they fell into arrears. She also ensured that her home was clean and that her children were brought up with manners.[14] On many occasions Thomas Morgan ate only because food was given to him at soup kitchens or mission halls.

Arthur Harding shared these experiences north of the Thames. In the 1890s his paternal aunts and uncles owned a public house,

41

several drinking shops and a large general store in Bethnal Green. His father also had been in business, but he had given up his work and become a waster who 'only lived for himself' and was absent from home a lot. This meant that Mrs Harding had the sole responsibility for feeding their children. Unfortunately she had a diseased hip and so she had to take in low-paid and arduous home work, like pasting eight gross of matchboxes for 1s 6d a day or making sacks, which was 'a terrible job for a woman – especially a half-nourished one'. Her meagre earnings were insufficient to provide meals consistently for her four children and so she had to 'forage'. Much of this foraging entailed making her 'poverty well known to the people who had the giving of charity. They noticed that mother was a dead cripple, and that father was a loafer, and that she had children to bring up. And so she got on the list for any of the gifts which came from wealthy families, to distribute among the poor. They made out she was "deserving".'[15] There can be little doubt that the poverty of the Hardings was the result of the laziness and self-indulgence of the father of the family, who had turned into a cadger and wastrel. His actions and lifestyle were despised by his son as much as they would have been by the majority of those whose poverty was no blame of their own.

Imprudence, thriftlessness, intemperance and selfishness were not faults inherent to the poor. Throughout the nineteenth century, plenty of aristocrats had a dissolute and prodigal way of life; and behind the façade of the much-vaunted values of the middle class, large numbers of men betted, caroused and made use of prostitutes.[16] Bad behaviour was not class specific, but the indolence and inconsiderate attitudes of some members of the poor were more obvious to society as a whole. This was because licentious living amongst the upper and middle classes mostly was hidden from view in private clubs. Contrarily, the lives of the poor became public property as a result of the host of investigations which spotlighted them. In particular, impressionistic reporters stressed the prevalence of immoral and dissipated lifestyles. It was left to the statistical enquirers to emphasise the impersonal forces which made people poor.

According to Rowntree's research these were sixfold for those in primary poverty. He noted, too, the proportion (expressed as percentages below) of people who were poor through each of the causes.

(1) Death of chief wage-earner [15.63%].
(2) Incapacity of chief wage-earner through accident, illness, or old age [5.11%].
(3) Chief wage-earner out of work [2.31%].
(4) Chronic irregularity of work (sometimes due to incapacity or unwillingness of worker to undertake regular employment) [2.83%].
(5) Largeness of family, i.e. cases in which the family is in poverty because there are more than four children, though it would not have been in poverty had the number children not exceeded four [22.16%].
(6) Lowness of wage, i.e. where the chief wage-earner is in regular work, but at wages which are insufficient to maintain a moderate family (i.e. not more than four children in a state of physical efficiency) [51.96%].[17]

Poverty and the unskilled

Rowntree's conclusions were shared by Bowley and Burnett-Hurst. They noted that in Stanley pay was 'relatively high' because it was a mining town. As a result, poverty there was caused mostly by the illness or old age of the chief earner. But in the other three towns surveyed the majority of the poor were pushed into their position by low wages. The two statisticians highlighted the serious implications of their findings. Most of those in poverty were victims of external factors and were not the creators of their own misfortunes. This understanding led to the declaration that the most pressing task in England was to raise the earnings of the worst-paid workers.[18]

The problem of low wages was most likely to affect those who were unskilled. In the Salford of Robert Roberts, this section of the population included various grades of labourers:

> split into plainly defined groups according to occupation, possessions and family connection, scavengers and nightsoil men rating very low indeed. Following these came a series of castes . . . first, the casual workers of all kinds – dockers in particular (who lacked prestige through the uncertainty of their calling), then the local street sellers of coal, lamp oil, tripe, crumpets, muffins and pikelets, fruit, vegetables and small-ware. Finally came the firewood choppers, bundlers and sellers and the rag and boners, often whole families. These people for some reason ranked rock-bottom among the genuine workers.[19]

General labourers formed the largest number of the unskilled. According to Rowntree, the average pay of such men in York was between 18s and 21s a week. These sums were too little 'to provide food, shelter and clothing adequate to maintain a family of moderate size in a state of bare physical efficiency'. Dr John Robertson, Birmingham's Medical Officer of Health, had the same view. In 1904 he conducted a study into the Floodgate Street area, which was typical of the poverty-stricken parts of the city. He found that the district was occupied by a large number of unskilled men and their families – labourers, street hawkers, barrow men and others. Their average incomes varied between 17s and 21s a week. This discovery prompted the unequivocal comment that it was 'impossible for a man living in the centre of the City, and employed as a labourer at the standard rate of wages, to keep a wife and family of three children without being in poverty'.[20] Research in Portsmouth and Oxford reflected these conclusions about incomes.[21]

Despite their low pay, labourers were not necessarily poor all their lives, a feature made clear by Rowntree. He outlined a poverty cycle, which was dynamic rather than static. According to this interpretation, the life of an unskilled man was distinguished by five alternating periods of want and comparative plenty. Unless his father was skilled, his childhood would be spent in poverty. When he and his siblings went to work their earnings would raise up the family's standard of living. These better times would continue through the early part of his marriage until his children were born. Once again he would be poor and his condition would not be bettered for at least ten years. After his older children found jobs, he would enjoy his last period of prosperity. This ended when he and his wife were left on their own and they became old.[22]

The poor were not members of a closed caste and their ranks were supplemented by those hundreds of thousands of people who had escaped hardships for a short time only. Yet there were those whose lives did not fit into neat notions of a poverty cycle. They did not enjoy periods of comparative prosperity and were poor constantly. In many cases this was because much unskilled work was casual. Born in Brighton in 1903, Albert Paul recalled that his father was a building-trade labourer. Jobs were very scarce at times and he was unemployed 'for at least 3 months out of every 12 months every year (and there was no dole money in those days)'.[23]

In Lancashire, Roberts recalled seeing such men 'follow a wagon laden with bricks from the kilns, hoping to find a job where the load was tipped'.[24] Insecurity dominated the lives of these workers, leading them into a web of debt out of which it was difficult to break free.

Work at unloading ships was also notorious for its irregularity. During the 1850s in London, Mayhew estimated that there were 12,000 dockers competing for jobs sufficient only for 4,000.[25] This oversupply of labour continued in the following decades. John Kemp's father told him that in the 1880s men gathered early in the morning at the dock gates of the capital. Only some of them would be given a few hours' employment. This made them desperate and they would be 'standing or climbing in the pockets of the man in front to grab the ticket to give him half a day's work' for the magnificent sum of 1s 3d.[26] The unhappy sight of so many dockers was drawn graphically by Robert R. Hyde. During the 1890s, he witnessed 'an endless stream of men, many of them half-famished' toiling with loads of fruit from the docks to the firms around Billingsgate Market. Many times he saw 'the utter physical collapse of a man under his load, whilst others similarly encumbered and unable to help would pass by with just a remark, "Poor old . . .", knowing full well that a like fate might befall them'.[27]

The prevalence of underemployment was marked in some places. This was stressed in 1907 by Edward G. Howarth and Mona Wilson, who carried out a detailed study into the industrial and social problems of West Ham. They noticed that irregular and casual work was as prominent in factories as it was on the docks – and that this situation had been prevalent for at least fifty years. Their conclusion was unambiguous. Underemployment was mainly responsible for the worst evils in the borough – the chief of which was chronic poverty (Document 5). This observation contrasted with Rowntree's results, which minimised the effects of casual work. The York investigator did qualify his figures, however. He noted that there were many irregularly employed men whose low earnings were supplemented by the incomes of wives and children. As a result, their families were raised above the primary poverty line.[28]

Stedman Jones has argued that 'London represented the problem of casual labour in its most acute form'. There is much to support this view, but it is important not to isolate the capital as a special and unusual case. It was not. Irregular employment was a major feature of other places.[29] In 1912, Frederic G. D'Aeth stated it was the dominant industrial problem of Liverpool, affecting 'some 25,000 workers, and involving a population of some 125,000'.[30] Nor was underemployment confined to ports. It seems that it was as evident in the poorer, central districts of other big cities – as Dr Robertson intimated for Birmingham. Certainly, Alan J. Kidd believed that this was the case for Ancoats and St George's in Manchester, which were 'more clearly characterised by casual labour than manufacturing districts like Gorton and Oppenshaw'.[31] This assertion was based partly on the research of Fred Scott, who carried out a survey for the Manchester Statistical Society in 1888–89. From a sample of 2,515 heads of families in Ancoats, he found that 20.7% were in irregular jobs. In a similar group in Salford, 40.4% were casual workers. Kidd mentioned that the nature and pattern of their employment was 'little understood before the end of the nineteenth century'. Still, it is likely that casual work had been a major problem for many years, as J. H. Smith indicated. He analysed the 1851 census for part of Deansgate in Manchester. His results showed that of the 1,821 inhabitants who were employed, over seventy per cent were engaged in low-paid, low-status and insecure trades.[31]

Even labourers with regular jobs could miss out on 'periods of comparative comfort' because of long lay-offs from work. In 1912, E. H. Kelly stated that in Portsmouth the announcement of cut-backs in naval spending 'is followed automatically by local distress, for the standard wage of unskilled men (21s. a week) allows little margin for provision for times of unemployment, and it is hard for such men to find other occupation until the welcome announcement is made of the laying down of a new "Dreadnought" and the hands are recalled'.[32] Labourers were not the only unskilled workers who could be affected by unemployment, casuality and low wages. So too could street traders. These were a sizeable section of the unskilled, as Mayhew showed. He was a great classifier of the people he studied, and in *London Labour and the London Poor* (1861–62) he divided the street folk of the capital into 'six distinct genera or kinds': sellers; buyers; finders; performers, artists and showmen; artisans or working pedlars; and labourers. In turn, they were subdivided – in the case of the sellers into eight portions.

Altogether, street traders numbered about 50,000, or one-fortieth of the capital's population.[33] Mayhew's work on them has been eulogised by Victor Neuberg as 'the fullest and the most vivid picture of the labouring people in the world's greatest city in the nineteenth century'.[34] The enquiry does include a great deal of direct reportage which gives it a liveliness missing from other studies. As the author himself put it, his was the first 'attempt to publish the history of a people, from the lips of the people themselves'.[35]

Today other researchers can hear the tapes of oral historians and check their sources. Listeners can ascertain if the respondents have been led and whether material has been used out of context. It is impossible to do this for Mayhew's evidence and so its accuracy cannot be verified. But it would be unwise not to be wary about his techniques. A contemporary stated that when the journalist was at the *Morning Chronicle* he had 'an array of assistant writers, stenographers and hansom cabmen constantly at his call'. Labourers of special interest, 'with picturesque specimens of the London poor', were brought to the offices of the newspaper. Here they told their tales to Mayhew, who 'redictated them, with added colour of his own, to the shorthand writer'. This account contrasts with the enquirer's own description of his methodology. He wrote that he called meetings where he conducted 'mass interviews', or else he went to an area under study to talk to six workers chosen at random. Then he acted upon the advice of two knowledgeable persons to find respondents who fitted specific categories of people.[36]

There is not necessarily any tension between the two versions of Mayhew's investigative approach. It is likely that both were applicable. But after he left the *Morning Chronicle* his research for *London Labour and the London Poor* had to rely more on interviewing people in their own homes and neighbourhoods. An evaluation of this material needs to take account of the crucial issue of class. Mayhew's interviewees might not have talked naturally to someone of his background, and they may have told him what he wanted to hear. His biographer, Anne Humphreys, agreed that he 'held to class separation' and this attitude may have come across. She added that the details surrounding his direct reportage 'sometimes show a condescension absent from the interviews themselves'. Still she believed that he 'came as close as anyone in

47

the period to revealing the inner lives of the working classes to his readers'.[37]

Any provisos about Mayhew's work cannot diminish the effect it had. He did bring to public notice the lives of many poor people. He did let his subjects speak – even though their words were filtered through him. If his writing is not the voice of the poor, it is a voice. For all the faults of his methodology, he does give the sounds, expressions and thoughts of many who were in poverty, notably street traders. Two pieces exemplify the power of language in *London Labour and the London Poor*. The first is a strong and vigorous description of the New-cut Market in Lambeth. Like a shopper, Mayhew's gaze scattered over a variety of traders, drawn hither and thither by the cries competing for custom in 'the scramble for a living'.[38] The second account was a more contemplative and solitary piece. It focused on the words of an old woman who sold tapes and cotton and whose husband was dying (Document 6).

The hardships of street traders were common throughout England. In 1850 a correspondent to the *Newcastle Chronicle* visited the poor in the east-end district of Sandgate. In one house he came upon a girl who sold herrings and fruit. Her income averaged about 3s 6d a week, out of which she paid 1s 9d for renting a 'hovel'. She shared this with her mother, a woman who gathered 'scarry' – the refuse of metal used in foundries.[39] Over forty years later and nearby in South Shields, Bessie Nichol experienced similar hardships. Her husband had abandoned his family and gave them no money. To feed her children, she worked at cutting up herrings in a factory. The job was seasonal and in the winter she survived by taking in washing and through the part-time employment of her daughters. The job of eight-year-old Francie was to walk the streets with 'a little sixpence ha'penny basket' in which there were strings of herring.[40] The vicar of St Laurence in Birmingham witnessed many of his parishioners scratching for a living in the same way. Amongst them were rag and bone collectors, wood choppers, sandstone sellers and hawkers of salt. This was bought for 2d a lump off coal barges. The block of salt was quartered and then sold for 1d. Although the income was desperately low, 'very many are engaged in this occupation, and if three lumps are sold in a day' they have done well.[41]

Poverty and the skilled

In his study of the Floodgate Street area of Birmingham, Dr Robertson found a large number of artisans 'who admitted receiving good wages, and who were apparently living in conditions of poverty from drink, gambling, or other unnecessary expenditure'.[42] The influence of these factors should not be discounted, but in many cases they were inapplicable. According to Treble, 'poverty amongst the urban able-bodied was primarily the product of a volatile, highly imperfect, and in certain areas, glutted labour market'.[43]

The possession of a skill was not always an insurance against these negative economic forces. In particular, trading slumps could lead to mass unemployment which affected all sections of the working class. Adshead revealed the force of this observation in his report on distress in Manchester in 1842. He included details about the suffering of out of work shoemakers, bricklayers, chemical workers and spinners.[44] The extensive implications of unemployment were widespread. John Foster's study of three English towns revealed that 1849 was a good year for the economy. In Oldham this meant that fifteen per cent of families were in poverty. This compared favourably with the situation two years before when trading conditions were bad. Then forty-one per cent of the town's families were poor.[45] In 1908 W. H. Beveridge indicated that unemployment continued to affect skilled workers. His famous study relied greatly on statistical information provided by some of their trade unions, which provided benefits to members who were out of work. Their numbers varied between 6.9% of their total in 1894 to as low as 2.4% in 1900.[46]

Most of these men were in trades which needed their skills. This was not the case for their fellows who had been involved in jobs which were eradicated by mechanisation. The handloom weavers were amongst this unfortunate group. Their trade was carried on in their homes and it deteriorated because of competition from cheaper cotton goods made in mills. At the same time their ranks were flooded by those who had lost out to mechanisation. Desperate to earn money, they accepted lower and lower prices for their products. A contributor to Adshead's work declared that they could earn only 5s to 6s a week when in full-time work. When only partially employed their condition was 'truly deplorable.'[47] The terrible plight of the handloom weavers was recorded in many songs, one of which was called 'The Four Loom Weaver'.

> I'm a poor cotton weaver
> As many one knows,
> I've nowt t'eat in the house
> And I've wore out my clothes.
> You'd hardly give sixpence
> For all I have on.
> My clogs they are broken
> And stockings I've none.
>> You'd think it were hard
>> To be sent into world
>> To clem and do t'best that you can.[48]

In London, the silk weavers of Spitalfields encountered similar hardships. Hollingshead recorded that there had been 25,000 looms in the district in 1824. Almost thirty years later they had dropped to 8,000, whilst the pay of the workers had declined catastrophically to no more than 7s 6d a week.[49] Similarly, the Coventry ribbon weavers had to contend with serious economic difficulties. One of their number was Joseph Gutteridge. A man steeped in his craft, his periods of comparative affluence were punctuated by stretches of joblessness. One of these came in the 1840s. He and his wife had to sell their furniture to raise money, but soon it ran out: 'For two days not a particle of food had passed our lips, and for nearly a fortnight, in this bitterly cold weather, we had slept on the bare boards huddled together to keep as warm as we could. How bitter my thoughts were no tongue can tell. I was maddened almost to suicide.' The Gutteridges survived with the help of kind neighbours and relatives until Joseph found a job paying 24s a week. His circumstances improved and he enjoyed a regular income until 1860, when the Cobden treaty lifted duties on French imports. The local employers were faced with cheaper foreign goods at a time when demand for ribbons had fallen because of a change in fashion. Wages were cut. In response the workers came out on strike and were then locked out. Faced with hunger, Gutteridge and his fellows had to take a hard decision: 'Hundreds of looms, the first cost of which was from £40 to £100, were sold to brokers for a mere song to enable weavers to obtain the means to sustain life, and were ultimately broken up for what the wood and metal would realise.'[50]

50

Over the next few years the number of ribbon manufacturers in Coventry plummeted from eighty to twenty, whilst the city's population fell by five thousand. Although his trade was in decline, Gutteridge was again fortunate to find good employment after the hard period of the early 1860s. In his ability to do so he differed from labourers, street traders and those skilled workers who often remained in constant poverty. Amongst them were the tailors of Liverpool and London as was revealed by Mackay and Mayhew in the *Morning Chronicle*.[51] Their trade was split into two sections – the honourable and the dishonourable. The latter part was in the ascendant and it was characterised by sweated labour – low-paid and arduous work in unhealthy conditions. Seeking the lowest possible price, contractors gave out jobs to middlemen. In turn, they made use of subcontractors – people who were both sweated and sweaters of those to whom they supplied work. By the time the employment reached the base of the system, payment had been pushed down as low as it could go. This problem was exacerbated because of piecework. Few employees made the whole garment, and the consequent subdivision of labour ensured that the trade became diluted with semiskilled and unskilled people.

Mayhew's letters had a deep effect. They led Charles Kingsley to write *Cheap Clothes and Nasty*, a pamphlet about the difficulties facing tailors in the dishonourable side of their trade. A vicar and Christian socialist, he followed this up with a novel, *Alton Locke* (Document 7). The leading figure was based on Thomas Cooper, a tailor and Chartist. In his book Kingsley emphasised that government agencies had led to sweating through their use of contractors. He also blamed Jewish tailors for their part in the system. Sharing the prejudices of others, he did not realise that they were as much the victims of the beating down of prices as were Gentiles. Unfortunately, racist condemnations continued throughout the century. Typical of them were the comments of Arnold White. In 1888 he wrote an article called 'The invasion of the pauper foreigners'.[52] He declared that there would be no sweating without East European Jews. White failed to acknowledge that the system had begun sixty years before, when few of these people lived in England. His arguments were countered effectively by Stephen Fox in a rejoinder in the *Contemporary Review*.[52]

A dual-sector system was apparent in other skilled occupations. As Mayhew made clear, they included hatters, boot makers and shoemakers, carpenters, joiners and cabinetmakers. Like the tailors in *Alton Locke*, many of them were becoming poor and losing their status within the working class. This was made visible by changes in their lifestyles. Their wives had to work to supplement their inadequate incomes, whilst their children had to avoid school because it was costly and took them away from earning money. Mayhew recognised the importance of artisan respectability and this phenomenon informed a later work, *Low Wages*. In it he maintained that earnings should be sufficient to provide for three things. First, the subsistence of a worker during his employment. Second, his subsistence when he was unable to work. Third, the present and future subsistence of his family and the education of his children.[53]

Because it took a long-term perspective, Williams praised this idea of 'super-subsistence' as a real conceptual innovation.[54] But he could not agree with Eileen Yeo that Mayhew's letters to the *Morning Chronicle* were 'the first empirical study into poverty *as such*'.[55] He contended that whilst the journalist investigated wages he did not calculate a poverty line. Nor did he cover a representative sample of the population. He neglected or ignored the two largest groups of workers – domestic servants and labourers – and he concentrated on a number of manufacturing trades.[56] Williams' argument is a strong one, as is his proposition that Mayhew endorsed the opinions of artisans and was concerned with their 'consciousness'. But the acceptance of this analysis does not mean that Mayhew's evidence should be dismissed. It brings out the economic pressures on many skilled workers and highlights that many of them could become poor.

Treble has noted that by the end of the nineteenth century, the numbers of handloom weavers and woolcombers had undergone a rapid contraction, and whole areas of sweated work had moved from homes and small workshops into factories.[57] These developments meant that large groups of poverty-stricken craft workers disappeared. At the same time, skilled workers in other sectors of employment were in regular and relatively well paid jobs. Combined with rising real wages, this meant that many of these men and their families enjoyed a rising standard of living. The same could be said for other workers like policemen, railwaymen and postmen, and even for those employed by local councils. Their wages might be low but they had security of employment. And as the most astute commentators pointed out there was 'no more prolific source of poverty than an uncertain and fluctuating income, the average of which cannot be struck'.[58]

Yet it would be unwise to diminish the economic difficulties which continued to beset many skilled workers. Sweating may have declined but it was still prominent in the tailoring trade. In other occupations there was also an oversupply of labour. As Arthur Harding remembered, cabinet-making was a precarious way of making a living because of 'the cut-throat competition of the vast number of out-of-work makers'.[59] Other skilled workers suffered because of seasonality of employment. Stedman Jones noticed that this was marked in those London trades connected to the 'season' of the upper class, which peaked between May and July. This meant that there was a slack time in the late summer, although for building workers their hard period came in the winter.[60]

Seasonality was not a phenomenon of the capital alone. It was evident in other major cities. So too were the effects of foreign trading conditions on industries which were dependent upon exports. Both these problems were spotlighted in 1891 when J. Gregory Mantle wrote a letter to the *Birmingham Daily Post*. He was a Wesleyan minister in the Summer Lane neighbourhood of Birmingham. This was seen as a very poor quarter, but many of its inhabitants were skilled workers whose incomes were insecure. Some of them were hit hard by bad weather and others were affected adversely by an American tariff. Amongst this latter group were gun makers and pearl-button makers ('pearlers'). Mantle noted one family of eight, all of whom were teetotallers. The father and son were unemployed pearlers. They were surviving barely on the earnings of the mother and younger children, who carded hooks and eyes. Still, they had been forced to sell their table to raise money for food, and in the corner of 'the desolate room' was a piece of wood. It was the remains of the bedstead, 'which was this week being sawn in pieces for firing'. The children were shivering in their rags.[61]

Poverty and people with disabilities

More than other neglected sections of the community, people with disabilities have been hidden from history. Ian Gregory has stated that it is often the case that 'increasing protests and agitation for change among a minority group in the present results in a surge of interest in the group's place in history'. He noted that this process had just begun for people with a disability. Gregory's own research focused on Derby in 1871. He found that not all such people had been born with their impairment; some of them had a better chance of earning money than others; and not all of them could be described as poor.[62] More work needs to be done on these people, but historians need to be alert to these three considerations. Notwithstanding this, within the working class it seems that those with disabilities were more likely to be poor than were the fit and healthy. The circumstantial evidence sustains this opinion.

In 1872 Blanchard Jerrold exclaimed that the aged, the orphan, the halt and the blind of London would fill an ordinary city. He believed that 'when the struggle for life is so severe as it is in England in the happiest of times, the wounded and disabled and the invalided must be in considerable numbers.'[63] Early in the next century, Fred Davies' blind father was one of this unlucky group. He and his family suffered privation in Hulme, Manchester – even though he had a brother who had an excellent job as a chief superintendent on the railways. As a child of ten in 1918, Fred was given the responsibility of leading his father to his pitches. These were 'places where he would stand every night, begging. He would carry a tin can and a notice on his chest saying he was blind and unable to find employment.' Sadly, Mr Davies died before his son was old enough to augment the family's income by going to work full time.[64] His life of poverty differed little from that of the blind street fiddler or from the blind man who read the Bible in the street mentioned by Hollingshead in 1861. The blind man read by 'feeling the raised letters with his hand, and he complained that he could do nothing now because "the touch was cold"'.[65]

There were many others who had unfortunate disabilities. At the turn of the twentieth century, Roberts mentioned that his village in Salford had 'its quota of feeble-minded, dummies (deaf mutes), hydrocephalics, grotesque cripples'.[66] Some of these people had sunk into poverty and never rose out of it again; others had been born poor and remained so all their lives. The same observations applied to those who suffered from mental illnesses and from diseases. In 1850 in Newcastle, a journalist came upon a nineteen-year-old woman whom he called 'an idiot'. She also had fits 'and is in consequence terribly deformed'.[67] Eleven years later Dr John Shaw described some of the tragic cases he found in his *Travels in England*. One poor invalid in Bradford was bedridden and frightfully afflicted: 'a fearful ulcerative process' had eaten away his skin and reduced his nose to a stump. In Brighton, Shaw met a girl of thirteen who had been rendered deaf, dumb and blind by disease, and who was laid prostrate by a spinal disease or some other problem. And in Birmingham he encountered 'a poor consumptive woman' and a 'dropsical man ... sweltering in his disease, with huge legs that, through their incapability of locomotion, literally fettered him to the place'. Both 'ought to have been in hospital receiving all the attention that medical science and good nursing could bestow, with fresh air and good food into the bargain, but were breathing a pestilential air, dying by inches, lolling their lives away like bad cabbages, or vegetable refuse rotting in a dark corner'.[68] It is impossible not to be moved by such stories of suffering.

People injured at work were also prone to poverty. Mayhew noticed a 'maimed Irish crossing sweeper', who had lost his leg when he fell from a scaffold whilst working as a bricklayer's labourer. He was thirty-six years old 'but looks more than fifty; and his face has the ghastly expression of death'.[69] In the same decade that this was written, Will Crooks' father lost an arm when he was oiling the machinery on a ship. His family's hardships dated from the day of this accident 'because he was forced to give up his work'. The only employment he could find was an odd job as a watchman, and so the brunt of responsibility for earning money fell onto his wife. Mrs Crooks 'used to toil with the needle far into the night and often all night long, slaving as hard as any poor sweated woman I have ever known, and I have known hundreds of such poor creatures'. The family was so poor that their meals consisted of 'bread and treacle for breakfast, bread and treacle for dinner, bread and treacle for tea, washed down with a cup of cold water'.[70]

Dangerous and unhealthy working conditions had an adverse effect on the lives of many working-class people. This point was emphasised by Robert Baker in Leeds in the 1830s, as it was three decades later by Sir John Simon. As Medical Officer to the Privy Council, he stated firmly that 'the canker of industrial diseases gnaws at the very root of our national strength'. Laws were passed which regulated employment in factories and mines, but Anthony S. Wohl has indicated rightly that ill health was 'an accepted part of working life'. He noted that miners, cutlery grinders and potters were prone to asthma, known colloquially as 'black spit' or 'potter's rot'; brassfounders were susceptible to an ague called 'Monday fever'; matchmakers were liable to suffer from necrosis, known as 'phossy jaw', whilst often chimney sweeps fell victim to a cancer called 'soot wart'.[71] Such illnesses were caused by bad working conditions and by the powder and dirt which was the result of so many manufacturing processes.

These problems were as obvious in 1914 as they had been in 1834. Vere W. Garratt made this plain. He worked in a small smelting shop in Birmingham. Here old gas meters were melted down in cupolas (furnaces), after which the metal was cleansed. Then it was recast and made up again. Garratt shrank from the brass shop, 'a whirling mass of machinery, where the men worked in deafening noise and dusty atmosphere with very inadequate ventilation'. But the worst part of the factory was the iron foundry, where the rough castings of the meters were filed smooth by hand and machine. The air was choked by 'a thick haze of filing dust', which was breathed in by the polishers. Garratt spoke to one of them. 'The irony of his job was that while he brightened the brasses he blackened his lungs in the process and made periodical visits to the sanatorium for treatment. A married man he told me he was condemned to an early grave.'[72] And in all likelihood, his family was condemned to poverty.

Poverty and age

Bell recognised that serious illness of the chief wage earner was likely to have a detrimental effect on a family.[73] Rowntree agreed. He also noted that injuries could have dire consequences, but like other statistical investigators he did not make clear the connection of poverty with disabilities. But he did recognise the bond with age. According to his poverty cycle a labourer would be poor for three periods in his life: in childhood, 'when his constitution was being built up'; in early middle age, 'when he should be in his prime'; and in old age. The investigator pointed out that poverty in childhood had lifelong effects on the health of a person. He noted another 'striking fact'. The proportion of children under fifteen who were poor was higher than their share of the total population of York.[74]

Bowley and Burnett-Hurst substantiated these observations. They found that 'in Northampton *just under one-sixth of the school children and just over one-sixth of the infants*; in Warrington *one-quarter of the school children and almost a quarter of the infants*; in Reading *nearly half of the school children and 45 per cent. of the infants*' were living in primary poverty. This was irrespective of exceptional distress caused by bad trade or short-time working. Unsurprisingly, they deemed these results 'a matter to cause the greatest alarm'. The two men went on to make it clear that the problem of childhood poverty was even greater than was indicated by their 'instantaneous' survey. They stated that there was a greater proportion of children and infants who '*at one time or another* have lived or will live below the standard taken as necessary for healthy existence'.[75] The hard lives of children such as these are highlighted by the memories of Will Thorne, Alice Foley, Jack Lanigan, Will Crooks and many others.

One of the greatest problems faced by all of them was an inadequate education. Until the 1870s, poor children went to school infrequently and found a job at very young ages. After school attendance became compulsory, some would play truant regularly to earn money – as did Francie Nichol in the 1890s.[76] Others worked before and after school. Their labours meant that they were often late for the register. One of them was W. Hobbs. On 9 March 1908 the head teacher of Ladypool Road National School wrote that 'since his admittance at February 24th he has never been early in the mornings, generally getting in at 9.20 or from that to 9.30 a.m. I understand that he sells papers for his father'.[77] Weekends brought no relief for children like this. The Saturday working experiences of one were quoted widely by social commentators. He rose at 6.30 a.m. and went to sweep the shop where he worked. Then he 'did the window out', had his breakfast, and 'started taking the orders that came in'. Later in the day he unloaded vegetables from the van of his employer and collected two tons of coal. After his dinner he rested for a few hours before returning to work, where he chopped wood until the shop closed. He went to bed at about midnight.[78]

When in class, such children would be tired whilst others would be weak from hunger. Both groups would be inattentive through fatigue. Their consequent inability to learn ensured that they would have to take unskilled and badly paid jobs when they left school. A life of poverty beckoned them, as it did for orphans. One of Mayhew's informants was certain that the loss of one or more parents was the cause of the large 'numbers of ragged, sickly and ill-fed children' who begged in the capital. The investigator himself described in detail the lives of two Irish sisters. They were both 'mother's children' and had never known their father. The elder was fifteen and had become responsible for her younger sister and brother eight years previously, when her mother died. Fighting against her dire poverty, this girl put herself and her siblings through school so that they could all read. Her brother had the added knowledge of writing, and she prayed 'to God that he'll do well with it'. He earned 1s 6d a week as a costermonger's boy, whilst his two sisters made enough to pay for their rent and their 'living'.[79]

In 1914, Arnold Freeman wrote about the similar hardships of a boy who was abandoned by his parents. His father had left home before he was born, 'when he knew this extra burden was coming into his life and died soon after'. The child's mother then went to live with a married daughter, so that from his infancy the boy had been looked after by 'kind neighbours'. Pale and weak-looking, he seemed destined to flit between jobs and to struggle.[80]

Average life expectancy did not alter much during the nineteenth century. In 1850 men could expect to live until they were forty and women up to the age of forty-two. By 1890 the respective years were forty-four and forty-seven.[81] It is not fanciful to suppose that the life expectancies of the poor were less than these averages. This could explain why Rowntree found that only 3.62% of those in primary poverty were over sixty-five. In York as a whole, 4.67% of the population was in this age group. The discrepancy between the two proportions occurred probably because affluent people were more likely to live longer than the poor.[82]

Throughout the period before 1918, there are many examples of old people suffering the poverty which had afflicted their childhoods. In common with the aged couple described by Mayhew (Document 6) they exemplified the adage 'you come into this earth with nothing and you go out of it with nothing'. Precluded by their poverty from saving money when they were younger, the aged poor had no chance of retirement. They had to labour. In 1905 this was made plain by Robert Sherard. Researching *The Child Slaves of Britain* he visited the Summer Lane neighbourhood of Birmingham. He came across a family where three children were carding hooks and eyes. They were aged eleven, nine and five and were 'in happy ignorance of the weight and stress of the years and years of drudgery to come'. The poignancy of their situation affected him deeply. They had no hope of relief 'till the grave'.[83]

Poverty and gender

The social investigators of the poor wrote largely in masculine terms. One who did not was Ralph Barnes Grindrod. In 1844 this surgeon described 'the distressed condition, moral and physical, of dress-makers, milliners, embroiderers, slop workers, &c'. He called his work *The Slaves of the Needle* and through it he sought to publicise the dreadful lives of these women. Grindrod estimated that in London alone there were 20,000 of them, with another 80,000 elsewhere in England. They were sweated as much as were the male tailors observed by Mayhew and Kingsley. Their employers were loath to take on enough workers to cope with high demand during the season. Consequently, too few women had to work long hours for little pay. Their plight led Thomas Hood to pen *The Song of the Shirt*, part of which reads:

> With fingers weary and worn,
> With eyelids heavy and red,
> A woman, sat, in unwomanly rags,
> Plying her needle and thread -
> Stitch – stitch – stitch!
> In poverty, hunger, and dirt,
> And still with a voice of dolorous pitch
> She sang the 'Song of the Shirt'.[84]

Faced with low incomes and terrible working conditions, some women became prostitutes. Frances Finnegan has cautioned that prostitution was not the inevitable outcome of poverty. Still, it was 'obvious that poverty in some form or another was the major reason for girls initially taking to the streets'.[85] This opinion is validated by contemporary surveys like that of the Reverend G. Merrick. Published in 1890, it studied those prostitutes imprisoned at Millbank, in London. More than ninety per cent of the women had fathers who were unskilled or semiskilled. Over half of them had been servants and the others had worked at charring, laundering or street selling.[86]

Judith R. Walkowitz has noted other features of prostitutes. An 'extraordinarily high percentage' of them had lost one or both parents. Most became prostitutes in their late teens and stayed on the streets only for a few years. The majority were local girls. And 'overwhelmingly they lived outside the family'.[87]

Prostitution was not an option for single women who were part of strong kinship networks. Nor was it a choice open to most married women. The strong moral codes of the poor precluded it. To earn money, such women continued to labour in sweated trades throughout the period before 1914, as Harding's reminiscences made clear. His mother's terrible life in Bethnal Green was replicated in many places.

In Birmingham, Sherard noted that female homeworkers did a variety of jobs. Some sewed the chains on to the leather chin straps of soldiers. Each strap had to have seventy-two links with four stitches to each link. For this the sempstresses might earn 2*d* an hour – although they had to pay for their own cotton, hemp and needles out of this sum. Deducting expenses and allowing for goods refused, Sherard calculated that two people could earn 1*s* 8*d* in two and a half days – if they strived from six in the morning until eleven at night. Another common occupation was carding hooks and eyes, four dozen of each to one card. In Tower Street the researcher came across a woman who did this task and was helped by her children after school. For a day's work she might earn 8*d*, out of which she paid 1*d* to a fogger. This was a woman who fetched the work from a factory and farmed it out.[88]

Booth, Bosanquet and others condemned the work of married women, in particular that which was carried on outside the home. It was asserted that children were neglected, homes became dirty, and husbands were forced to the pub by wives who did not attend to their domestic responsibilities. More than this, they were accused of causing high infant mortality rates in poorer working-class neighbourhoods. This was because women who worked were more likely to bottle-feed their babies and it was believed that this method of nourishment was inferior to breast-feeding. Overall it was. There was no powdered milk until just before the First World War and the bottles used had long necks in which germs could collect. It was difficult to keep them sterilised in a poverty-stricken home where fuel was low and costly. Life-threatening diarrhoea was often the result. But amongst the poor it was found that it mattered little whether a woman breast-fed or bottle-fed her baby. As Robertson stated in 1910, this was because poverty itself had 'such an evident pernicious influence on the health of the mother and her offspring'. His comments were based on the findings of Dr Jessie Duncan, who carried out an inquiry for Birmingham's Health Department. She concentrated on St Stephen's and St George's wards, both of which were densely populated. They were characterised further by bad housing, an unhealthy environment, high infant mortality rates and large numbers of women at work. A total of 1,212 homes were visited regularly by Duncan and two female health visitors during 1908. Including earnings from all sources, forty-five per cent of the households received less than 20s a week, whilst in twenty per cent of them the income was 10s a week or less. The extent of poverty was great even with the money brought in by wives and children. It was found that fifty-four per cent of the mothers worked before or after childbirth. Amongst them the infant mortality rate was 190 per 1,000 live births. This compared with a rate of 207 for those mothers who were not industrially employed.[89]

Five years later, a study in Manchester came up with similar results. The researcher was W. Elkin and she wondered whether 'when the income is small, the disadvantages of married women's employment are counteracted or not by the additional comfort derived from the wages'.[90] The same question had preoccupied Robertson. He pointed out that the money gained by working mothers 'was an important influence in the prevention of poverty which is one great cause of a high infant mortality'. The harmful effects of low earnings were emphasised by an examination of the weights of the live babies in the Birmingham survey. Those belonging to the poorest families weighed the least (Document 8).

Of the married women who had jobs, eighty-one were the sole or main sources of income for their families, 556 had jobs to supplement the small wages of their husbands, and only twenty worked because they had a preference to do so. Average earnings were 8s 5d a week.[91] A comparable situation prevailed in West Ham, where large numbers of women did homework making shirts, blouses and underclothing. E. G. Howarth and M. Wilson obtained information about 294 of them. They discovered that of their husbands fifty-three per cent had casual jobs, whilst 'many of the artisans and others were either out of work or employed irregularly'.[92] Research elsewhere in the country corroborated these conclusions. In 1915 it was reported that in Liverpool 'the wives are at work because their husbands are often casual labourers and sometimes drunkards'. The same year in Yorkshire, a study of married women who were employed showed that over eighty per cent of them were labouring because of economic necessity.[93]

This investigation concentrated on the occupation of women in the woollen and worsted trades. The majority of them were single. So too were many of the female cotton workers in Lancashire and Cheshire – or else they were young married women with no or few children. Some of them could earn up to 20s a week, although in Birmingham the wages for female factory workers rarely exceeded 11s.[94] This sum was considerably less than the amount which even an unskilled man could earn, but it was much better than the wages for homework, charring, and the taking in of washing. These sectors of employment were dominated by mothers of large families who had to fit their work around their domestic responsibilities. Prominent amongst them were widows.

Rowntree noted that in York the primary poverty of almost one in seven people was caused by the death of the chief wage earner. Amongst this group there were 389 widows, two-thirds of whom were over fifty years old. Figures like these made explicit the connections between poverty, gender and age. Rowntree added these people to those who were poor because of the incapacity of the chief wage earner. They totalled 549 families, of which 367 were earning money at an average of 10s 11d a week. The householders in these cases were mostly women: 165 went out charring, seventy-eight took in washing, twenty-eight had lodgers and eighteen were dressmakers.[95]

It is likely that abandoned wives made up another significant proportion of women in these types of employment. Desertion by husbands was a problem that was not enquired into statistically, but the circumstantial evidence suggests that either it led to poverty or else it deepened that condition. In 1849, Reach noticed in Leeds a number of poor women with four or five children who had been deserted by their husbands.[96] Almost sixty-five years later, Freeman gave an account of one such Birmingham woman. Her problems were the same as many others'. She received no money from her husband to help her raise seven children. She 'tried to keep the house together by charing' (*sic*), but her dire situation was such that she felt sure 'there ain't no God or 'E wouldn't let me suffer as I've suffered'.[97]

Not all men were selfish and unthoughtful of their responsibilities. In her study of Lambeth published in 1913, Maud Pember Reeves included details about husbands like Mr H., who gave his wife all his wages. Another woman said that 'My young man's that good ter me I feel as if somethink nice 'ad 'appened every time 'e comes in'.[98] But no matter how considerate or loving the husband, the main responsibility for rearing a family fell on the woman. Robertson stated strongly that amongst the poorer classes 'mothers live more exacting and self-denying lives than probably any other group in the community'. He stressed that they lived in semi-starvation, foregoing food so that their husbands and children could eat. Their hardships were distressing, especially when they were expectant or nursing mothers.[99]

These views were shared by Margaret Llewellyn Davies. An upper-class woman with a keen social conscience, she was a general secretary of the Women's Co-operative Guild. This organisation pressed for women's suffrage, better housing, maternity benefits and the reform of the divorce law. Its membership was made up mostly of the wives of better-paid working-class men. In 1915 the Guild published the correspondence of some of them in *Maternity Letters from Working Women*. On reading them, Davies declared that 'the suffering and waste of life, the overwork and poverty, must be tenfold and twentyfold where wages are less and employment more precarious'. This was substantiated by a number of the letter writers (Document 9). Rowntree's delineation of a poverty cycle for labourers had shown that 'the women' were poor 'during the greater part of the period they are in pregnancy'.[100] This realisation and the revelations of the Guild women led Davies to formulate a poverty line based on the needs of mothers. It had to be in excess of 30s a week. That sum was regarded as good wages, yet it was 'utterly inadequate for rearing a large or even small family'. The result was an 'excessive burden' upon women.[101]

Poverty and ethnicity

It would be foolish to assert that all members of ethnic minorities were poor. They were not. Colin G. Pooley made this plain in relation to Irish migrants to Britain. Using nineteenth-century census data, he analysed the socio-economic structure of the Irish-born who were living in seven British towns. He found that between seventeen and forty per cent of them were in skilled jobs or higher-status employment. Still, in each of the towns studied by Pooley no fewer than 57.4% of the Irish-born were in semiskilled or unskilled occupations. These figures make it difficult to disagree with Jeffrey G. Williamson's opinion that most Irish people arrived in Britain illiterate and unskilled. Once settled, they manifested a slow rate of upward mobility because they were discriminated against occupationally, or because 'they could ill afford the investment in acquiring skills either for themselves or their children'.[102]

Irish migration to Britain had been going on for centuries, but the scale of this movement increased enormously in the later 1840s following the failure of the potato crop. Forced from their land by starvation and foreign landowners, poverty-stricken Irish peasants fled their country. In five months during 1847 alone, 300,000 of them arrived in Liverpool – a city of a quarter of a million inhabitants. Nationally, the Irish in Britain peaked at 805,717 in 1861 – 3.5% of the total population. These migrants were largely from rural areas but they settled mostly in urban districts. Every major town and city had a substantial number of them, but in only a few did they make up a significant proportion. As Roger Swift mentioned, most of the unskilled Irish crowded into long-established and already overcrowded districts of settlement in Lancashire and London.[103]

In Liverpool the Irish represented 22.3% of the population in 1851, although this proportion dropped later in the century as migration lessened. Many of them were casually employed dock workers.[104] It was a similar situation elsewhere. Jennifer Davis' work on Jennings' Buildings, Kensington, showed that the majority of the residents were Irish Catholics by birth or descent. Most were 'employed in the poorly-paid seasonal trades which dominated west London: market gardening and laundry work for the women, building work for the men'.[105] Poverty stalked such people, as it did many of the Irish in the cotton towns of Lancashire. Their hardships were described by Reach in the *Morning Chronicle*. He visited a 'low Irish' quarter in Oldham and went into the home of a 'haggard man and woman'. They were making brooms from ling, 'almost the only work of the adult Irish population' in the town. In a good week the couple might make 4s from hawking their products.[106]

Over fifty years later in Manchester, Mick Burke's Irish mother also had to hawk goods to make a living. She sold fish 'out of a three-wheeled truck with skinned rabbits hanging from the handles'. Her run was 'round Ancoats, up Ashton New Road and round Openshaw and Clayton'. Because she was 'out in the pouring rain' her hands 'were all twisted with rheumatism'. Each morning she was at Smithfield Market for five o'clock to buy her goods. She skinned the rabbits herself and sold their skins for hide to make gloves, trilbies and hard hats. Her hard work and thoughtful coping strategies were typical of many poor women of all ethnicities. Unable to read and write, she was an intelligent person who contrived the survival of her family.[107]

Nearby in Salford, Irish women were noticeable as spinners in the mills, an occupation that was worse paid than weaving, drawing and winding-in. Roberts recalled that they and their countryfolk 'formed the lowest socio-economic stratum' in the city.[108] Racism against them was rooted deep. According to the *Report on the State of the Irish Poor in Great Britain* (1836), migrants from Ireland were 'an example of a less civilised population spreading themselves, as a kind of a sub-stratum, beneath a more civilised community, and, without excelling in any branch of industry, obtaining possession of all the lowest departments of manual labour'.[109]

Engels had similar opinions. He castigated the Irish for surviving on the minimum necessaries of life and for bringing with them filth and drunkenness. His researches were based partly on his visits to poorer areas of Manchester and Salford. In these his main guide was his Irish working-class lover, Mary Burns. This relationship did not lead the German factory owner to discard the prejudices of his class. His views were also affected by his political thinking. He hoped that the capitalist system would be overthrown by a proletarian revolution. But he feared that this might not occur because of the competition of Irish workers. They were willing to work for lower wages and this had two negative effects: first, the hindering of working-class consciousness; and second, the degrading of English workers to such a low level that they would become incapable of political action. Engels' work is characterised by its contradictions, however. As Williams discerned, 'The *Condition* is a quarrelsome text; it is not a unitary whole but plural, polysemic, and dispersed'.[110] This feature is obvious in Engels' attitudes towards the Irish. Whilst he held that they were 'little above the savage', he felt also that their 'fiery' temperament could have a positive effect on the English working class.[111]

Ideas that the Irish were a corrupting force were widespread. These beliefs were informed by a conscious racism. The Irish were demeaned and made to appear subhuman. Like others who were poor, they battled against their poverty. Their humanity cannot be hidden. Nor can their influence on the English working-class movement. Some of the greatest Chartist and trade-union leaders were Irish. They and their fellows did not debase English workers. Nor did they lower their living standards significantly. In a revisionist approach Williamson concluded that 'British incomes were little affected' by Irish migrants. The unskilled did suffer to some extent from their competition, but landlords and capitalists gained from their presence.[112]

Italian immigrants were also affected by discrimination and poverty. As the pioneering research of Lucio Sponza has shown, those in London were settled mostly in the notorious rookery of Saffron Hill, the area 'chosen by Charles Dickens as the thieves' den in *Oliver Twist*'. This part of Holborn was popular with Italians for two reasons. First, it had many lodging houses, which provided cheap accommodation. Second, 'it secured an easy access to the town centre as well as to the open grounds of the London fairs to those engaged in itinerant trades', whilst 'it also offered good infrastructures for petty manufacturing and trading to the artisans'.[113] The majority of the Italians in the capital came from valleys around Parma in northern Italy. By contrast, in St Bartholomew's, Birmingham, most of their countryfolk were *Nobladans* – speakers of Neapolitan dialects. Their numbers had increased after 1870 because the economic system had collapsed in southern Italy following its unification with the north.[114] Mostly illiterate and unable to speak much English, the emigrants had little choice other than unskilled work. Some resorted to labouring to earn money – as did a few of their better-educated children. One of these was Salvatore Miele. He was born in 1891 near Monte Cassino, which he left when he was about six. In common with other Italians he and his family entered England at Bristol. From there they went to Barnstaple 'and went busking around Devon and Cornwall as work was unattainable'. By the early years of the twentieth century they had made their way to Birmingham, where Salvatore became a labourer for terrazzo floor-laying firms. Most of these were owned by more prosperous northern Italians. Salvatore's daughter remembered him going to his job 'with a sack over his shoulder, with a few tools needed. The terrazo [*sic*] used to be manually polished with a stone, it was hard and long work, using a lot of water, which in freezing weather had to be broken off thick ice before work could begin'.[115]

Other southern Italians were prominent as hawkers of plaster figures and as organ grinders who travelled the streets collecting coppers off listeners who appreciated the music they played. David Green has stated that in Victorian Holborn pushing barrel organs was 'a precarious occupation and the rewards were relatively small'. The instruments were expensive to buy and so many grinders rented them at between 1s 4d and 2s 6d a day. Even in the summer season they would be fortunate to earn more than 14s a week, 'which left them precious little on which to live'.[116] In 1905, Russell noted similar rentals in Manchester, but he felt that the grinders might clear between 2s 6d and 8s a day. He pointed out that the work was hard. The machines were heavy 'and a considerable amount of exertion is undertaken' by those who played them.[117] By contrast, the making and tuning of the organ barrels was a skilled job, paying about 25s a week in the early 1900s.[118]

Accordion playing was also favoured by *Nobladans*. In Birmingham one family famed for its musical talents was the Tamburros. Like many of their fellows they came from the area of Sora near Monte Cassino. When they arrived in England they busked from Bristol to Lancashire before settling in the Midlands city.[119] The final trade associated with southern Italians was ice-cream making. This was another occupation which was dependent upon good weather, and in the winter its sellers changed over to providing baked potatoes and hot chestnuts. Not all the Italian street traders stayed poor. Some of them prospered and became *padroni* – patrons. These men returned to their villages to recruit teenage boys to work for them in England. Their parents were given money and the youngsters were indentured with their *padrone* until he deemed that the debt had been paid off. In the 1860s and 1870s there was an outcry about this system, which was compared to a form of slavery.[120] The 'evils' of the *padroni* appear to have been exaggerated and their operations continued at least until the First World War.[121]

There were a few Chinese people in England before 1914, gathered in Limehouse, London and in Liverpool. The majority were males and they were paid low wages as sailors and as workers in laundries. Similarly, there were black and south Asian seamen in both cities. As Colin Holmes showed, they were liable to joblessness because of the hostility of white sailors. Once they became unemployed it was difficult for them to find work again.[122]

After the Irish and ahead of the Italians, the largest ethnic minority in England was the Jews. These were split into two main groups. Sephardi were the descendants of Spanish Jews. They were long established in England and included well known families like the Disraelis and Montefiores. Ashkenazi Jews from Germany and Holland had been arriving since the 1700s, and by the mid-nineteenth century many of them were noticeable as businessmen and craftsmen.[123] A few were Anglicised street traders. One of them was interviewed by Mayhew. He was about twelve years old and sold sponges. His daily income fluctuated from nothing to a little more than 1s.[124]

From the 1840s Ashkenazi from Eastern Europe began to come to England. They were escaping from persecution and the worsening economic conditions in the Russian Empire. Their numbers later increased greatly as pogroms were mounted against them. About 150,000 of these Jews settled in Britain between 1881 and 1914. They came to three cities in particular. In London they gathered in Whitechapel, St George's in the east, and the adjoining districts; in Leeds they made Leylands their home; whilst in Manchester their neighbourhood was Redbank. Bill Williams has described this Ashkenazi community in the 1860s as 'poor, squalid, gauche, inarticulate, fearful, lacking membership of respected institutions, out of step with the major intellectual and political trends in Western Europe'.[125] All three cities were associated with the textile industry and tailoring – a skill which many East European Jews possessed. Many of them became victims of sweating, as they did in other trades like the making of shoes, cigars, and furniture. Willy Goldman grew up in the Jewish East End of London around the time of the First World War. At the age of fourteen he went to work in a sweat shop for twelve a hours a day. Here he was 'under the constant glare of an electric light, in an atmosphere that was thick with cigarette-smoke and the dust raised by treadle-machines, a room inhabited by crooked bodies and crooked minds, whose language was of a kind unheard of in any schoolroom'. Like other English-born sons of East European Jews, he was unhappy with his prospects.

> Now it seems as though for several years you have been the victim of a huge hoax. Your parents' emigration emerges as a waste of valuable time and money. They might as well have stayed where they were. You are no better off than they thirty years ago. If your father had spent his life sitting cross-legged in a Russian workshop you weren't much better off doing the same in an English one. If he had hawked fruit round the back streets there, it was not more profitable doing it here. If he had, in short, passed most of his life in a European ghetto, everything pointed to you duplicating his existence in an English one. History was a monotonous cycle. The only 'change' was in your respective attitudes: he was inured to his fate; while you would have to suffer a slow, back-breaking readjustment before you acquired his tragic and age-long resignation.[126]

Goldman's experiences contrasted with the remarks of Beatrice Potter (later Webb). In Booth's survey she noticed how quickly a 'greener' immigrant could become a 'guv'nor', in the process moving from Whitechapel to Willesden.[127] Still, large numbers of Jews remained poor, working as street traders or sweated artisans. Like all those in poverty, they lived in a hostile environment.

Notes

1 'Poverty, and how we treat it, or "shabby genteel"', *Jackdaw*, 31 October 1879, cited in R. Iliffe and W. Bagueley, *Victorian Nottingham. A Story in Pictures, Volume 11*, Nottingham, 1973, pp. 37–8.

2   H. Mayhew, *London Labour and the London Poor, Volume 3*, London, 1861–62, pp. 433–7.

3   W. J. Dalley, *The Life Story of W. J. Davis, J.P. The Industrial Problem. Achievements and Triumphs of Conciliation*, Birmingham, 1914, pp. 3-5.

4   J. Mack and S. Lansley, *Poor Britain*, London, 1985, p. 206.

5   P. Townsend, *Poverty in the United Kingdom*, Harmondsworth, 1979, p. 429.

6   A. M. McBriar, *An Edwardian Mixed Doubles. The Bosanquets versus the Webbs. A Study in British Social Policy 1890–1929*, Oxford, 1987, p. 55.

7   H. Bosanquet, *The Strength of the People: A Study in Social Economics*, first published 1903, New York, 1980 edn, p. 57.

8   'Present conditions of the people. By the author of "Old Bailey Experience". Class I. Labourers in cities and towns', *Fraser's Magazine*, 9, 1834, p. 72.

9   W. L. Sargent, *Economy of the Labouring Classes*, London, 1857, pp. 315 and 349.

10   J. H. Treble, *Urban Poverty in Britain 1830–1914*, London, 1983, p. 110.

11   Cited in D. Thompson, *The Chartists. Popular Politics in the Industrial Revolution*, Aldershot, 1986 edn, p. 226.

12   J. Lanigan, 'Incidents in the life of a citizen', in J. Burnett (ed.), *Destiny Obscure. Autobiographies of Childhood, Education and Family from the 1820s to the 1920s*, Harmondsworth, 1984 edn, pp. 96–7.

13   A. Foley, 'A Bolton childhood', in Burnett (ed.), *Destiny Obscure*, pp. 100–7.

14   'Thomas Morgan', in T. Thompson, *Edwardian Childhoods*, London, 1981, pp. 13–29.

15   R. Samuel, *East End Underworld. Chapters in the Life of Arthur Harding*, London, 1981, p. 24.

16   C. Chinn, *Better Betting with a Decent Feller: Bookmakers, Betting and the British Working Class 1750–1990*, Hemel Hempstead, 1991, pp. 72–3.

17   B. S. Rowntree, *Poverty. A Study of Town Life*, first published 1901, New York, 1980 edn, pp. 119–20.

18   A. L. Bowley and A. R. Burnett-Hurst, *Livelihood and Poverty*, first published 1915, New York, 1980 edn, pp. 41–2.

19   R. Roberts, *The Classic Slum. Salford Life in the First Quarter of the Century*, first published 1971, Harmondsworth, 1973 edn, pp. 21–2.

20   City of Birmingham Health Department, 'The Floodgate Street area', *Annual Report of the Medical Officer of Health*, Birmingham, 1904, pp. 14–16.

21   E. H. Kelly, 'Portsmouth', and C. V. Butler, 'Oxford', in H. Bosanquet (ed.), *Social Conditions in Provincial Towns*, first published 1912, New York, 1985 edn, pp. 2 and 62–3.

22   Rowntree, *Poverty*, pp. 136-7.

23   A. Paul, *Poverty – Hardship but Happiness. Those Were the Days 1903–1917*, first published 1974, Brighton, 1981 edn, p. 9.

24 Roberts, *The Classic Slum*, p. 88.

25 H. Mayhew, *London Labour and the London Poor, Volume 3*, London, 1861–62, pp. 300–12.

26 J. Kemp, *Memories*, unpublished, no date, p. 3 (thanks to Val Preece).

27 Robert R. Hyde, *Industry was my Parish*, London, 1968, p. 13.

28 Rowntree, *Poverty*, pp. 119-121.

29 G. Stedman Jones, *Outcast London. A Study in the Relationship Between the Classes in Victorian Society*, London, 1984 edn, p. 20

30 F. G. D'Aeth, 'Liverpool', in Bosanquet (ed.), *Social Conditions*, p. 40.

31 A. J. Kidd, 'Outcast Manchester', in A. J. Kidd and K. W. Roberts (eds), *City, Class and Culture. Studies of Cultural Production and Social Policy in Victorian Manchester*, Manchester, 1985, pp. 50–1.

32 E. H. Kelly, 'Portsmouth', in Bosanquet (ed.), *Social Conditions*, p. 2.

33 Mayhew, *London Labour and the London Poor, Volume 1*, pp. 5–6

34 V. Neuberg, 'Introduction', in Mayhew, *London Labour and the London Poor*, first published 1861–62, Harmondsworth, 1985 edn, p. xix.

35 Mayhew, *London Labour and the London Poor, Volume 1*, p. xv.

36 G. Himmelfarb, *The Idea of Poverty. England in the Early Industrial Age*, London, 1984, pp. 319–21.

37 A. Humphreys, *Travels into the Poor Man's Country*, Athens, Georgia, 1977, pp. 3 and 201.

38 Mayhew, *London Labour and the London Poor, Volume 1*, pp. 12–15.

39 *Inquiry into the Condition of the Poor of Newcastle-upon-Tyne, from the Newcastle Chronicle*, Newcastle, 1850, p. 14

40 J. Robinson, *The Life and Times of Francie Nichol of South Shields*, London, 1975, p. 15.

41 T. J. Bass, *Everday in Blackest Birmingham. Facts not Fiction*, Birmingham, 1912, pp. 9–10.

42 City of Birmingham Health Department, 'The Floodgate Street area', p. 16.

43 Treble, *Urban Poverty*, p. 13.

44 J. Adshead, *Distress in Manchester. Evidence (Tabular and Otherwise) of the State of the Labouring Classes in 1840–42*, London, 1842, pp. 26-39.

45 J. Foster, *Class Struggle and the Industrial Revolution*, London, 1974, p. 96.

46 W. H. Beveridge, *Unemployment. A Problem of Industry*, first published 1908, New York, 1980 edn, pp. 17–18.

47 Adshead, *Distress in Manchester*, p. 33.

48 'The Four Loom Weaver', probably late 1830s, in J. Raven (ed.), *Victoria's Inferno. Songs of the Old Mills, Mines, Manufactories, Canals and Railways*, Wolverhampton, 1978, pp. 128–30.

49 J. Hollingshead, *Ragged London in 1861*, first published 1861, New York, 1985 edn, p. 76.

50 V. E. Chancellor (ed.), *Master and Artisan in Victorian England. The Diary of William Andrews and the Autobiography of Joseph Gutteridge*, New York, 1969, pp. 122–3 and 178.

51 C. Mackay, 'Letter VII. Tailors and the slop trade – the sweating system', *Morning Chronicle*, 1 July 1850; H. Mayhew, 'Letter XVI and Letter XVII. The operative tailors', *Morning Chronicle*, 11 and 14 December 1849.

52 A. White, 'The invasion of pauper foreigners', *Nineteenth Century*, 23, 1888, 414–22; S. Fox, 'The invasion of pauper foreigners', *Contemporary Review*, 53, 1888, 855–67.

53 H. Mayhew, *Low Wages, Their Causes, Consequences and Remedies*, London, 1851, pp. 16–17.

54 K. Williams, *From Pauperism to Poverty*, London, 1981, p. 255.

55 E. Yeo, 'Mayhew as a social investigator', in E. P. Thompson and E. Yeo (eds), *The Unknown Mayhew. Selections from the Morning Chronicle 1849–50*, London, 1971, p. 54.

56 Williams, *From Pauperism to Poverty*, p. 253.

57 Treble, *Urban Poverty*, pp. 185–9.

58 'Pictures of the people drawn by one of themselves. No. III. – How they live (continued)', *Birmingham Morning News*, 1871, Birmingham Library Services.

59 Samuel, *East End Underworld*, p. 99.

60 Stedman Jones, *Outcast London*, pp. 33–51.

61 J. Gregory Mantle, Wesleyan Minister, 66, Trinity Road, Aston, *Birmingham Daily Post*, 7 January 1891.

62 I. Gregory, 'The disabled in the nineteenth century', *Local History Magazine*, 45, July/August 1994, pp. 14–15.

63 G. Doré and B. Jerrold, *London. A Pilgrimage*, first published 1872, New York, 1978 edn, p. 179.

64 F. Davies, *My Father's Eyes. Episodes in the Life of a Hulme Man*, Manchester, 1985, p. 8.

65 Hollingshead, *Ragged London*, pp. 26–8 and 47.

66 Roberts, *The Classic Slum*, p. 80.

67 *Inquiry into the Condition of the Poor of Newcastle-upon-Tyne*, pp. 15–16.

68 J. Shaw, *Travels in England: A Ramble with City and Town Missionaries*, first published 1861, New York, 1985 edn, pp. 156–7, 159, 186–7 and 217.

69 Mayhew, *London Labour and the London Poor, Volume 2*, pp. 559–60.

70 G. Haw, *The Life Story of Will Crooks MP*, London, 1917, pp. 2–4.

71 A. S. Wohl, *Endangered Lives. Public Health in Victorian Britain*, London, 1984 edn, pp. 264–5.

72 V. W. Garratt, *A Man in the Street*, London, 1939, pp. 78–9.

73 F. Bell, *At the Works*, first published 1907, London, 1985 edn, p. 47.

74 Rowntree, *Poverty*, pp. 137, 209–221 and 381.

75 Bowley and Burnett-Hurst, *Livelihood and Poverty*, pp. 44–5.

76 Robinson, *The Life and Times of Francie Nichol*, pp. 12–15.

77 Ladypool Road National School, *Log Book*, 9 March 1908, Birmingham Library Services.

78 R. Bray, 'The boy and the family', in E. J. Urwick (ed.), *Studies of Boy Life in Our Cities*, first published 1904, New York, 1980 edn, p. 24.

79 Mayhew, *London Labour and the London Poor, Volume 1*, London, pp. 277–8 and 141–2.

80 A. Freeman, *Boy Life and Labour. The Manufacture of Inefficiency*, first published 1914, New York, 1980 edn, p. 39.

81 J. Benson, *The Working Class in Britain 1850*–1939, Themes in British Social History, Harlow, 1989, p. 98.

82 Rowntree, *Poverty*, pp. 381–2.

83 R. Sherard, *The Child Slaves of Britain*, first published 1905, cited in P. Keating (ed.), *Into Unkown England 1866–1913. Selections from the Social Observers*, Glasgow, 1976, p. 188.

84 R. B. Grindrod, *The Slaves of the Needle. An Exposure of the Distressed Condition, Moral and Physical of Dress-Makers, Milliners, Embroiderers, Slop Workers &c.*, London, 1844, pp. 3–30.

85 F. Finnegan, *Poverty and Prostitution*, Cambridge, 1979, p. 213.

86 G. Merrick, *Work among the Fallen, as Seen in the Prison Cells*, London, 1890, pp. 26–7.

87 J. R. Walkowitz, *Prostitution and Victorian Society. Women, Class and the State*, Cambridge, 1982 edn, p. 19.

88 Sherard, *The Child Slaves of Britain*, pp. 183–8.

89 City of Birmingham Health Department, *Report on the Industrial Employment of Married Women and Infantile Mortality*, Birmingham, 1910, pp. 1–8.

90 W. Elkin, 'Manchester', in C. Black (ed.), *Married Women's Work*, first published 1915, London, 1983 edn, pp. 175–6.

91 City of Birmingham Health Department, *Report on the Industrial Employment of Married Women*, pp. 8–11.

92 E. G. Howarth and M. Wilson (eds), *West Ham. A Study in Social and Industrial Problems*, first published 1907, New York, 1980 edn, p. 268.

93 B. L. Hutchin, 'Yorkshire' and S. N. Fox, 'Liverpool', in Black (ed.), *Married Women's Work*, pp. 135 and 183.

94 Elkin, 'Manchester', in Black (ed.), *Married Women's Work*, p. 165; E. Cadbury, M. C. Matheson and G. Shann, *Women's Work and Wages: A Phase of Life in an Industrial City*, first published 1906, New York, 1980 edn, pp. 119–44.

95 Rowntree, *Poverty*, pp. 122–4.

96 A. B. Reach, 'Letter XVII', *Morning Chronicle*, 13 December 1849.

97 Freeman, *Boy Life and Labour*, p. 35.

98 M. P. Reeves, *Round About a Pound a Week*, first published 1913, London, 1979 edn, pp. 16 and 149.

99 City of Birmingham Health Department, *Report on the Industrial Employment of Married Women*, p. 18.

100 Rowntree, *Poverty*, p. 137.

101 M. Llewellyn Davies (ed.), *Maternity Letters from Working Women*, first published 1915, London, 1978 edn, pp. 6–7.

102 C. G. Pooley, 'Segregation or integration? The residential experience of the Irish in mid-Victorian Britain' and J. G. Williamson, 'The impact of the Irish on British labor markets during the industrial revolution', in R. Swift and S. Gilley (eds), *The Irish in Britain 1815–1939*, London, 1989, pp. 60, 68–71 and 139.

103 R. Swift, *The Irish in Britain 1815–1914. Perspectives and Sources*, London, 1990, pp. 20–1.

104 Pooley, 'Segregation or integration?', in Swift and Gilley (eds), *The Irish in Britain*, p. 74.

105 J. Davis, 'Jennings' Buildings and the Royal Borough. The construction of the underclass in mid-Victorian England', in D. Feldman and G. S. Jones (eds), *Metropolis. London. Histories and Representations since 1800*, London, 1989, pp. 14–15.

106 A. B. Reach, 'Letter VIII. The low lodging houses of Manchester', *Morning Chronicle*, 12 November 1849.

107 M. Burke, *Ancoats Lad. The Recollections of Mick Burke*, Manchester, 1985, pp. 3–5.

108 Roberts, *The Classic Slum*, pp. 20–3.

109 *Report on the State of the Irish Poor in Great Britain*, Parliamentary Papers, London, 1836, 34, xxxiv, pp. 456–7.

110 Williams, *From Pauperism to Poverty*, p. 296.

111 F. Engels, *The Condition of the Working Class in England*, first published 1845, Harmondsworth, 1987, pp. 123–6 and 150–1.

112 Williamson, 'The impact of the Irish', in Swift and Gilley (eds), *The Irish in Britain*, pp. 134–60.

113 L. Sponza, *Italian Immigrants in Nineteenth-Century Britain: Realities and Images*, Leicester, 1988, pp. 19–23.

114 C. Holmes, *John Bull's Island. Immigration & British Society 1871–1971*, Basingstoke, 1988, p. 30.

115 C. Chinn Letters Archive, Miss Miele, November and December 1992.

116 D. Green, 'Little Italy in Victorian London: Holborn's Italian community', *Camden History Review*, 15, 1988, pp. 2–6.

117 C. E. B. Russell, *Manchester Boys. Sketches of Manchester Lads at Work and Play*, first published 1905, Manchester, 1984 edn, p. 13.

118 C. Alberici, *A Book of Sorts*, unpublished manuscript, no date, pp. 1–4 (thanks to Pam Overthrow).

119 C. Chinn Interviews, Jackie Tamburro, 21 December 1992.

120 'The Nightside of Birmingham – No. 5. Organ boys and their owners', *Birmingham Sketches*, 3 December 1863, and 'Italian beggar children in Birmingham', *Aris's Birmingham Gazette*, 13 September 1877 (thanks to Doreen Hopwood).

121 C. Chinn Letters Archive, Mrs J. W. Evans, November 1992; Digbeth and Deritend Project Interviews, Mrs Nimmons, 1986, Birmingham Library Services.

122 Holmes, *John Bull's Island*, pp. 52–5.

123 V. D. Lipman, *A History of the Jews in Britain since 1858*, Leicester, 1990, pp. 1–13.

124 Mayhew, *London Labour and the London Poor, Volume 2*, pp. 136–7.

125 B. Williams, *The Making of Manchester Jewry 1740–1875*, Manchester, first published 1976, 1985 edn, p. 334.

126 W. Goldman, *East End. My Cradle*, first published 1940, London, 1988 edn, pp. 60–2.

127 D. Englander, 'Booth's Jews: The presentation of Jews and Judaism in *Life and Labour of the People in London*', at Charles Booth's *Life and Labour of the People of London* Conference, Milton Keynes, 15 April 1989, p. 16.

3

The environment of poverty

Poverty and housing

The urban poor lived in areas which offended the senses. A gloomy outlook, vile smells, harsh sounds, rough textures and bitter tastes were their lot. Their dreadful environment was revealed starkly in 1889 in the *Sunday Chronicle*. Writing under the pseudonym of 'Nunquam', Robert Blatchford made a 'voyage of discovery among the working-class dwellings' of Manchester. He was appalled by 'the miles of narrow, murky streets, the involuted labyrinths of courts and passages and covered ways, where a devilish ingenuity seems to have striven with success to shut out light and air'. Everywhere there was filth, broken pavements, ill-set roads covered with rubbish, stagnant pools of water, and 'dark, narrow, dilapidated, built-in hovels'.[1] Commentators on other places shared Blatchford's disgust. In 1901, J. Cuming Walters was indignant that the poor of Birmingham had to live 'near the ill-smelling canal; or in the vicinage of factories which pour out their fumes in billowing masses from the throats of giant stacks'.[2] Three years later the Reverend Bass explained that the city possessed an Oxygen Street. With incredulity he exclaimed, 'ye gods, what a name for a street where atmosphere, polluted by neighbouring works, made my throat and nose smart and my eyes run'.[3]

Throughout history, low and insecure earnings had driven the poor into the least salubrious spots. But the unprecedented urbanisation of the early nineteenth century increased vastly the scale of this residential segregation. Demarcated by main roads, railways and canals, large and populous neighbourhoods came to be the preserve of those in poverty. This phenomenon was noted in 1844 by Engels. He stated that the central business district of Manchester was collared by a ring of workers' quarters, outside of which were the suburbs of the middle class (Document 10). His analysis was followed by detailed and vivid descriptions of the living conditions which prevailed in the working-class streets. These were hidden from general view, lying as they did behind the major shopping thoroughfares.

Stephen Marcus has praised this section as a *tour de force*. He maintained that it was the only representation of an industrial city which 'achieves such an intimate, creative hold upon its living subject'.[4] It is hard to disagree with this assessment. Engels' writing may have manifested incongruities, as Victor Kiernan has admitted.[5] He may have been influenced by his socialist beliefs and his antagonism towards the bourgeoisie, as his critics professed. His selection of the evidence may have been biased.[6] Still, his chapter on residential segregation is a perceptive insight into social relations and the setting of poverty. For as Marcus stated, Engels read Manchester with his eyes, ears, nose and feet.[7]

By the mid-nineteenth century the flight of prosperous families to fresher districts outside the city was even more pronounced. According to Arthur Ransome and William Royston, the result was that the poor were left as 'almost the sole possessors of the township of Manchester and the greater part of Salford'. This development meant that it was difficult to compare the two cities with London and Birmingham, 'which still count within their borders a considerable number of well-to-do inhabitants'.[8] Manchester was bounded to the west and the north by other manufacturing cities. Consequently, its middle class tended to move south, towards rural Cheshire. In other towns affluent families settled on the western edges. This location was upwind of the smoke and smells of the industries collected in the central neighbourhoods. Conversely, the influence of the prevailing winds ensured that eastern areas might also become homes to those in poverty. This was the case in Sunderland. Its east end was situated between the docks, the fish quay and the city centre. Here was found casual work, overcrowded tenements and heavy airs.[9]

The gathering of the poor was affected not only by geographical factors but also by physical features. In particular, their dwellings were sited in low-lying sectors which were damp and liable to flooding. Sheffield's east end was in the Don valley; the poorest portions of Manchester were by the Irwell, Irk and Medlock; whilst the most poverty-stricken people of Birmingham found their shelter in the valleys of the River Rea and Hockley Brook. Even in a town like Bath, the link between homes of the poor and low ground was evident. Graham Davis' research showed that the area between the Abbey and the River Avon featured 'small-scale industry and working-class housing' and that it was 'frequently inundated with flood water'.[10] Contrarily, in most towns the middle class inclined towards higher and better-drained spots.

By the mid-nineteenth century about 10,000 people lived in the Avon Street neighbourhood of Bath. This was one-fifth of its residents. In common with other poorer people they crowded into too few houses. Nationally, the surplus of families over dwellings more than doubled between 1801 and 1871, but the inadequacy of the housing stock was at its worst in those places which grew spectacularly. As Richard Rodger made plain, of the twelve largest cities in Britain in 1871, eight 'had experienced their most rapid acceleration in the 1820s; Bristol grew by 70%, Bradford 66%, Salford 56%, Leeds 47%, Liverpool 46%, Manchester 46%, Birmingham 42% and Sheffield by 41%'.[11]

The influx of people to these places created a high demand for homes. Motivated by the prospect of a quick and sizeable profit, some landlords subdivided their properties. Still there was not enough accommodation for the poor. This insufficiency encouraged speculative builders to throw up shoddy structures wherever they could. In 1880 Dr Alfred Hill, Birmingham's first Medical Officer of Health, explained that jerry-built houses 'may be built on an impure foundation with mortar consisting of dirt instead of sand, and only enough lime to "swear by"'.[12] His observations were supported by his counterpart in Manchester. Dr Leigh was certain that whilst 'the old houses are rotten from age and neglect' the new dwellings 'often commence where the old ones leave off, and are rotten from the first'.[13]

Inferior workmanship and improper and insubstantial materials were the trademarks of the jerry-builders. Constructing in haste for a short-term gain, they filled in open spaces and formed new slums. According to Robert Williams in 1893, these were areas in which each dwelling was hemmed in by others of the same type. All were dilapidated, badly drained, small-roomed, wanting in light and air and 'wholly unfit for human habitation'.[14] The unskilled, the sweated, the seasonally employed, widows, the injured and the chronically ill were drawn to this housing because it was the most inexpensive. But it was not cheap. In 1913, Pember Reeves explained that in Lambeth 4s a week was the rent for one room which was fifteen feet by twelve feet in size. With rates and taxes the sum paid out on shelter could be doubled. This meant that a man on 24s a week had to lay out a third of his earnings on his housing. She compared this situation with that of a rich man who paid £250 a year in rent, rates and taxes for an eighteen-roomed property in Kensington. Such a sum was equivalent to one-eighth of his income. Pember Reeves' conclusion was stark. A poor man paid more per cubic feet of space than did a rich man.[15]

Poverty-stricken people had no bargaining power. They had to pay the rents that were charged by property owners because they had to live in densely populated neighbourhoods. Here were the opportunities for street traders of every kind to scratch a living. Here were the businesses which gave out irregular employment to men, women and children. Here where the many fought to stay alive was the chance of survival. Economic forces compelled the poor to live where they did. This was made plain in 1884–85 by the Royal Commission on the Housing of the Working Classes (Document 11). Tormented by low earnings and insecure jobs, the predicament of those in poverty did not change much before the First World War. It was explained graphically by one Birmingham woman: 'Why don't I leave? Because I can't get a house any better near to my husband's work . . . . We've got no choice. We're obliged to take the house we can afford.'[16]

The dwellings of the urban poor were varied in their type but were uniform in their low quality. At the base of the hierarchy of housing were common lodging houses, where a person could rent a bed for a few coppers a night. Often they were the resort of newcomers or those who were almost destitute, friendless and kinless. They were used by families as much as they were by single people. The consequent mixing of genders and ages offended the moral sensibilities of most middle-class Victorians. Their concerns were exacerbated by the communal sleeping arrangements and cooking facilities of lodging-houses. It was feared that these facilities encouraged promiscuity. The reality was less racy. Raphael Samuel has pointed out that numerous travellers tramped England in search of work. For these 'footsore wanderers', lodging houses 'offered warmth and a cheerful shelter' and an 'atmosphere that was companionable'.[17]

These features did not impress the authorities. A series of Acts was passed between 1851 and 1853 which regulated lodging houses and made them open to inspection. Minimum standards of cleanliness, space and ventilation were laid down, and single people were separated according to their gender. In London alone nearly 11,000 common lodging houses came under these laws. The condition of some of them was described in 1854 by George Godwin, an editor of *The Builder*. In the vicinity of Gray's Inn Lane, London, there 'was a clump of fourteen small houses' which had been limewashed and cleansed. They had space for seventy-five lodgers, each of whom paid 3*d* a night for a bed. If fully let, the income from these premises totalled £6 11*s* 3*d* a week. These lodging houses compared favourably with one in Church Lane, St Giles. Here, in an apartment fifteen feet square, thirty-seven men, women and children were 'all huddled together on the floor'. In another small room near the Tower of London, 'fourteen adults were sleeping on the floor without any partition or regard to decency'.[18]

Godwin accepted the general good of measures aimed to improve situations like these. Still, his support was qualified. He observed that sanitary inspectors could close down premises and push the poor out of dreadful living quarters. But 'no adequate provision has been made for their reception elsewhere'. Unable to afford the higher charges of better-maintained lodging houses, the destitute poor could only overcrowd those inferior premises 'not at present discovered by the police'. Town councils and similar governing bodies were empowered by the 1851 Act to levy a rate for the building of 'lodging houses for the labouring classes'. Godwin urged the City of London to take up this provision immediately so that premises could be erected where the charge for shelter would be no more than 2*s* a week.[18] His plea went unheeded. Twelve years later, Huddersfield was the only local authority in England which had acted positively. Nearby in Leeds, a model lodging house was paid for by a local philanthropist, whilst in London a charitable body had built similar structures.

Praiseworthy as they were, such initiatives had little effect on the overall problem.[19]

Common lodging houses continued to draw notice. As in the past, it was feared that they encouraged sexual immorality and crime, and there were worries that they were supervised inadequately. In 1901, Cuming Walters described those in the Park Street area of Birmingham. He was a journalist with the *Birmingham Daily Gazette*, and his article was one of a number in which he sought to arouse middle-class opinion about the terrible housing of the poor. Like other socially concerned observers, his writing was distinguished by the way he blended 'facts and figures' and compassion for those in poverty with descriptions about drunken men, dissolute women, and unintelligent children.[20] Partly this was a technique to gain the notice of readers; partly it was influenced by the belief that the apparent degeneracy of the poor was connected to bad housing conditions. It is instructive to compare his racy account with the more sober thoughts of Francie Nichol. After she married Johnny Robinson, she went to look after her father-in-law's Thrift Street lodging house. In a poor part of South Shields, it was a 'rough place' full of 'tough people'. Still, some of the lodgers 'were ordinary, quite decent and fairly respectable'. None of them were there by choice, 'only out of necessity'. But as Nichol emphasised, lodging houses were better than the workhouse for 'there was room for a little pride'.[21]

In 1840 the members of the Select Committee on the Health of Towns had also argued that 'moral evils' arose from housing which was in a deplorable state. But in common with Cuming Walters, their rectitude was matched by their genuine concern for the health of those condemned to live in slum conditions. Some of the worst properties they came across were cellar dwellings, most of which were below terraced housing. In Liverpool, there were 7,800 of these premises occupied by 39,000 people – one-fifth of the city's population. Most were 'dark, damp, confined, ill-ventilated and dirty'.[22] Dr Duncan, later the Medical Officer of Health of the city, stated that sometimes 'the fluid matter' from ground-floor communal privies oozed into the cellars. In others, the floors were so wet that their residents had to walk on doors which were taken off their hinges and laid flat on bricks.[23]

Many of the cellar dwellings of Manchester were as unpleasant. Jacqueline Roberts has shown that they remained in use until the early 1870s, when they were closed down by John Leigh, the city's Medical Officer of Health. One cellar was below number four John Street. This was the home of John McCormick, a mat maker who had lost his sight. In 1871 his room was shared with his three daughters and four lodgers, all of whom were widowed and aged between forty-three and seventy. Nearby, at number eight, lived an Irish cabinet-maker, his wife, six children, his mother-in-law, a lodger and her son. Below them in the cellar were the Flahertys, a family of seven.[24] There were cellar dwellings in some other northern cities, especially in Leeds. As in Manchester, the majority of them consisted of one small room rented at about 1s to 1s 6d a week. They were described by James Hole in 1866 as having 'no space for ventilation, for ordinary convenience of movement, nor even for the requirements of common decency. It is kitchen, bedroom, living room – all in one.' He felt strongly that such places were utterly unsuited for the bringing up of a family.[25]

By this date, the greater number of cellar dwellings in Liverpool had been closed by the council. Though well meant, the effects of this action were not wholly positive. Those who lost their homes were not given alternative accommodation. Consequently, they crowded into the cheapest housing they could find. As Hugh Shimmin explained, these were back-to-backs built in courtyards.[26] This was the dominant form of housing for the poor in the West Midlands, West Yorkshire and south-east Lancashire. John Burnett has mentioned that until the 1840s back-to-backs constituted up to seventy per cent of the total housing stock in Liverpool, Nottingham, Leeds, Huddersfield and Keighley.[27] In Birmingham, the proportion was as large. By 1914, the city had 43,366 back-to-backs grouped in about 6,000 courts. As late as 1960, there remained over 25,000 of them – the last of which were not demolished until the end of that decade.[28]

The building of back-to-backs maximised the number of dwellings on a small plot of land. Most were in terraces which ran at right angles from the street. They shared their backs with a parallel line of houses, from which they were separated by a wall only the thickness of one brick. These terraces were approached via a narrow entry between and below two dwellings which had roadside frontages. Each row faced a courtyard which had communal facilities – lavatories, wash-houses, and 'miskins', where the rubbish was put. A vivid description of one yard is given by Kathleen Dayus, who grew up in poverty before 1914 in Hockley, Birmingham (Document 12).

Most back-to-backs were no more than fifteen feet square. Some had a cellar, whilst on the ground floor the majority had a tiny scullery and one main room. This was multifunctional. It served as a living room, kitchen, dining room, and often as an additional bedroom as well as a place for mothers and children to do homework. This is shown by one of the few photographs of an interior of a back-to-back (Document 13). Cooking was on an open fire, and later on a range. Often the flooring was quarry tiles, covered with peg rugs – hessian sacking on to which women 'bodged' (stitched) old rags. In one corner of the ground floor was a door leading to a steep set of stairs. This went up to the second storey where there were two bedrooms. Other back-to-backs had three storeys, each with one room. In Birmingham these were called 'attic-high'. They were a slightly better form of accommodation because the space in them was greater than in a two-storey back-to-back. For both types, the rent was about 3s 6d a week by the turn of the century.

Above back-to-backs in the housing hierarchy were 'two-up two-down' terraced dwellings. These were through-houses which were unattached to any others at their rear. They were common in 'The Boroughs', the poorest part of Northampton, as they were in Manchester and Salford. Few were well planned, and by the early 1900s many had deteriorated.[29] Bill Horrocks recalled those in Bolton. The 'mortar between the bricks was a breeding ground for little brown bugs which were a constant menace to householders'. On the floor were flag stones 'uneven after a century of wear and tear', whilst 'the walls were covered in whitewash, which often flaked off owing to the vibration caused by passing coal carts, making a mess on the floor'. The typical living room was about ten feet square. It had a jutting-out fireplace, an oven at the side, a kettle constantly on the hob, and a table taking up most of the rest of the room. On the ceiling was a contraption which acted as a clothesline and which could be pulled up and down. The back kitchen was tiny. It had a small table for scrubbing and washing, a boiler, and shelves attached to the walls. Coal was kept under the staircase. The bigger bedroom 'was just large enough for two full size beds', whilst the smaller had room only for a single bed. Families of twelve lived in such places, 'which must have made mothers' lives hellish'.[30]

'Two-up two-downs' and back-to-backs were characterised by the residence of one family – although finding it difficult to pay the rent, widows and others often took in lodgers to help them survive. The situation was different in tenements. These were buildings which were subdivided for multiple occupancy. Theoretically, they were unlike lodging houses because the minimum tenancy was for a week. In practice, the distinction between the two was slight. Some tenement owners offered rooms for rent on a daily basis, whilst many allowed their properties to become vastly overcrowded. The structures themselves were of two types: those which had been constructed specifically for the poor; and those which had been the properties of prosperous families. These had moved out because their dwellings were engulfed in the urban sprawl or because their facilities had become outdated. By 1850 such a process had transformed All Saints in Newcastle from 'the residence of the local aristocracy' to a poverty-stricken district. Places like these were called 'rookeries' because towering and tottering tenements were packed in 'narrow streets and narrow entries'.[31] In London, the most infamous were those of St Giles, Saffron Hill, Seven Dials, and Jacob's Island in Bermondsey – about which Mayhew and Dickens also wrote.

Many rookeries were cleared during the mid-nineteenth century, but tenements remained a feature of the housing of the poor in London. Peter Sanders' family lived in one of them in Bethnal Green, where Booth indicated that 44.6% of the population were suffering poverty. The home of the Sanders family was in a courtyard lying off the street. It was a large terraced house which was three storeys high and had been built originally for weavers. The Sanders family rented the one room on the upper floor for 2s 6d a week. Entry was through a trap door at the top of a staircase. Below them was a family sharing two rooms, as there was on the ground floor. The tenancies of these larger accommodations cost about 5s a week. Water was fetched from a tap in the small back garden, where there was a communal lavatory.[32] Nearby, in the Nichol, Arthur Harding lived in even worse conditions. In the late 1880s his home was Keeve's Buildings, Boundary Street. This was a three-storey tenement 'which contained twelve rooms, let to twelve different families'. There was a basement for washing, a yard in which to put the rubbish, and a water tap on each landing.

Each room had 'an ordinary flimsy door that you could kick open', and rent was about 3s a week.[33]

During the same decade, Lord Shaftesbury stated that 'however great the improvement of the condition of the poor in London has been in other respects, the overcrowding has become more serious than ever it was'.[34] Yet tenements crammed with people were not restricted to London. In 1851 Dr Hector Gavin wrote *The Habitations of the Industrial Classes*. Much of his book included evidence from doctors across urban England. Those from Stockton-on-Tees, Doncaster, Tewkesbury, Gainsborough and Torquay stressed that overcrowding was a 'very great evil' in their towns. Numerous examples were given. One was the case of two men, four women and three children. They slept in three beds in a room which was just twelve feet by nine feet.[35]

Over thirty years later the Royal Commission on the Housing of the Working Classes also noticed that the most aggravated forms of overcrowding could be seen in smaller centres of population. Amongst those mentioned were the mining town of Camborne in Cornwall and Alnwick in the North East. The packing of too many people into too little space was as prevalent in the tenements of Bristol and Newcastle upon Tyne. Consequently the commissioners felt that overcrowding was less conspicuous in towns dominated by back-to-back and 'two-up two-down' housing.[36] Official statistics appeared to corroborate this assumption. In Manchester in 1904 there was the 'comparatively low' number of 4,516 overcrowded houses, with 34,137 residents. Marr was convinced that these figures did not reflect the real situation. They were based on the census definition of overcrowding as 'more than two people to a room'. He emphasised that a better criterion was provided by the model bye-laws of the Local Government Board. These laid down a requirement of 400 cubic feet of air for every person over ten years of age in any room not used exclusively for sleeping. Marr affirmed that there was much overcrowding in Manchester, 'and not infrequently gross instances are to be found'.[37] Researchers in Birmingham made the same point.[38]

In 1897, Arthur Sherwell showed that St Anne's in Soho was one of the most overcrowded districts in the capital. Not only did an average of just over thirteen people squeeze into each dwelling, but also 232 persons thronged into each acre. The population density was even more excessive in parts of south London and the

East End, peaking at a massive figure of 365 in Bethnal Green (North).[39] At first sight the poorest parts of Manchester compared favourably with these statistics. The Reverend J. E. Mercer recorded that Angel Meadow had 200 people to each of its thirty-three acres. But the investigator cautioned that these figures were not indicative of the true compactness of the population. He explained that 'when we take into account that one end of the district is almost wholly occupied by works, warehouses, and railways, the density of the residential portions may be reckoned as half as much again, or 300 to the acre, and is quite on a par with the metropolitan slum'.[40] Robertson indicated a like situation in the Birmingham wards of St George's and St Stephen's.[41]

The housing plight of the poor was recognised by some commentators early in the nineteenth century. In 1840 members of the Select Committee on the Health of Towns recommended that the slum problem should be tackled by the passing of a Building Act. This was to apply to towns of a certain population and to houses constructed for the working class. Its provisions were to include the banning of back-to-backs, of terraces in close courts and of most cellar dwellings. Another intended rule required that behind and before every terrace there should be space proportionate to the height of the dwellings. Further, proper lavatories were to be erected, better facilities for the disposal of rubbish were to be provided, and party walls were to be of a specified thickness. The Committee thought that it was a matter of great regret that such legislation had not been enacted at the beginning of the century, 'before our great towns were so densely populated, and so many dwellings for the working classes had been built in contravention of the proposed rules'. They were certain that such action would have prevented 'much of the discomfort and sufferings' which prevailed in England.[42]

Their recommendations were ignored. So were similar proposals made by Hole in 1866. These were even more far reaching. He advocated that the repression of bad housing should be accompanied by the provision of new homes for the poor. This could be effected only if the state loaned money at a low rate of interest to builders.[43] It is important to be aware that such courses of action were suggested. They dispel claims that the English authorities can be absolved from blame for the dreadful housing of the poor. Such arguments assert that rapid and immense urbanisation was a novel and exceptional situation. In these circumstances governments could be excused for not knowing how to react to the social problems which confronted them. This line of reasoning cannot be sustained. The members of the Select Committee on the Health of Towns made it plain that there was an awareness of the difficulties facing the poor. They and Hole made it clear that there was a strategy which could be implemented to alleviate these problems.

Their urgings foundered on the rocks of laissez faire ideology and the self-interest of so many who were wealthy. The building of better houses for industrial workers would have led to increased rents. As H. J. Dyos and D. A. Reeder have perceived, there was a tacit acceptance that this development meant the payment of higher wages. Businesspeople feared this 'would have raised the costs of exports and reduced the capital being sent abroad, which in turn would have held back the growth of exports'. Actually, the reverse may have happened, 'but it did not look that way at the time'.[44] Slum dwellers were essential in creating England's wealth but they were excluded from the benefits of their labour. They provided workers who could be paid cheaply and who could be taken on and laid off whenever it suited an employer. Accordingly, they were as important to the domestic market as they were to exporters. Jenifer Davis has highlighted this in Kensington. The poverty-stricken inhabitants of Jennings' Buildings were integral to local structures of power and profit. Landlords secured high dividends from their tenancies; builders gained from having a reservoir of labour; and local publicans and other traders secured a useful source of cash-paying customers.[45]

Slums could have been eradicated only with radical and decisive government policies. This was not to happen. As a result, local authorities which wished to alleviate the housing problems of the poor were forced to be reactive and restrictive instead of proactive and constructive. For example, in Manchester the building of back-to-backs was banned through a bye-law as early as 1844 – although it was not until 1909 that they were forbidden by national legislation. Yet as Godwin and Shimmin showed, initiatives like this could lead to a deterioration in the conditions of life for the urban poor. It was a point with which Thomas Beames concurred. He noted that the forming of the spacious New Oxford Street had necessitated the demolition of a large part of the rookery of St Giles. Indignantly he proclaimed that no 'poor man has gained by the change' nor had any section of the working class 'reaped an advantage'. To bolster this bold statement Beames quoted the findings of a Statistical Society report. These indicated that the poor who had been 'expelled' from their homes had no alternative but 'to invade the yet remaining hovels suited to their means'. The result was that 'the circle of their habitations is contracted while their numbers are increased, and thus a large population is crowded into less space'. Beames declared that slum clearance had to be accompanied by the building of 'habitable dwellings for the population you have displaced, otherwise, you will not merely have typhus, but plague'.[46]

His urgings went unheeded. Demolition of slum properties continued to lead to congestion in adjacent areas, as J. A. Yelling has verified.[47] The result was a deterioration in the living conditions of the capital's poor – a point affirmed by the Royal Commission on the Housing of the Working Classes.[48] Many clearances were carried out by railway companies, which needed land for stations, lines and works. According to J. R. Kellett, these developments took up between five and a half and nine per cent of the space in the central zones of major cities.[49] On a personal level, Jack Simmons has shown that more than 76,000 Londoners had to move from their homes between 1853 and 1901 for the land hunger of the railways.[50] Other demolitions were by owners who wished to improve their properties, or who wanted ground for the construction of docks and works. Until 1885 there was no legal requirement to rehouse the people who lost their homes in any of these ways.

The loss of space for the urban poor was ubiquitous. In Birmingham, the poverty stricken were pushed out of their homes to make way for the building of the Town Hall (1830s), of New Street Station (1840s), for the financial sector around Colmore Row (1860s) and for Corporation Street (1870s and 1880s). The forming of this 'Parisian-style boulevard' cut a swathe through some of the worst slums in the city, destroying 855 decrepit houses. It was carried out by the council under the auspices of the Artisans and Labourers' Dwellings Improvements Act of 1875. This enabled the clearance of an insanitary area and it allowed for the rehousing of those who were displaced. In Birmingham, this latter provision was not taken up. Those who had lost their homes overflowed into the adjoining streets. There were too few dwellings for them. Demand was high and landlords put up rents. Birmingham's improvement scheme failed the poor. Under heavy criticism, the council belatedly built 104 dwellings. Their minimum weekly rental of 5s was too great for people who could not earn more than 17s 6d in a week.[51] Instances such as these justify Martin Gaskell's claim that the intervention of local authorities in housing had a disastrous effect on the lives of the poor.[52]

Poverty and health

Bad housing was a major problem. It was compounded by the inadequate facilities of the slums. This was illustrated in 1840 by a description of a populous district in Leeds. It was unpaved and 'more or less deficient in sewerage'. The roads were full of holes and they were intersected by deep channels formed by the rain. Sometimes these streets were 'rendered untenable by the overflowing of sewers and other more offensive drains'. Ash-holes were exposed to public view and were never emptied. Rubbish was everywhere. It accumulated in cellars, it was piled up against walls, and it was thrown into the streets. The same insanitary conditions prevailed elsewhere. In Manchester 'the streets may be full of pits, brimful of stagnant water, the receptacles of dead dogs and cats', and there was no public park or ground where 'the population can walk and breathe the fresh air'. London had numerous houses, courts and alleys without privies, whilst those for the back-to-backs of Liverpool were 'in the most abominable state of filth'. They gave off odours so foul that it was almost impossible to remain near them 'for any time'.

Throughout urban England, repulsive reeks were added to by 'noxious businesses'.[53] In 1847 in London, Hector Gavin shrank from 'accumulations of filth in nightmen's yards, collections of dung for sale, swine-pens, slaughter houses, knackers' yards, cow-sheds, pig-sties, gut spinning, tallow boiling, the burning of animal and vegetable matters, such as animal charcoal by the sugar refiners, the dessication of nightsoil, and a thousand others'. The air was polluted and defiled further by 'a vast variety of offensive trades, manufactories, chemical works, and gas manufactories'. These were most destructive to the health and comfort not only of

89

the work people engaged in them, but of those who were exposed to their extended influence.[34]

Another source of bad smells was the 'burial places in the midst of populous neighbourhoods'. In 1837, Dr John Hogg stated that each year in London over 45,000 people died. Most of them were interred in small churchyards. Hogg exclaimed with horror that 'thousands of tuns [*sic*] of decomposing human remains are deposited within a few feet of the surface'. In many instances, the bodies 'are not allowed to rest long enough to turn to earth before they are again tossed up to cover the accumulating dead'.[35] The problems arising from insanitary and unhealthy burial places were compounded by the practice of laying out the dead in their home for up to seven days. This custom was induced by poverty. The poor did not have the money to pay for their deceased to be put in a funeral home; nor could they afford to have time off work for burials, so that of necessity these took place mostly on Sundays. In 1843, it was reported from Chorlton-on-Medlock that 'in the summer it frequently happens that when the bodies are brought for interment they are quite offensive, and it cannot but happen that mischief must be caused to those who are compelled to live in the same room with a decomposing corpse'.[36] Poverty ensured that this practice continued until the inter-war years. In back-to-backs, the dead were laid out on the table in the one ground-floor room, with a saucer full of onions to dispel the smells.

Another cause of 'mischief' to the poor was unhealthy water for drinking, cleaning and washing. In many places this was sold by private companies via taps in streets, but the supply was intermittent. Consequently, in some poor neighbourhoods the water firms filled communal butts. They were 'made of wood from which the paint has often decayed; sometimes the wood itself is decayed; they commonly have no cover on top, and a film of blacks and dust forms on the surface of the water'. This was taken into homes in tubs or earthenware vessels which were uncovered, and 'frequently a green scum is found in them'.[37] Where there was no supply of tapped water, butts were used to collect rain water. Elsewhere, water was taken from streams and rivers polluted with sewage, or as in Birmingham it was drawn via pumps from a well in a yard. Writing in the *Morning Chronicle*, Mackay found it 'painful to witness little girls of eight or nine years of age struggling along the court, and up ladders, with loads of water far

too heavy for them to bear'. In another yard he discovered that
between 300 and 400 people shared one pump. The water was 'of
a greenish colour, and smelling as strongly as if a gas-pipe had
burst'.[58] The city's wells were close to midden privies, from which
'filthy liquids' soaked into the ground and thence to the water. This
problem was so bad that in 1873 it was reported that the water
from one well was so polluted that it 'would make excellent
manure'.[59]

Unastonishingly, ill health and diseases were prevalent in these
districts. This was demonstrated in a poem called 'King Cholera'.

> What is my court? These cellars piled
>   With filth of many a year;
> These rooms with rotting damps defiled;
> These alleys where the sun ne'er smiled,
>   Darkling and drear!
>
> What are my perfumes? Stink and stench
>   From slaughter house and sewer;
> The oozing gas from open'd trench.
> The effluvia of the pools that drench
>   Courtyards impure.[60]

The cholera outbreak of 1831 was concentrated in the poorest
urban areas. Aware of this, some people enquired into the
statistical connection between disease and poverty. After 1837 their
efforts were aided by the Office of the Registrar General. This body
provided global figures on crude death rates and causes of death.
Supervised by William Farr, it provided numerous reports which
were crucial to the realisation that poverty killed. Its operations
were supplemented by the local investigations of doctors like
Southwood Smith. In 1838 he reported there were 14,000 cases of
'fever' in twenty of the capital's areas. Out of this total, 9,000
occurred in just seven places: Whitechapel; Lambeth; Stepney; St
George the Martyr, Bethnal Green, Holborn and St George's in the
East. These were some of the poorest parts of London. They were
associated with the unskilled, the sweated and ethnic minorities.
The same dreadful scenario was found in Liverpool. Here 'the
proportion of cases of fever occurring among the inhabitants of
cellars is about thirty-five per cent, more than it ought to be'
according to their number in the city's population.

Such statistics affected the deliberations of the members of the Select Committee on the Health of Towns in 1840. They were moved with a humanitarian concern for the poor who suffered ill health and premature death. At the same time they were concerned that these problems were costly. The nation needed healthy workers.[61] This point was emphasised by Edwin Chadwick in 1842 in the *Report on the Sanitary Condition of the Labouring Population in Great Britain*. Its 457 pages of text and appendices presented evidence from 1,000 Poor Law medical officers. This displayed the utter shortcomings of the nation's systems of drainage, sewerage and water supply. Chadwick emphasised that this situation was at its worst in overcrowded districts. Consequently, epidemics were 'caused, or aggravated, or propagated chiefly amongst the labouring classes'. The solution was better drainage and sewerage, the regular and effective removal of refuse from houses and roads, and improved water supplies.[62]

As A. S. Wohl has explained, Chadwick 'skilfully wove the most lurid details and evocative descriptions, damning statistics and damaging examples into a masterpiece of protest literature'.[63] Chadwick's aim was to emphasise that public health reform was in the interests of his upper- and middle-class readers. He contended that those who were exposed to disease were 'less susceptible of moral influences' and the effects of education than were those who were healthy. A dirty environment produced adults who were 'short-lived, improvident, reckless, and intemperate, and with habitual avidity for sensual gratifications'. Moreover, diseases could spread from the poor to those who were more prosperous. Chadwick and others believed that this happened through the miasma – the fetid air which arose from damp mounds of animal and human excreta, putrefying rubbish, dead people and slaughtered beasts. This theory was not discounted until the 1880s, when the significance of germs in the transmission of diseases was acknowledged. Yet as Michael Flinn has noted, the 'eradication of miasma was a sound instinct, and could do nothing but good'.[64]

Chadwick's report sold 100,000 copies. It was followed the next year by that of the Commission on the Health of Towns, which also advocated sanitary engineering. Despite this publicity, 'there was no great increase in general public support'. As C. H. Hume indicated, this failure led Chadwick to inaugurate a propaganda campaign.[65] It was co-ordinated via the Health of Towns

Association, which was founded in 1844. Prominent amongst its members were the future Lord Shaftesbury, Slaney and Southwood Smith. Another was Gavin, who in 1847 wrote *Unhealthiness of London*. He highlighted the lower life expectancy of townsfolk compared with rural dwellers. In Surrey 'the mean duration of life' was forty-five years, in London it was thirty-seven, and in Liverpool it was only twenty-six. Even members of the gentry could expect to die younger if they lived in a major city.[66] But as Gavin demonstrated, the poor were the worst affected by the overcrowding of towns and by an insanitary environment. In Bethnal Green, the average life expectancy of a labourer was just sixteen years; that of one of the gentry was forty-five (Document 14).

Some local authorities heeded the calls to act on public health. One of them was Liverpool. According to E. C. Midwinter, this city's Sanitary Act of 1846 was the first comprehensive health legislation in England. It was followed by a number of initiatives: the appointment of Dr W. H. Duncan as the country's first permanent municipal medical officer of health; the purchase by the Corporation of the two private companies which supplied the city with water; the building of the Rivington Pike Reservoir; and the construction of a proper sewerage system. National government was more tardy in its response to the environment of poverty. It did not pass a Public Health Act until 1848 – another year in which cholera raged across the country. This allowed the creation of local boards of health. They were empowered to levy a rate out of which they would cleanse, pave, sewer, and drain their areas. But the Act was permissive – except in those districts where the annual death rate was exceptionally high. The effects of this legislation were patchy, so much so that Midwinter was justified to call it 'a failure'.[67]

Throughout the mid-Victorian years the poor continued to live in dire surroundings which made them ill and killed them. In 1865 it was recounted that in Hunslett, Leeds, the ashpits were full 'not of ashes, but of fluid matter, up to the seat, so that the women in the houses said they had to empty everything in the streets'. One yard had twenty-six dwellings, 'two privies only, and an open drain down the centre', whilst another was 'saturated with disgusting matter'. Watercourses like the Hol Beck had become open sewers which 'spread their foul exhalations in the neighbourhoods through which they pass'. Other districts were polluted by pigsties and by works like that which boiled Russian tallow. This 'produced such an effect on those in the neighbourhood that they were unable to eat, and suffered from sore throats'.[68]

Even in progressive Liverpool, the lot of the poor was unenviable. In 1864 Shimmin reported that a fifth of the city's population lived in 3,273 courts. Some of the most atrocious were in Thomas Street. This was the residence of 'chip-sellers, rubbing-stone dealers, fruit-hawkers, cotton-pickers, saltheavers, and dock labourers, with their dependants'. In Number Six Court a widow and her five children lived in a house that was darkened by its proximity to others and which had been without water for nine months. 'The poor woman lighted a candle in order to show us what she had to put up with by reason of *the filth from the adjoining midden breaking through into her cupboard*'. In Wright Street one of the walls of a large biscuit works adjoined the privies and ashpits of Number Seven Court. Shimmin recoiled in disgust from the awareness that the heat from the factory's boiler 'must keep the filth in a state of constant fermentation'.[69]

Conditions in London were as bad, and they were exacerbated by the spread of typhus from 1861. Recently Anne Hardy argued strongly that this disease was associated with grave social dislocation.[70] She agreed with Stedman Jones that the 1860s was a time of economic crisis in the East End. The decade had begun with widespread building strikes, which had a devastating effect on the earnings of many people; silk weaving entered its final decline; and in the mid-1860s the ship-building industry collapsed. The consequences of these misfortunes were erratic employment, nutritional deficiencies and insecure living standards. These difficulties were compounded by widespread demolitions for factories, warehouses, railways and improvement schemes – all of which increased overcrowding. At same time, there was a high level of immigration 'of people with no previous experience of urban life'. The combination of these negative factors led to an 'artificial' subsistence crisis, which was not related to food shortages and excessively high prices. In these circumstances typhus thrived.

The disease was as noticeable in the cotton towns of Lancashire. These were also examples of urban crisis. They exhibited terrible distress because of mass unemployment resulting from the interruption of cotton imports from a United States of America beset by civil war. In the north-west and elsewhere, typhus declined in the 1870s. This development led Hardy to state that in epidemic terms 'life became considerably more secure for the urban poor'. The major exception to this betterment was Liverpool. Here the disease continued to be endemic, 'if generally submerged', until the later 1890s at least. It appeared mostly within older and generally low-lying districts, in which lived the poorest and most casually employed of the city's population – many of whom were Irish.[70]

For the urban poor, the mid-Victorian boom was a chimera. They did not enjoy rising living standards. Indeed, it is probable that their position deteriorated. As Ransome and Royston stated in 1866 about Manchester and Salford, 'there are good reasons why the sanitary conditions of the cottage-dwellings of the town should get worse instead of better'.[71] Their comment was as relevant to the lives of those in poverty elsewhere. Schemes which raised civic pride encroached on their limited living space and forced them to cram together ever more tightly. Their neighbourhoods were littered with more rubbish and were awash with more sewage because of overcrowding. They continued to be supplied with dank and brackish water. Their ageing, jerry-built houses became even more decrepit. Many trades became extinct. Sweating extended. Unemployment was widespread. Casual work continued unabated. And the poor continued to die at a disproportionate rate to those who were prosperous.

A limited improvement did follow. National government recognised that interference was necessary if the lives of millions of citizens were to be ameliorated. In 1872 another Public Health Act divided England into sanitary authorities, each of which had to appoint a medical officer of health. Three years later sweeping legislation laid down rules for water supply, sewage disposal, the lay out of streets and buildings, removal of nuisances, inspection of food, notification and suppression of diseases, procedures for burial, and for the control of markets, lighting and offensive trades. Acting upon these laws and on their own initiatives, a large number of local authorities became examples of municipal socialism. They took over gas and water companies and brought light and fresh drinking supplies to the neighbourhoods of the poor; they built proper sewerage systems; they closed cess pits and cess pools and replaced them with dry-pan privies or water closets; and they began to cleanse their streets and take away rubbish more effectively.

Birmingham was foremost amongst the active councils of England. It was lauded as 'the best governed city in the world'.[72] But behind the façade of Corporation Street and civic pride lay a hidden city of poverty and deprivation. In the city's west-end district of Edgbaston, each house was supplied with fresh water; in the neighbourhoods of the poor, there was just one communal tap in each yard. Rubbish was still put in ramshackle miskins (wooden sheds). And as Kathleen Dayus showed, dry-pan privies and bad housing remained common until 1914 (Document 12). Confined by their poverty in insanitary and unhealthy districts, the poor of Birmingham continued to die more often than their more prosperous fellow citizens. In 1898 in St Bartholomew's ward, over fifty per cent of the dwellings had a weekly rental of 3s 6d or less. The annual death rate in the area was 37.6 per 1,000 people. This figure dropped to 32.7 in places where the proportion of low-rent houses was between twenty-five per cent and fifty per cent. It fell drastically to 17.1 in districts where there were no houses let at 3s 6d or less a week. Six years later another report showed similar correlations for infant mortality rates.[73]

These findings were substantiated in the survey into the Floodgate Street area. Other important inferences were drawn. From 1899 to 1903, the mean annual death rate for the district was 31.57 per 1,000 people. This was ninety per cent higher than that for the artisan ward of All Saints. But even within the poor neighbourhood, life expectancies fluctuated between streets. In Fazeley Street the mean mortality rate was 21.8 per year; nearby in Park Street, the site of many lodging houses, it was a massive 63.5.[74] Research from Salford corroborated the implication that the working class was stratified by the statistics of ill health and life expectancy.

In 1904, Marr publicised a table which was compiled by Dr Howson, the Medical Officer of the Salford School Board. It gave the height, weight, chest and head circumferences of boys from three local schools. These were compared with similar measurements for public schoolboys and for boys of artisan families. The differences were striking. Poorer children were conspicuous as shorter and lighter than their counterparts in the prosperous working class and the upper class. But there were also variations between the boys of the three Salford schools. Howson attributed this situation to a variety of factors. Amongst them was the availability of light and fresh air in the neighbourhood of the schools, and the influence of a healthy diet.[75] Recent research has confirmed that physical wellbeing is important in assessments of standards of living. In particular, Roderick Floud has explained that heights and the speed of growth in childhood and adolescence are the best indicators of nutritional status. This is 'the state of the human body as it balances nutrient intake with growth, work and the defeat of disease'. Changes in nutritional status are indicated by shifts in average height, which in turn are attributed to alterations in the environment. Floud examined the average heights of males recruited to the British Army from 1750. He noted that this was a biased sample because most recruiters sought taller men, but he made allowances for this problem in his calculations. These showed that heights rose in the late 1700s and early 1800s, but declined in the second quarter of the nineteenth century. Floud suggested that physical growth was retarded 'as children struggled to combat endemic and epidemic diseases in the crowded housing of the period'. His study indicated that heights rose gradually later in the century. Still, he noted one other period when nutritional status did not seem to improve. That was towards the end of the 1800s, when there was strong evidence for rising real incomes. He surmised that this paradox could be explained by the 'severity of unemployment' and the prevalence of disease.[76] Whatever the cause, it is apparent that such factors would have been at their worst amongst the urban poor. Similarly, they would have suffered most from the inferior environmental factors which were evident earlier in the century.

In 1904 Marr indicated that for the decade 1881–90, the average expectation of life at birth was 28.78 years for a Manchester man. This was an improvement on the situation half a century before. Yet such a realisation is diminished by a comparison with the national average of 43.66 years, and one for the rural districts of 51.48.[77] Moreover, Marr's figure was not class specific. It is likely that the life expectancy of poorer Mancunians was even less than his average. They and their urban fellows continued to be excluded from the benefits of industrialisation. They worked and lived in a land which denied them a fair share of wealth, a fair share that would have given them better food, decent housing, a cleaner environment, and regular work.

The urban poor knew that they were disfranchised economically. Arthur Potts emphasised this. He lived in Whitsters Lane, Pendleton, and 'reckoned that no country in the world had worse conditions than we had'. He and his people starved and lived in places where 'hygiene was only a word'. In his neighbourhood, four dry-pan privies served seventy people. At the top of their lane was a cleansing department depot, from which fifty or sixty carts used to set out three nights per week to empty the excreta bins and the dustbins. Once collected, 'all this excreta from thousands of homes had to be carted down the Lane to the "muck docks"'. Here it was loaded onto barges and taken to be processed into fertiliser. In 1904, Potts saw his first flush toilet: 'to me as a young boy it was the eighth Wonder of the World!'[78]

Notes

1   Nunquam, 'Modern Athens. A city of slums', *Sunday Chronicle*, 5 May 1889 (thanks to Dr Mike Harrison).

2   J. C. Walters, 'No. 2. A second glance around', *Scenes in Slumland. Pen Pictures of the Black Spots in Birmingham*, articles reprinted from *Birmingham Daily Gazette*, March 1901.

3   T. J. Bass, *Down East Among the Poorest*, Birmingham, 1904, p. 22.

4   S. Marcus, 'Reading the illegible', in H. J. Dyos and M. Wolff (eds), *The Victorian City. Images and Realities, Volume II. Shapes on the Ground and a Change of Accent*, first published 1973, London, 1976 edn, p. 272.

5   V. Kiernan, 'Foreword', in F. Engels, *The Condition of the Working Class in England*, first published 1845, Harmondsworth edn, 1987, pp. 15–6.

6   W. O. Henderson, *The Life of Friedrich Engels*, two volumes, London, 1976, p. 70.

7   Marcus, 'Reading the illegible', p. 258.

8   A. Ransome and W. Royston, 'Report upon the health of Manchester and Salford during the last fifteen years', *Transactions of the National Association for the Promotion of Social Science*, London, 1866, pp. 462–3.

9   East End History Project, *Them Were the Days . . . or Were They? Life in Sunderland's East End in the 1930s*, Sunderland, 1985, p. 1.

10   G. Davis, 'Beyond the Georgian façade: the Avon Street District of Bath', in M. Gaskell (ed.), *Slums*, Leicester, 1990, p. 147.

11   R. Rodger, *Housing in Urban Britain 1780–1914*, Studies in Economic and Social History, Basingstoke, 1989, p. 7.

12 City of Birmingham Health Department, *Annual Report of the Medical Officer of Health*, Birmingham, 1880, p. 45.

13 Nunquam, 'Modern Athens'.

14 R. Williams, *London Rookeries and Colliers' Slums: A Plea for More Breathing Room*, first published 1893, New York, 1985 edn, p. 13.

15 M. P. Reeves, *Round About a Pound a Week*, first published 1913, London, 1979 edn, pp. 22-3.

16 Walters, 'No. 1. A first glance round', *Scenes in Slumland*.

17 R. Samuel, 'Comers and goers', in H. J. Dyos and M. Wolff (eds), *The Victorian City. Images and Realities, Volume I. Past and Present and Numbers of People*, first published 1973, London, 1976 edn, pp. 127–8.

18 G. Godwin, *London Shadows. A Glance at the 'Homes' of the Thousands*, first published 1854, New York, 1985 edn, pp. 20–1 and 45–6.

19 J. Hole, *The Homes of the Working Classes with Suggestions for Their Improvement*, first published 1866, New York, 1985 edn, pp. 51–5 and 161–3.

20 J. C. Walters, 'No. 10. The city of the dreadful night', *Further Scenes in Slumland. Pen Pictures of the Black Spots in Birmingham*, articles reprinted from *Birmingham Daily Gazette*, 1901.

21 J. Robinson, *The Life and Times of Francie Nichol of South Shields*, London, 1975, pp. 53–4.

22 Select Committee on the Health of Towns, *Report*, first published 1840, New York, 1985 edn, p. 39.

23 M. W. Flinn (ed.), *Report on the Sanitary Condition of the Labouring Population of Great Britain* (Chadwick's report), first published 1842, London, 1965 edn, p. 93.

24 J. Roberts, *Working-Class Housing in Nineteenth Century Manchester. The Example of John Street, Irk Town 1826–1936*, Manchester, no date, p. 18.

25 Hole, *Homes of the Working Classes*, p. 49.

26 H. Shimmin, *The Courts and Alleys of Liverpool*, first published 1864, New York, 1985 edn, pp. 3–6.

27 J. Burnett, *A Social History of Housing, 1815–1970*, Newton Abbot, 1978, p. 74.

28 C. Chinn, *Homes For People. 100 Years of Council Housing in Birmingham*, Birmingham, 1991, p. 12.

29 Northampton Arts Development, *In Living Memory. Life in 'The Boroughs'*, Northampton, 1987, pp. 68–75 (thanks to Gillian-Marie Burdett); T. H. Marr, *Housing Conditions in Manchester and Salford*, Manchester, 1904, p. 37.

30 B. Horrocks, *Reminiscences of Bolton*, Manchester, 1984, pp. 5–6.

31 *Inquiry into the Condition of the Poor of Newcastle-Upon-Tyne*, from the *Newcastle Chronicle*, Newcastle, 1850, pp. 7–8.

32 P. Sanders, *The Simple Annals. The History of an Essex and East End Family*, Gloucester, 1989, pp. 92, 107 and 119.

33 Samuel, 'Comers and goers', in Dyos and Wolff (eds), *The Victorian City*, pp. 2–3.

34 Royal Commission on the Housing of the Working Classes, *First Report*, London, 1885, pp. 7–8.

35 H. Gavin, *The Habitations of the Industrial Classes*, first published 1851, New York, 1985 edn, pp. 32–4.

36 Royal Commission on the Housing of the Working Classes, *First Report*, p. 8.

37 Marr, *Housing Conditions in Manchester and Salford*, pp. 28–33.

38 City of Birmingham Health Department, 'Sanitary condition of the city', in *Annual Report of the Medical Officer of Health*, Birmingham, 1890, p. 30.

39 A. Sherwell, *Life in West London. A Study and a Contrast*, London, 1897 edn, pp. 15–24.

40 J. E. Mercer, 'The conditions of life in Angel Meadow', *Transactions of the Manchester Statistical Society*, Manchester, 1897, p. 161

41 City of Birmingham Health Department, *Report on Industrial Employment of Married Women and Infantile Mortality*, Birmingham, 1910, p. 3.

42 Select Committee on the Health of Towns, *Report*, first published 1840, New York, 1985 edn, p. 51.

43 Hole, *The Homes of the Working Classes*, pp. 49 and 96.

44 H. J. Dyos and D. A. Reeder, 'Slums and suburbs', in Dyos and Wolff (eds), *The Victorian City. Volume I*, p. 361

45 J. Davis, 'Jennings' Buildings and the Royal Borough. The construction of the underclass in mid-Victorian England', in D. Feldman and G. Stedman Jones (eds), *Metropolis. London. Histories and Representations since 1800*, London, 1989, pp. 16–7.

46 T. Beames, *The Rookeries of London, Past, Present and Prospective*, London, 1851, pp. 41–3.

47 J. A. Yelling, *Slums and Slum Clearance in Victorian London*, London, 1986, pp. 34, 65–6, 123–5.

48 Royal Commission on the Housing of the Working Classes, *First Report*, p. 19.

49 J. R. Kellet, 'The railway as an agent of internal change in Victorian cities', in R. J. Morris and R. Rodger (eds), *The Victorian City. A Reader in British Urban History 1820–1914*, London, 1993, p. 185.

50 J. Simmons, 'The power of the railway', in Dyos and Wolff (eds), *The Victorian City. Volume I*, p. 297.

51 C. Chinn, *Homes For People*, Birmingham, 1991, pp. 5–6.

52 S. M. Gaskell, 'Introduction', in M. Gaskell (ed.), *Slums*, Leicester, 1990, p. 12.

53 Select Committee on the Health of Towns, *Report*, pp. 39–47.

54 H. Gavin, *Unhealthiness of London*, first published 1847, New York, 1985 edn, p. 40.

55 Select Committee on the Health of Towns, *Report*, p. 47; J. Hogg, *London As It Is*, first published 1837, New York, 1985 edn, pp. 237–8.

56 Royal Commission on Large Towns, *First Report*, London, 1844, pp. 210–1.

57 Gavin, *The Habitations of the Industrial Classes*, pp. 42–3.

58 A. Mackay, 'Letter II. Sanitary conditions', *Morning Chronicle*, 14 December 1850.

59 Special Meeting of the Balsall Heath Local Board of Health, *Report of Dr Ballard*, 11 January 1873.

60 G. Godwin, *Town Swamps and Social Bridges*, first published 1859, Leicester, 1972 edn, p. 49.

61 Select Committee on the Health of Towns, *Report*, pp. 34–49.

62 Flinn (ed.), *Report on the Sanitary Condition of the Labouring Population*, pp. 192–5.

63 A. S. Wohl, *Endangered Lives. Public Health in Victorian Britain*, London, 1984 edn, p. 147.

64 Flinn (ed.), *Report on the Sanitary Condition of the Labouring Population*, pp. 63 and 192–5.

65 C. H. Hume, 'The public health movement', in J. T. Ward (ed.), *Popular Movements, c. 1830–1850*, Basingstoke, 1970, p. 195.

66 Gavin, *The Habitations of the Industrial Classes*, pp. 5–11.

67 E. C. Midwinter, *Victorian Social Reform*, Seminar Studies in History, Harlow, 1968, pp. 33–6.

68 Hole, *The Homes of the Working Classes*, pp. 129–30.

69 Shimmin, *The Courts and Alleys of Liverpool*, pp. 16 and 55.

70 A. Hardy, 'Urban famine or urban crisis? Typhus in the Victorian city', in Morris and Rodger (eds), *The Victorian City*, pp. 209–40.

71 Ransome and Royston, 'Report upon the health of Manchester and Salford', p. 463.

72 A. Briggs, *Victorian Cities*, Harmondsworth, 1968, pp.194–206, 217–32.

73 City of Birmingham Health Department, *Annual Report of the Medical Officer of Health*, Birmingham, 1899, p. 8; City of Birmingham Health Department, *Special Report of the Medical Officer of Health on Infant Mortality in the City of Birmingham*, Birmingham, 1904, pp. 10–11.

74 City of Birmingham Health Department, 'The Floodgate Street area', *Annual Report of the Medical Officer of Health*, Birmingham, 1904, pp. 7–8.

75 Marr, *Housing Conditions in Manchester and Salford*, pp. 21–2.

76 R. H. Floud, 'Standards of living and industrialisation', in A. Digby and C. Feinstein (eds), *New Directions in Economic and Social History, Volume 1*, Basingstoke, 1989, pp. 117–29.

77 Marr, *Housing Conditions in Manchester and Salford*, p. 20.

78 A. Potts, *Whitsters Lane. Recollections of Pendleton and the Manchester Cotton Trade*, Manchester 1985, pp. 21–2.

4

Reactions to poverty

Poverty: punishment and philanthropy

Poverty evoked different reactions. The poor had no option but to
cope as best they could with low incomes, bad housing, ill health
and an insanitary environment. Upper- and middle-class people
were more fortunate. They could choose their response. As Gavin
regretted, some were apathetic and indifferent 'to the sufferings
and frightful devastation of life, which are proved to be constantly
going on'.[1] Others took a negative interest. They supposed that
most of the able-bodied poor were lazy people who had to be
forced to earn a living. This assumption underlay the provisions of
the Poor Law Amendment Act of 1834.

The legislation grouped parishes into unions. Each was
empowered to levy a rate on property owners, out of which relief
was to be given to applicants. But no longer were paupers to
receive this help in their own homes. They had to go into a
workhouse, which each union was required to build. Once inside
these institutions, paupers were put into one of seven groups
according to their age, gender and physical wellbeing. This meant
that families were split up, as Will Crooks recalled with bitterness.
During the 1850s his father lost his arm in an industrial accident,
and his mother was unable to support the family despite her
strenuous efforts. She asked for help from the 'parish'. It was
refused. Her husband and children had to go into 'the big
poorhouse down by the Millwall Docks'. Here 'they were put into

102

a bare room like a vault, the father and two sons, while the three sisters were taken they knew not where'. The next day, Will and his brother were separated from their father. A few weeks later, the two young boys were taken to a 'poor law school' and were parted from each other. In later life Crooks swore that 'every day I spent in that school is burnt into my soul'. Fortunately, his mother strove to increase her income so that the guardians would allow her family out of the workhouse.[2]

Anne Digby has recognised that the cruelty of the workhouse system was rooted not in its material deprivation but in its psychological harshness.[3] It stripped paupers of their self-respect and tore from them their dignity. They ceased to be individuals and were treated as inmates. Their lives were subjected to strict rules, which aimed to 'enforce industry, order, punctuality and cleanliness'. To pay for their food and shelter, they were given hard jobs like breaking stones, picking oakum, cleaning floors and washing clothes. It was felt that this austere regime would deter most labourers from applying for relief and so encourage them to support themselves. Only the truly destitute would knock at the workhouse doors. Here paupers would be separated and be unable to spread their bad habits to others amongst the working class.

Karl Marx proclaimed that the new Poor Law made pauperism a crime to be suppressed and punished. Workhouses were 'the *revenge* of the bourgeoisie upon the poor who appeal to its charity'.[4] It is difficult to dismiss this opinion. It is one that was held by the poor themselves. They hated workhouses. In 1865 Thomas Archer explained that their utter repugnance 'may be inferred from the sufferings to which they continually submit' rather than apply for indoor relief.[5] Some twenty-five years later, the same loathing was evident in Summer Lane, Birmingham. During a bad winter, Reverend Mantle visited the homes of unemployed men. They and their families were starving, cold and weak, and 'have nothing but the workhouse before them unless the weather changes'. But Mantle was impressed by 'such an aversion to the "house" as I should not have credited, had I not heard it with my own ears'.[6]

By this period workhouse authorities had become more humane. They realised that most of those entering their institutions were not able-bodied adults. They were orphans, abandoned children, deserted wives, widows, the sick, the maimed, the mentally ill and the aged. According to M. A. Crowther, in order to cope with the needs of these people, workhouses became 'an embryonic social service'.[7] They had to provide hospitals, schools and facilities for the elderly. At the same time, in their casual wards they gave shelter on a nightly basis to the homeless and for those tramping in search of jobs. Yet whether or not conditions in workhouses became better, they were institutions founded on the principles of punishment, deterrence, humiliation and the loss of independence. These features continued to be prominent.

Robert Roberts recalled that workhouse was 'a word that rang like a knell' among the working class of Salford in the early years of the twentieth century.[8] It tolled most for the elderly who entered its gates. If they were married, they were separated from their partners. The experience of seeing this happen to his grandparents led a Mr Ingle to write a music-hall song which protested at their treatment. William Boxall remembered that the artist 'stood at the footlights' to sing the last verse, which was 'a vitriolic attack on the Board of Guardians'.[9] Elderly paupers were condemned to a life sentence with no remission. Death was the only escape, and even then there was the ultimate degradation of a burial in a pauper's grave. But the aged were not the only ones who continued to suffer the indignities enforced by the new Poor Law. So too did children. Doreen Molloy's father had vivid memories of life in the Birmingham workhouse in the early 1900s.

> After his mother was widowed, she was sent there, with her four young sons, but she disappeared, leaving them there. He wrote about those awful years, the dreadful food, the sack like clothes he had to wear, that made his body sore. How he was made to witness his little brother being stripped naked and being caned with a thin stick, because he tried to run away. He was always having to say prayers, thanking God for having a roof over his head and for his food.[10]

Even now, elderly working-class English people recall the workhouse gates as 'The Archway of Tears'.

In 1834 there were about 1.26 million paupers in Britain, making up 8.8% of the population. By 1900 only 2.5% of Britons were in receipt of Poor Law relief. These figures suggested that poverty was a minor problem. It was not, as was shown by the researches of Booth, Rowntree and others, and by the memories of those who were poor. A fall in the number of paupers can be explained by the working-class loathing of workhouses as much as it can by rising standards of living. But if the new Poor Law resulted in fewer paupers officially, it did not cause an end to outdoor relief. The practice continued, especially in industrial parishes. Here the number of able-bodied paupers was small when trade was good but became large during a depression. On these occasions it was impossible to relieve them all in a workhouse, as Rose showed.[11]

Outdoor relief was common in London up to 1914. In her autobiographical novel set in Bermondsey, Kathleen Woodward recalled the indignities faced by those who applied for help from the parish. Her father was a skilled man but was 'sick with an illness which left him half invalid for the rest of his life'. Consequently her mother contrived the survival of her family by assiduously cleaning the clothes of those who were better off. But 'the slightest falling-off of the supply of washing threatened our slender resources'. On these occasions, an application for relief was made to the local board of guardians. Woodward remembered that the help given was a weekly sum of rice, which the family ate 'until we were sick'. Her mother 'modestly appealed for a little change', and she and her five children were 'summoned peremptorily' before the local board. The twelve men and women 'fired question after question' at Ellen Woodward. She 'grew more dogged' and was told rice was very nutritious. Her request for a variation in the family's diet was in vain. Woodward commented that life 'might have been less difficult for my mother if she had been able to relax her pride, if she had been more hesitating, more diffident in the presence of her "superiors"'. Independent, strong-willed and determined, Ellen Woodward resented the patronising attitudes of the guardians. They 'provoked her to the utmost contempt and impatience, and ground a fine edge to her tongue'.[12]

From the 1870s the inspectors of the Local Government Board pressed guardians to end the practice of outdoor relief. Digby indicated that they were helped by the activities and publicity of the Charity Organisation Society (COS).[13] This was started in the capital in 1869, at the end of a decade of economic distress, bread riots and a fear of disorder amongst the unemployed. According to W. A. Bailward in 1895, the COS was based on two beliefs: first, that the destitute should be dealt with by the Poor Law; and second, that charities should help 'those cases in which the application of the workhouse test would be unduly harsh'.[14]

There was a proliferation of philanthropic bodies in England. In 1872, Jerrold stated that those in London attested 'by their income and various forms, the zeal with which the Rich come to the side of the wounded in the fight' for life. He listed hospitals, refuges, orphanages, soup kitchens, 'retreats kept for the old by the heroic Little Sisters of the Poor', and institutions for the blind, the deaf and dumb, discharged prisoners, and fallen women.[15] Led by C. S. Loch, the members of the COS were concerned that 'crafty paupers' could survive by gaining help from various charities, none of which investigated properly the circumstances of those who appealed to them for aid. According to this view, overlapping and indiscriminate alms giving was an evil. It abetted the undeserving poor and led respectable workers to imitate their bad example.

The COS aimed to overcome these problems by co-ordinating the philanthropic activities in each Poor Law union. Claimants for help were registered and assessed by officers. Their information was passed to a committee on which the local charities were represented. This body decided whether the applicants were deserving of help. The role of the officers in the operations of the COS was vital. It was thought that they would establish a personal relationship between the giver and the receiver of charity. In so doing, it was felt that they would re-establish a bond between the rich and poor in working-class areas. And through the influence and guidance of the officers, it was maintained that the beneficiaries of charity would learn to become independent. As Derek Fraser has recognised, 'the belief in self-help as the supreme virtue, coupled with the notion that most poverty was the result of personal failing, was central to the COS outlook'.[16] This interpretation is underlined by the recollections of Margaret Mabey. She worked voluntarily for the COS in south London in the 1930s. In retrospect she thought that her committee was concerned with 'the maintaining of strict moral standards' and not with the relief of suffering.[17] This is a point Stedman Jones has made.[18] But as Alan J. Kidd stressed for Manchester, the official theory of Poor Law relief and charity 'never completely dominated the practice of private giving by individuals or societies'. The language of deserving and undeserving poor may have been authoritative, but some charities 'relieved categories of the poor who should, according to the orthodox theory of social policy, have been dealt with by the Poor Law'. A prime example of this nonconformity was the Wood Street Mission. Set up during the urban crisis of the 1860s it aimed to redeem destitute and neglected children. Like many others, its motivators were certain that crime was connected to bad housing and a lack of education and moral guidance. Yet from the 1880s the Mission 'responded to what was increasingly seen as the major social problem of the late Victorian city, that of adult male unemployment'. Meals were provided for these men and from 1902 a night shelter was available for those of them who were homeless. By this time the Wood Street Mission had become notorious for acting in a way contrary to the tenets of the Manchester and Salford District Provident Society – the equivalent of the COS. Despite this unorthodox approach, Kidd argued that the Mission refined and strengthened 'the middle-class response to social crisis'. This was for two reasons. Its aid staved off unrest in winters of high unemployment and distress; and its policies were aimed at the religious and moral redemption of the outcast poor.[19]

A similar situation was obvious in Summer Lane, Birmingham. Here the Reverend Mantle of the Hatchett Street Mission organised soup kitchens for jobless men in the harsh winter of 1891. Like its Manchester counterpart, this place did not require a work test of the unemployed. Similarly, it was associated with evangelicalism and Wesleyan Methodism.[20] Other charities in the city were more in tune with COS philosophy. In 1888, a girls' night shelter was opened at Bath Row. It offered a temporary home 'to any girl requiring immediate help – to await investigation, and be returned to her friends, or placed in one of the homes already existing'.[21]

Rose emphasised that charity was a major Victorian growth industry, 'providing aid for an increasing number of specialist needs and unpaid employment for middle-class ladies'.[22] In 1872, Jerrold observed that some of these women were motivated by vanity, but many others were impelled by more positive reasons, and often they became active in social reform.[23] As with Elizabeth Gaskell in the 1840s, some of them believed that it was their Christian duty to help those in poverty. They were impressed by Biblical stories like those of Dives and Lazarus. This personalised the split between the rich and the poor and showed that the wealthy would be punished by God if they did not help their less fortunate fellows.[24] Other women became involved in social matters for the same reasons as Octavia Hill. She had 'an unshakeable belief in the moral superiority of the middle and upper classes', feeling that the working class needed to be taught good standards of living. Peter Malpass explained that this authoritarian approach informed her work with the COS and in the housing field.[25] Beatrice Webb was another person who had elitist notions, but in a crucial respect she differed from Hill. She was affected by 'a consciousness of sin', a conviction that 'the industrial organisation, which had yielded rent, interest, and profits on a stupendous scale, had failed to provide a decent livelihood and tolerable conditions for the majority of Great Britain'.[26] As Harris has pointed out, often Webb's thinking was muddled, but she was devoted to the salvation of humanity.[27] This was to be achieved through socialism.

Thousands more middle-class women helped the poor, not because of religious, political or moral beliefs but because it was the right thing to do. One of them was Mrs Caswell. In the early 1900s she was active in setting up an infant welfare centre in poverty-stricken Floodgate Street, Birmingham (Document 15). She was helped by Jessie Lloyd, of the Quaker banking family. They were supported by local councillors and the city's medical officer of health, and they were given cod-liver oil, Cow and Gate dried milk, Glaxo and other medical supplies by Southall Brothers – another of the city's firms which was owned by Quakers. The centre started off more as 'a social', where there was help for local mothers 'in caring for their babies, hygiene, simple remedies, first aid etc'. Later it employed a trained nurse and doctor. At first, their presence led to a dwindling in the numbers of mothers who came for advice. They 'did not like authority' or the 'babies to be stripped, weighed and have Drs. comments on feeding, clothing'. This reluctance wore off. The infant welfare centre came to provide a valuable service in the area, as did the Women's Settlement in Summer Lane from 1899.[28] This building housed a medical care committee, a crippled children's union, and clubs for girls; and from it, voluntary helpers made Provident collections for saving purposes. The settlement had close associations with the local COS and with the University of Birmingham, providing a base for trainee social workers.[29]

There were similar places elsewhere. In London, there was a women's university settlement in Blackfriars; the Victoria Women's Settlement was in Liverpool; and in Leeds there was the Red

House.[30] There were also a large number of settlements aimed at men. All were modelled on an institution named after Arnold Toynbee, who coined the term the 'industrial revolution'. He saw this as a process which had created middle-class wealth at the cost of working-class suffering. According to Donald Read, his guilt at this state of affairs led him to 'put his social concern to the test in the East End of London'.[31] He went to work in the parish of St Jude's, Whitechapel, but died at a young age in 1883.

Samuel Barnett was the vicar of this area. He was determined that neither Toynbee nor his example should be forgotten. It was his belief that there should be a permanent place of residence in the East End at which upper- and middle-class men could settle for a time. Their presence would have a dual effect. They could help the working class and learn of their problems, whilst the local people would be raised up socially and intellectually by the example of the settlers. Barnett's vision was shared by others, especially at Keble College, Oxford University. With their financial backing he was able to open Toynbee Hall in 1884. The settlement's supporters had three main objectives: the provision of 'education and the means of recreation and enjoyment for the people in the poorer districts of London and other great cities'; the investigation 'into the condition of the poor'; and the advancement of 'plans calculated to promote their welfare'.[32] Toynbee Hall was followed soon after by Oxford House in Bethnal Green, linked to Baliol College. It was more religious in tone, whilst its emphasis was more on clubs for the working class rather than on educational activities. By 1914 there were another twenty-five settlements in the capital, with twelve elsewhere in England.

During the 1840s the writings of Mrs Gaskell and Disraeli showed that there was a concern to re-establish social intercourse between the rich and the poor. This belief was most evident amongst clergymen like Kingsley and Frederick Denison Maurice. Both of them were Christian socialists. They wanted to act as mediators between the classes and they called for social reforms. Still, Stedman Jones has maintained that the ideas behind the settlement movement 'grew out of the crisis of the 1860s'.[33] In that decade a number of middle-class people had also felt that it was important to break down the barriers which separated the classes. One of them was Edward Denison. He argued that the East End needed a resident gentry. As Briggs and Macartney have put it, 'this class of well-to-do people with leisure had a responsibility to help the less fortunate by living alongside them'.[34]

Denison himself settled in Stepney. But according to Stedman Jones, 'the character of East End life filled him with disgust' and after eight months he abandoned the place.[35] Others agreed with his feeling that middle-class people should live amongst the poor, and they were more firm in adhering to his philosophy. K. S. Inglis has stated that there were a number of clergymen 'whose family, education and acquaintance could easily have won them cosy rural livings,' yet they chose to work in the parishes of the poor.[36] Amongst them was J. R. Green. In the late 1860s he settled as a vicar in Stepney rather than in the West End. Another was Barnett himself. He moved to St Jude's in 1874, and within a few years he was encouraging Oxford University undergraduates to visit his parish.

For all their dedication, these men were few and their impact was limited. According to Hennock, this situation changed because of the resurgence of publicity about poverty in the early 1880s. This 'created the widespread concern and desire for action that provided Barnett with a receptive audience for his views and enabled him to place the settlement of university men amongst the poor on a regular and more permanent basis'.[37] The results of this action were impressive. Settlements became important centres of social work, helping to improve the health and welfare of those in poverty. At the same time, many settlers were affected profoundly by their experiences. Robert R. Hyde was one of them. A vicar in Hoxton, he was also active in the Maurice Hostel Settlement for ten years from 1906. During his time there, 'no day was ever dull, no two days ever alike, and the tasks demanded the whole of one's physical, mental and spiritual powers'. Hyde made another point. Many settlers went on to make important contributions to social good and to hold 'positions of authority in every walk of life'.[38] Some of these people were to have a significant influence on the formulation and implementation of social policy. William Beveridge, the man credited as the architect of the Welfare State, was a subwarden of Toynbee Hall; whilst E. G. Howarth, co-author of the study on West Ham, was 'head of the house for residents' at Stratford, a place connected to Trinity College, Oxford.

Yet the settlement movement was based on a certainty of social superiority. This was made clear by the word 'settlement' itself. It resonated with the assurance that the poor had to be raised up to the standards of middle-class people. This language differed little from that of religious missionaries who felt that they had to civilise and Christianise the poor. Its implications were deep. Indigenous working-class culture was demeaned, whilst the responses of the poor themselves to poverty were ignored. Most settlers subscribed readily to the view that they knew best. In George Lansbury's opinion, they gained more from the settlement movement than did the poor.[39] This interpretation is too scathing, but certainly not all residents were motivated by a concern with the plight of the poor. Some were caught up in the vogue of slumming. In the words of D. B. McIlhiney, 'partly from a real desire to help, partly to satisfy their own voyeuristic curiosity, fashionable West Enders descended on the East'.[40]

These people were ridiculed by the novelist Arthur Morrison in *A Child of the Jago* (1896). The focus of his disdain was the People's Palace on the Mile End Road. This building was the inspiration of Walter Besant, another novelist, who had written about the East End of London in 1882 in *All Sorts and Conditions of Men*. Constructed with funds from the Beaumont Trust, the People's Palace had sporting clubs and 'the finest gymnasium in London'. In addition it gave cheap musical concerts and occasional exhibitions 'of arts and crafts of all kind'. Besant wanted it to be a cultural beacon in a district which was 'unparalleled in its meanness and its monotony'.[41] In the words of Deborah E. B. Weiner, the structure itself gave visual form to the contribution of West End charity to the East End. Similarly, its operations were run by the middle class and not by local people, whilst many of those who used its facilities were not the poor but were the skilled of the working class and members of the lower middle class.[42] Morrison attacked these features with biting wit. He himself had worked for a time at the People's Palace, and knew it well. In his novel it became the East End Elevation Mission and Pansophical Institute (Document 16).

Poverty: physical inefficiency and social reform

In *Mary Barton* (1848) Elizabeth Gaskell described 'a thorough specimen of Manchester man'. John Barton was 'born of factory workers, and himself bred up in youth, and living in manhood, among the mills'. In height he was 'below the middle size and slightly made; there was almost a stunted look about him; and his wan, colourless face, gave you the idea, that in his childhood he had suffered from the scanty living consequent upon bad times, and improvident habits'. The female factory workers of the town were as marked out by their appearance. They had sallow complexions and irregular features, but they also manifested 'an acuteness and intelligence of countenance, which has often been noticed in a manufacturing population'.[43]

The urban poor did tend to be small, slightly built and pallid of skin. They were made that way by their inadequate diet, by the polluted environment in which they had to live and by their dreadful working conditions. Their look continued to impress observers, amongst them John Edward Morgan. He was a physician at a hospital in Salford and Honorary Secretary of the Manchester and Salford Sanitary Association, in which position he drew up weekly and quarterly reports on the health of the local people. In particular, Morgan felt that the urban poor were distinguished by 'a want of stamina', underdeveloped muscular systems, an 'impoverished state of blood', an unbalanced nervous system, decaying teeth, enlarged glands, dry and parched skin, and scanty and withered hair. He attributed their degeneracy to town life, emphasising the healthiness of rural dwellers by comparison. In 1865 he presented his findings to the Social Science Congress, calling his paper *The Danger of the Deterioration of Race from the Too Rapid Increase of Great Cities*.[44]

Morgan's ideas inspired interest but not too much anxiety. At the time of his writing, Britain was the greatest industrial, economic and imperial power in the world. But in the 1880s this supremacy was threatened, and beliefs in physical inefficiency became more apparent. Five years into the decade, James Cantlie worried that London's 'puny and ill-developed' poor would have an adverse effect on Britain's imperial standing.[45] In 1889, J. Milner Fothergill extended this argument and infused it with social Darwinian theory and racist thought. He declared that urban life was so deleterious to the physique that the children and grandchildren of 'town denizens' became successively more degenerate. Measuring this downward progress, by the seventh generation 'they would be tiny little objects – mannikins merely, a

112

race of dwarfs'. Left to itself, nature would kill off these people, and their place would be taken by fresh rural migrants. But the course of natural selection was perverted by the interference of man. In the past, 'plague, pestilence and famine killed off the weak'; now they survived because 'philanthropy has insisted on protecting delicate organisms'. Fothergill was convinced that the urban poor were 'a physically inferior race', which had reverted to an earlier and lowlier ethnic form. Small and dark, they were akin to the Celto-Iberians. Unlike them, 'the rustic remains an Anglo-Dane'. By their blonde hair and blue eyes they were connected to the Norse, 'the highest type of mankind'.[46]

The theory of urban degeneration influenced many people. Amongst them was Llewellyn Smith, a contributor to Booth's survey. He believed that the inferior physical condition of townsfolk meant that they were dominant in the casual market and were more likely to be poor. Conversely, he felt that rural migrants were prominent in skilled and responsible work. As a result, he proposed that the wide extent of poverty in the East End was connected to 'the comparatively low proportion of provincial immigrants in the district'. Stedman Jones showed the fallacies in these arguments. First, there was 'no correlation between skill, responsibility, and provincial upbringing'. Second, in the older, inner industrial perimeter of the capital there was a higher incidence of London-born people – but this 'was a symptom of a pre-existing malaise'. The area was home to most of the capital's traditional crafts, many of which were declining or becoming sweated trades. Consequently, rural migrants avoided the district and favoured the suburbs.[47]

Still, the idea persisted that town life was a harmful influence. Philanthropists like Dr Barnardo took orphans and abandoned children and sent them to the open spaces of Canada and Australia. Social imperialists like the journalist Arnold White also advocated the emigration of those who had not 'sunk into the semi-nomadic conditions of casual labour in the great cities'. To improve the health of the children of the poor who stayed behind, they called for gym training in schools, the opening of parks in urban areas, and free school meals. They proposed further government interference in housing and sanitary matters. Like White, they were certain that overcrowded dwellings and the one-room system 'forges incest, illegitimacy, juvenile prostitution, drunkenness, dirt, disease and a death-rate higher than that of Grosvenor Square'. They also supported negative eugenics, arguing that the quality of the race could be improved by the sterilisation of the unfit and by the ending of alien immigration. It was held that these measures were essential if Britain were to maintain its power.[48]

As Helen Jones has explained, the concern over the physical, mental and moral deterioration of the British race became an obsession in the early years of the twentieth century.[49] The catalyst for this transformation was the Boer War. In 1901 White wrote that in Manchester 11,000 men volunteered for army service in a ten-month period from the outbreak of hostilities. Eight thousand of them 'were found to be physically unfit to carry a rifle and stand the fatigues of discipline'. Of the 3,000 who were accepted for the military, 'only 1,200 attained the moderate standard of muscular power and chest measurement required'.[50] These figures inspired apprehension, as did the sentiment that the city-bred British troops performed badly against the country-raised Boers. There seemed to be other indications that Britain was becoming a nation of physical inefficients. It was believed that large numbers of healthy people were emigrating, whilst the birth rate of the fit middle class was declining. Ironically, only the urban poor were doing their national duty by having large families. The decay of the Empire appeared likely, especially in the face of intense competition from Germany, which had healthy workers and soldiers.

In these circumstances the idea of national efficiency cut across political boundaries, and it was subscribed to by socialists like Jack London (Document 17). In 1901 this American 'went down into the under-world' of the capital 'with an attitude like that of an explorer'. Dressed as a working man he travelled through the East End, stopping in the casual wards of workhouses and in rented rooms. He described the urban poor as unintelligent, animal-like and 'unable to render efficient service to England in the world struggle for industrial supremacy'.[51] They were the people of hell, the people of the abyss. His language resembled that of Engels. In the 1840s this German socialist was certain that 'only a physically degenerate race, robbed of all humanity, degraded, reduced morally and physically to bestiality, could feel comfortable and at home' in the slums of Manchester.[52] Both men blamed capitalism for the degradation of the urban poor. Still, Engels did believe that urbanisation was a positive force because it polarised society into the bourgeoisie and the proletariat. Inevitably this development would lead to a revolution by the workers and the overthrow of capitalism. But for London, city life was an unnatural existence for humans.

Following the Boer War, the Conservative government set up an Inter-Departmental Committee on Physical Deterioration. As Harris has indicated, 'this body aired many degenerationist fears', but the vast majority of its witnesses 'came down in favour of an environmentalist point of view'. This is an important recognition. Whilst the effects of 'drink, pollution, malnutrition and disease *were* perceived as hereditary, they were also seen as reversible by wise social policies – and the effects of the latter were seen as in turn transmissible to future generations'.[33] Such thinking led to a recognition that the State needed to act. The Committee recommended that there should be medical inspections of school children and the provision of meals for those who were poor. But these proposals did not indicate that the poor were to be exonerated from blame for the ill health of their children. In particular, the members of the Committee cast guilt on mothers. They were declared to be ill prepared in home management, and they were castigated for going out to work and neglecting their domestic responsibilities. Such reactions manifested a striking inability to understand both the family economy of the poor and the coping strategies which necessitated female employment. They were patronising, based on ignorance, and redolent of class prejudice.[34]

Many school boards were involved already in social work with children. In the Liberal government of 1906 there was an increasing number of politicians who were amenable to an extension of such operations. They felt that as the birth rate fell so the value of children as assets to the nation increased. According to J. R. Hay this meant that 'priority should be given to ensuring the health and efficiency of the next generation'.[35] At the same time, the Liberals had to react for the first time to the demands of a significant group of Labour MPs, called by Fraser 'the symbol of the distress of the masses'.[36] They tended to represent the organised, skilled and men of the working class, but they were firm in pressing for social reform. In 1906 they persuaded the Liberal government to introduce the Education (Provision of Meals) Act. The next year a clause in the Education (Administrative Provisions) Act authorised school medical inspections. This latter measure was the result largely of the efforts of Sir Robert Morant, Permanent Secretary of the Board of Education, a former settler and someone who was concerned with national efficiency. Read stated that, in retrospect, the two pieces of legislation marked a new beginning in British social legislation.[57]

These measures were followed in 1908 by the introduction of old-age pensions, at 5s a week for individuals who earned less than £21 a year. This was a limited response to poverty which was caused by old age. The poor had shorter lives than those who were better off financially, yet the benefit was given only to those who were aged seventy and over. There had been agitation for such a measure since the 1880s, and Hay believed that it was a product partly 'of statistical investigation which proved the extent of poverty among the old and the impossibility of attributing it solely to moral failure'.[58] Yet whilst the reform may have been motivated mostly by humanitarianism, there was a practical consideration behind it. It was hoped that pensions would reduce the number of aged paupers and so lessen pressure on boards of guardians. For all these provisos, the benefit was non-contributory and it was paid through the Post Office. Fraser made plain the importance of these features. They meant that pensions were 'quite separate from the Poor Law and immune from its moral stigma'.[59]

In some respects, a more radical piece of legislation was the Trades Board Act of 1909. This fixed minimum wages and maximum hours of work in four sweated occupations: tailoring; box making; lace making; and chain making. It resulted from the pressure of women's organisations, a campaign by the *Daily Mail*, and the urgings of politicians like the Labour MP Ramsay MacDonald. But it should not be forgotten that since the late 1840s there had been a concern about sweating and calls to act against the system. In the same year as this legislation, the Chancellor of the Exchequer put forward a budget to raise money 'to wage implacable war against poverty and squalidness'. The proposals of Lloyd George indicated a shift from indirect to direct taxation, and they signified that the rich would have to contribute more to the State. John Grigg stated that this initiative was 'truly progressive'. The sums raised were to pay for old-age pensions and 'to make some further provision for the sick, for the invalided, for widows and orphans'.[60] Because of a depression in certain industries, the unemployed were added to this list of those who needed help from the state. There was pressure from trade unionists and Labour MPs to alleviate the problems caused by joblessness, and Lloyd George's personal beliefs led him to sympathise with their calls. Influenced by Beveridge, now a senior civil servant at the Board of Trade, the Liberals introduced voluntary labour exchanges in 1910.

The following year, Part I of the National Insurance Act gave unemployment benefit to workers in industries which were prone to cyclical depressions, such as shipbuilding and construction. The scheme was paid for by contributions from employees, employers and the State, and it gave those out of work 7s a week for a maximum of fifteen weeks in any twelve months. It did not respond to the problems caused by underemployment, casual work and irregular earnings.

Part II of the Act applied to all regularly employed manual workers who were over sixteen and who earned less than £160 a year. It gave sickness benefit for thirteen weeks at a weekly rate of 10s for men and 7s 6d for women. For both genders, these sums dropped to 5s a week for the next thirteen weeks, and thereafter to a weekly disability allowance of 5s. The measure also provided medical and sanatorium care, and it gave a lump-sum payment of 30s to the expectant wives of insured men. Although small, at least this amount was enough to pay for the attendance of a doctor or a midwife at the birth of a child. The benefits were paid for by weekly contributions of 4d from employees, 3d from employers, and 2d from the State. Helen Jones has made the pertinent point that 'roughly 90% of women were not part of the formal economy' and so were excluded from the scheme.[61] So were self-employed street traders, many of whom suffered from low incomes. The measure was inspired by notions of relief and not of prevention. In the words of the Labour leader Keir Hardie, 'insurance was a porous plaster to cover the disease that poverty causes'. The Act could also be seen as a political ploy. As Fraser put it, social insurance 'was deliberately used as a means of making socialism less likely'.[62]

Poverty and the residuum

Helen Jones argued convincingly that the National Insurance Act was aimed at promoting the physical efficiency of the male

117

breadwinner and the avoidance of pauperism.[63] Hay has added another important observation. Just as old-age pensions were denied to those 'who habitually failed to work according to his ability, opportunity and need', so too was insurance benefit refused to workers who were dismissed for misconduct. These clauses made clear 'the desire to provide decent treatment and social incentives for the respectable, and to separate them from the residuum'.[64] According to Himmelfarb, this term was noticeable from the 1840s. She stated that 'it is significant that the same words – 'residuum', 'refuse', 'offal' – were used to denote the sewage waste that constituted the sanitary problem and the human waste that constituted the social problem'. In her opinion, Mayhew's investigations into the street folk 'gave evidence of the persistence, in the midst of the greatest metropolis of the world, of an archaic, anarchic, barbaric people'. Uncouth and immoral, they were distinguished by a 'culture of poverty'. They flouted the values of society by their licentiousness and their unwillingness to work regularly, and they passed on their deviant behaviour to their children.

Himmelfarb showed that Mayhew was not alone in identifying a group of people who were poor because of pathological rather than economic reasons. Mary Carpenter was a leading supporter of reformatory schools, and in 1852 she stated that there was a very strong dividing line 'between the labouring and the "ragged" class, a line of demarcation not drawn by actual poverty'. The latter group was marked out not only by their worn and tattered clothes but also by dirty homes and a seedy lifestyle.[65] Archer described the 'ragged' in 1865. He called them a dangerous class, 'occupying a position between the pauper and the convict'. The young men were 'half casual labourer half thief', and the young women were 'half street hawker half prostitute'.[66] For Marx, these people were part of the lumpenproletariat. This was 'the social scum, that passively rotting mass thrown off by the lowest layers of the old society'. It was the antithesis of the proletariat, and was potentially counter-revolutionary.[67]

Observers robbed the so-called 'ragged' of their membership of the working class and they stole from them their humanity. Hollingshead wrote that they 'are always oozing onto the pavements and into the gutters' from their 'colonies'. One such was New Court in Whitechapel. It was 'a nest of thieves, filled with thick-lipped, broad-featured, rough-haired, ragged women, and hulking, leering men'. These people seemed un-English. The faces that peered out of the narrow windows 'are yellow and repulsive; some are the faces of Jews, some of Irishwomen; and some of sickly-looking infants'.[68] Previous observers had also stressed the supposed racial inferiority of the 'ragged'. In 1853, John Garwood was certain that 'wherever in London what has expressively been called a "*Rookery*" exists, we may be sure that it is inhabited by Irish'. He was firm in his belief that they brought with them poverty, quarrels, drunken disturbances, dirt and excessive crowding.[69] Amongst the rookeries associated with the Irish were Seven Dials, St Giles, Ratcliff and The Mint. All were infamous for an apparently criminal and vicious population.

The writers on the 'residuum' had much in common with the proponents of the theory of urban degeneration. They asserted the significance of hereditary characteristics, yet they believed that these factors could be overcome by positive environmental influences. James Greenwood exhibited this mixture of approaches and arguments. In 1869, he declared that the philanthropic action of religious missionaries and school teachers could not solve the problem of 'Alley-bred Arabs'. Such children 'might be tamed and taught to feed out of our hands, and to repeat after us the alphabet, and even words of two or three syllables'. They might even be induced to shed 'their bedraggled feathers and adopt a more decent plumage; but they can never be other than restless and ungovernable, and unclean birds, while they inhabit the vile old parent nest'. Greenwood felt that there was only one way 'to diminish the race of the children of the gutter'. This was the abolition of 'the breeding places of disease and vice and all manner of abomination'.[70]

By the time of Greenwood's writing, many of the rookeries of London had been demolished. This process continued. But such developments led to overcrowding and to a seemingly worse problem. According to George Sims in 1883, 'the poor – the honest poor – have been driven by the Artisans' Dwellings Act, and the clearance of rookery after rookery to come and herd with thieves and wantons, to bring up their children in the last Alsatias, where lawlessness still reigns supreme'.[71] One of these was The Nichol. For Archer in 1865, this latter spot was 'as foul a neighbourhood as can be discovered in the civilised world (savage life has nothing to compare to it)'. Its people were 'depressed almost to the last stages of human endurance'. The children were ragged and dirty, whilst the women were gaunt and 'from their faces almost all traces of womanliness have faded'.[72] Thirty years later, the district was the setting for Morrison's *A Child of the Jago*. He agreed with his predecessor's condemnation, declaring that 'what was too vile for Kate Street, Seven Dials and Ratcliff Highway in its worst day, what was too useless, incapable and corrupt – all that teemed in the Old Jago'. The Nichol was cleared in the 1890s as part of the Boundary Street Clearance Scheme carried out by the London County Council. Like Sims, Morrison feared the consequences of this process. The 'dispossessed Jagos had gone to infect the neighbourhoods across the border, and to crowd the people a little closer'. Another Jago was growing slowly, 'teeming and villainous'.[73]

Since the 1850s there had been a concern that the 'residuum' could contaminate the industrious poor with their bad habits and low morals.[74] But in the context of the 1880s this worry became more widespread. The housing crisis in London meant that artisans were having to live in 'low' neighbourhoods. They could also become infected with incorrigible behaviour. It appeared that the dangerous classes were growing. As Stedman Jones has put it, the dissolute poor seemed 'large enough to engulf civilised London'. These worries were exacerbated by the revival of socialism, by widespread unemployment and by the West End riots of 1886 and 1887. Consequently, Stedman Jones argued that the interest and reactions of the upper and middle classes to poverty were prompted as much by fear as by guilt.[75]

The notion of a menacing and numerous 'residuum' informed the debate about urban degeneration and it affected the investigations of Booth. He divided the population of London into eight classes, of which 'A' was the lowest. This was made up of some occasional labourers, street sellers, loafers, criminals and semi-criminals. According to Booth, their life was that of savages, their food was of the coarsest and their only luxury was drink. They were 'the battered figures who slouch through the streets, and play the beggar or the bully, or help foul the record of the unemployed'. Such people 'render no useful service, they create no wealth; more often they destroy it'. They degraded whatever they touched and were 'perhaps incapable of improvement'. Their character was hereditary, although their ranks were added to by others, who drifted down 'from the classes of casual and irregular labour'. They were mixed up with class B, but they numbered only about 11,000 or 1.25% of the capital's population. Hennock has explained that this finding allowed Booth to demonstrate conclusions that were socially reassuring.[76] The investigator maintained that 'the hordes of barbarians of whom we have heard, who issuing from their slums, will one day overwhelm modern civilisation, do not exist. There are barbarians, but they are a handful, a small and decreasing percentage: a disgrace but not a danger.'

Class B was more numerous, about 100,000 people. This was 'a deposit of those who from mental, moral and physical reasons are incapable of better work'. Its members were the very poor who relied on casual earnings. They were uncivilised, physically inefficient, shiftless, helpless, idle and prone to drunkenness. Their competition was a crushing load to the people of classes C and D. This meant that class B had to be swept away so that their work could be done by the deserving poor. Such a result could be achieved by the establishment of State-run labour colonies away from London.[77] Fabian socialists agreed that governments had a duty to eliminate the unfit. Amongst them were H. G. Wells and George Bernard Shaw. They shared the view of the right-wing journalist White that 'failures' should be sterilised. In the wake of the Boer War, proposals for coercive State action against the 'residuum' became more noticeable. But they were not implemented. They clashed with the belief in the rights of the individual and with the acknowledgement that the environment was more important than eugenics in the shaping of character.

Stedman Jones has emphasised that the problems of casual labour and the 'residuum' disappeared in the First World War. The needs of a war economy meant that the underemployed obtained full-time, regular work. It was impossible to find 'unemployables'. This development showed that the casual poor were 'a social and not a biological creation'.[78] It is an indictment on English society that it took the tragedy of conflict to make it clear that poverty was caused mostly by economic conditions. It is as perturbing that it needed a terrible war to make it obvious that the urban poor were people and not some subhuman species. Words like 'residuum', 'undeserving' and 'ragged' obliterated the humanity of the poor. They destroyed their individual personalities. They ignored their relationships with each other. They disregarded the vitality and compassion that was evident amongst those who battled against poverty daily. Such terms fell from use amidst the recognition of the efforts of poor men and women on behalf of the nation. The urban poor fought and worked for a country which had denied them the full rights of citizenship and which had degraded them. They did not fail England. England had failed them.

Notes

1   H. Gavin, *The Habituations of the Industrial Classes*, first published 1851, New York, 1985 edn, p. 19.

2   G. Haw, *The Life Story of Will Crooks MP*, London, 1917, pp. 9–12.

3   A. Digby, *The Poor Law in Nineteenth-Century England*, the Historical Association General Series, London, 1985 edn, p. 17.

4   Cited in Digby, *The Poor Law*, p. 31.

5   T. Archer, *The Pauper, the Thief and the Convict*, first published 1865, New York, 1985 edn, p. 16.

6   J. G. Mantle, Wesleyan Minister, 66, Trinity Road, Aston, 'Letter', *Birmingham Daily Post*, 7 January 1891.

7   M. A. Crowther, *The Workhouse System. The History of an English Social System*, London, 1983 edn, p. 269.

8   R. Roberts, *The Classic Slum. Salford Life in the First Quarter of the Century*, Harmondsworth, 1973 edn, pp. 84–5.

9   C. Chinn Letters Archive, William Boxall, 3 March 1993.

10   C. Chinn Letters Archive, Doreen Molloy, 4 July 1992.

11   M. E. Rose, *The Relief of Poverty 1834–1914*, Studies in Economic and Social History, Basingstoke, 2nd edn, 1986, pp. 17 and 12.

12   K. Woodward, *Jipping Street*, first published 1928, London, 1983 edn, pp. 15–7.

13   Digby, *The Poor Law*, pp. 25–6.

14   W. A. Bailward, 'The Oxford House and the organisation of charity', in J. M. Knapp (ed.), *The Universities and the Social Problem*, first published 1895, New York, 1985 edn, pp. 164–5.

15   G. Doré and G. Jerrold, *London. A Pilgrimage*, first published 1872, New York, 1978 edn, pp. 179–91.

16   D. Fraser, *The Evolution of the British Welfare State*, Basingstoke, 1984 edn, p. 132.

17   M. Mabey, 'The Charity Organisation Society, Elephant and Castle Branch, 1936', C. Chinn Letters Archive, 10 March 1992.

18   G. Stedman Jones, *Outcast London. A Study in the Relationship Between the Classes in Victorian Society*, London, 1984 edn, pp. 251–3.

19   A. J. Kidd, '"Outcast Manchester": voluntary charity, poor relief and the casual poor 1860–1905', in A. J. Kidd and K. W. Roberts (eds), *City, Class*

and Culture. Studies of Cultural Production and Social Policy in Victorian Manchester, Manchester, 1985, pp. 48–67.

20 Mantle, 'Letter', *Birmingham Daily Post*.

21 The Girl's Night Shelter, *Minutes*, 18 June 1888 (thanks to Daphne Agnew, Admission Manager, Lydia Rogers House, Birmingham).

22 M. E. Rose, 'Poverty and self-help: Britain in the nineteenth and twentieth centuries', in A. Digby, C. Feinstein and D. Jenkins (eds), *New Directions in Economic and Social History, Volume II*, Basingstoke, 1992, p. 156.

23 Doré and Jerrold, *London. A Pilgrimage*, pp. 188.

24 E. Gaskell, *Mary Barton. A Tale of Manchester Life*, first published 1848, Harmondsworth, 1970 edn, pp. 45 and 475.

25 P. Malpass, 'Octavia Hill 1838–1912', in P. Barker (ed.), *Founders of the Welfare State*, London, 1984, p. 32.

26 B. Webb, *My Apprenticeship*, cited in P. Adelman, *The Rise of the Labour Party 1880–1945*, first published 1972, Harlow, 1986 edn, p. 3.

27 J. Harris, 'The Webbs. Beatrice Webb 1858–1943. Sidney Webb 1859-1947', in Barker (ed.), *Founders of the Welfare State*, p. 53.

28 Mrs Caswell, 'Sparkhill and Greet Maternity and Infant Welfare Centre, 1920', unpublished manuscript supplied by Ivy Caswell.

29 J. Rimmer, *Troubles Shared. The Story of a Settlement 1899–1979*, Birmingham, 1980, pp. 1–51.

30 C. E. B. Russell, *Social Problems of the North*, first published 1913, New York, 1980 edn, pp. 121–4.

31 D. Read, *England 1868–1914. The Age of Urban Democracy*, Harlow, 1979 edn, p. 298.

32 A. Briggs and A. Macartney, *Toynbee Hall. The First Hundred Years*, London, 1984, p. 9.

33 Stedman Jones, *Outcast London*, p. 259.

34 Briggs and Macartney, *Toynbee Hall*, p. 4.

35 Stedman Jones, *Outcast London*, pp. 258–9.

36 K. S. Inglis, *Churches and the Working Classes in Victorian England*, London, 1961, p. 144.

37 E. P. Hennock, 'Poverty and social theory in England: the experience of the 1880s', *Social History*, 1, 1976, p. 90.

38 Robert R. Hyde, *Industry was my Parish*, London, 1968, pp. 30 and 36.

39 Cited in M. E. Rose, 'The Manchester University Settlement in Ancoats, 1895–1909', *Manchester Region History Review*, 7, 1993, p. 61.

40 D. B. McIlhiney, *A Gentleman in Every Slum*, Ann Arbor, Michigan, 1976, p. 26.

41 W. Besant, *East London*, first published 1899, New York, 1980 edn, pp. 15 and 312–3.

42 D. E. B. Weiner, 'The People's Palace. An image for East London in the 1880s', in D. Feldman and G. Stedman Jones, *Metropolis. London. Histories and Representations since 1800*, London, 1989, pp. 45 and 49.

43 Gaskell, *Mary Barton*, p. 41.

44 J. E. Morgan, *The Danger of Deterioration of Race from the Too Rapid Increase of Great Cities*, first published 1866, New York, 1985 edn, pp. 2–9.

45 J. Cantlie, *Degeneration Amongst Londoners*, first published 1885, New York, 1985 edn, pp. 33–7.

46 J. M. Fothergill, *The Town Dweller. His Needs and His Wants*, first published 1889, New York, 1985 edn, pp. 113–4.

47 Stedman Jones, *Outcast London*, pp. 130–51.

48 A. White, *The Problems of a Great City*, first published 1886, New York, 1985 edn, pp. 60–1, 68 and 226.

49 H. Jones, *Health and Society in Twentieth Century Britain*, Themes in British Social History, London, 1994, p. 22.

50 A. White, *Efficiency and Empire*, London, 1901, pp. 102–3.

51 J. London, *The People of the Abyss*, first published 1903, London, 1977 edn, p. 94.

52 F. Engels, *The Condition of the Working Classes in England*, first published 1845, Harmondsworth, 1987 edn, p. 100.

53 Harris, 'The Webbs', in Barker (ed.), *Founders of the Welfare State*, p. 243.

54 *Report of the Inter-Departmental Committee on Physical Deterioration*, London, 1904, Parliamentary Papers.

55 J. R. Hay, *The Origins of the Liberal Welfare Reforms, 1906–1914*, Studies in Economic and Social History, Basingstoke, 1983 edn, p. 44.

56 Fraser, *The Evolution of the British Welfare State*, p. 149.

57 Read, *England 1868–1914*, p. 462.

58 Hay, *The Origins of the Liberal Welfare Reforms*, p. 47.

59 Fraser, *The Evolution of the British Welfare State*, p. 153.

60 J. Grigg, 'Lloyd George 1863–1945', in Barker (ed.), *Founders of the Welfare State*, p. 71.

61 Jones, *Health and Society in Twentieth Century Britain*, p. 26.

62 Fraser, *The Evolution of the British Welfare State*, pp. 163–4.

63 Jones, *Health and Society in Twentieth Century Britain*, p. 27.

64 Hay, *The Origins of the Liberal Welfare Reforms*, pp. 34–5 and 54.

65 G. Himmelfarb, *The Idea of Poverty. England in the Early Industrial Age*, London, 1984, pp. 358–71, 378 and 381.

66 Archer, *The Pauper, the Thief and the Convict*, pp. 23–4.

67 Cited in Himmelfarb, *The Idea of Poverty*, p. 378.

68 J. Hollingshead, *Ragged in London in 1861*, first published 1861, New York, 1985 edn, p. 44.

69 J. Garwood, *The Million-People City*, first published 1853, New York, 1985 edn, p. 314.

70 J. Greenwood, *The Seven Curses of London*, first published 1869, New York, 1984 edn, pp. 80–2 and 457.

71 G. R. Sims, *How the Poor Live and Horrible London*, London, 1889 edn, p. 11 (articles first published in *The Pictorial World*, 1883).

72 Archer, *The Pauper, the Thief and the Convict*, pp. 11–12.

73 Arthur Morrison, *A Child of the Jago*, first published 1896, London, 1946 edn, pp. 6, 10, 73–4 and 233.

74 Himmelfarb, *The Idea of Poverty*, p. 387; Hollingshead, *Ragged London in 1861*, p. 14.

75 Stedman Jones, *Outcast London*, pp. 283–5.

76 Hennock, 'Poverty and social theory', *Social History*, p. 75.

77 C. Booth, *Life and Labour of the People in London, Volume 1*, London, 1889, pp. 39 and 150–4.

78 Stedman Jones, *Outcast London*, p. 336.

5

Living in poverty

The abyss

The urban poor looked different to outsiders. Many were not tall, well built, blond haired and blue eyed. They were short, slight, dark haired and sallow skinned. Their actions were not reserved. They swirled along their streets, noisy and raucous. Their areas seemed strange. They were heavy with unhealthy smells. They were loud with the shriek of machines, the clatter of horses' hooves and the clamour of people. They were dark from the smoke which billowed from factory chimneys, from the crowding of houses which seemed to push out fresh air and light, and from too few streetlamps. In the frantic imagination of many upper- and middle-class people, the urban poor seemed to be a peculiar tribe who lived in a foreign place.

This view was sustained by journalists and impressionistic writers. In 1849 Mayhew explained that 'in passing from the skilled operative of the West-end to the unskilled workman of the Eastern quarter of London, the moral and intellectual change is so great that it seems as if we were in a new land and among another race'.[1] This form of writing became more popular as Europeans took over huge parts of Africa and Asia. Self-assured in their racial superiority, explorers and colonisers wrote of their discoveries. They forgot that they had been preceded by indigenous peoples. These arrogant assumptions were shared by comfortable and prosperous readers, who were thrilled by accounts of exotic places.

To draw their attention to the problems in their own country, some reformers felt compelled to use the language of exploration. As Peter J. Keating has explained, the result was the development of 'a distinctive branch of modern literature in which a representative of one class consciously sets out to explore, analyse and report upon the life of another class lower on the social scale than his own; the reverse procedure being, of course, not really possible, except in satire'.[2]

One of the contributors to this genre was George Sims, a person who was concerned deeply with the overcrowding of the poor in London. In 1883 he was commissioned by Gilbert Dalziell to write a series of articles for 'a new illustrated paper', the *Pictorial World*. Accompanied by an artist called Fred Barnard, Sims went south of the Thames into the Borough. The two men 'smoked like furnaces the whole time, but we did not smoke cigars or silver-mounted briars'. So as 'to avoid all suspicion of swank and to make the inhabitants feel more at home in our company, we smoked short clay pipes and coloured them a beautiful black in the course of our pilgrimage through Poverty Land'.[3] Sims emphasised that his work was 'a book of travel', and in it he compared the Borough to a 'dark continent' full of 'wild races' (Document 18).

General William Booth of the Salvation Army imitated Sims' approach. In 1890 he had published *In Darkest England and the Way Out*. This title made specific reference to Stanley and his descriptions of 'Darkest Africa'. Booth appealed to his readers not to forget that England had its 'forests' and their 'denizens'. As much as the pygmies of Africa, the disinherited and outcast of England needed spiritual salvation and material help.[4]

London began his book in a similar way. He wrote that he approached the travel agents Thomas Cook and Sons to arrange for him a tour of the East End. They could not do so. Pathfinders and trail clearers, 'living sign posts to all the world, and bestowers of first aid to bewildered travellers – unhesitatingly and instantly, with ease and celerity, could you send me to Darkest Africa or Innermost Thibet [*sic*], but to the East End of London, barely a stone's throw from Ludgate Circus, you know not the way'.[5] Like Hollingshead and Besant before him, London emphasised the monotony, melancholy and misery in the poorer parts of the capital.[6] And in common with many others, he highlighted the immorality and debauchery which he believed was rampant in these places. It was these features which stunned the readers of the short pamphlet *The Bitter Cry of Outcast London*. It was published in 1883 but there has been controversy over its authorship. Some historians agree with Fishman that it was written by the Reverend William C. Preston.[7] Others concur with John D. Beasley that the Reverend Andrew Mearns 'was solely responsible for conceiving the idea of *The Bitter Cry*, for the planning and organisation of the research, the final editing, and much of the writing'.[8] Whoever was the author, Bentley B. Gilbert felt that the pamphlet was 'perhaps the most influential single piece of writing about the poor England has ever seen'.[9] Its impact was assured by W. T. Stead, editor of the *Pall Mall Gazette*. He republished it 'in adroitly condensed form'. As Read has showed, these extracts highlighted the depravity which was thought to be associated with overcrowded and bad housing conditions.[10]

Much of the information in *The Bitter Cry* referred to the Collier's Rents district of Bermondsey, a place of 'reeking courts, crowded public-houses, low lodging-houses and numerous brothels'. Here there were 123 dwellings with a population of about 3,250. Mainly the people were 'costermongers, bird catchers, street singers, liberated convicts, thieves and prostitutes'. Mearns made it clear that he came across much courage and kindness amongst these folk. He stated that 'there is something unspeakably pathetic in the brave patience with which the poor not seldom endure their sufferings, and the tender sympathy which they show to each other'. But these positive qualities did not impress his readers. What gained their notice were the assertions of licentiousness. According to Mearns, amongst the poor marriage was not 'fashionable', 'incest is common; and no form of vice and sensuality causes surprise or attracts attention'.[11]

Poorer areas were not only outlandish. They seemed to be hellish. This gloomy and depressing picture was reinforced by novels like George Gissing's *The Nether World*. Published in 1889, it was infused with pessimism. As Allen indicated, Gissing 'did not like the working class'. In particular, he loathed the poor. This was made evident in his version of 'a disagreeable quarter, a street of squalid houses, swarming with yet more squalid children'. On all the doorsteps sat little girls, 'themselves only just out of infancy, nursing or neglecting bald, red-eyed, doughy-limbed abortions in every stage of babyhood, hapless spawn of diseased humanity, born to embitter and brutalise yet further the lot of those who unwillingly gave them life'.[12] Even sympathetic observers viewed the slum as an abyss in which physical and moral degradation was rife. William Booth used the term 'abyss'. So did London. And so did the future Liberal minister C. F. G. Masterman, in *From the Abyss* (1902).

Some members of the working class used the same language and agreed with its implications. It was Wright's firm belief that many of the poor had existences 'little better than a hell upon earth'. The home life of these people was 'something simply horrible'. It put 'decency, morality, and religion, as well as physical health and comfort out of the question; and so degrades and brutalises those condemned to it that they live as well as die like the beasts in the field'. In a vile setting, the industrious and respectable poor tried in vain to maintain standards. Those who were reckless made no such attempts. They were the 'charity-hunting poor'. The men were loafers and roughs, the women were viragos. Their language was ribald and blasphemous, and they brought up their ragged children in a 'horrible' way. They were taught nothing of virtue, 'but immorality both in word and deed is openly practised before them', whilst 'the sexes mingle together promiscuously'.[13]

Charles Shaw recalled that in the 1840s in Burslem, north Staffordshire, there was a neighbourhood which was seen as full of such people. It was called 'Th' Hell Hole'. Shaw exclaimed that 'in squalor, in wretchedness, in dilapidation of cottages, in half-starved and half-dressed women and children, in the number of idle and drunken men, it was as terribly dismal as its name would suggest'. It was the home of bullies and their victims, 'and for unsanitariness and immorality I should think it could not have been surpassed in all England'.[14] Fifty years later in London, the Nichol was as infamous. Harding remembered that it was 'something like a ghetto'. A stranger 'wouldn't chance his arm there', and 'the whole district bore an evil reputation'. The other working-class people of Bethnal Green saw it as so disreputable that they avoided contact with those who lived there.[15]

Nearby in Hoxton, 'the Nile' was another place which was notorious for its 'wickedness'. Charles Booth wrote that if a wall had been placed around the district 'it would shut in nine-tenths of the thieves in London'. Hyde perceived that this was an exaggeration, 'but it was of value to those skilful compilers of appeals, who sought support for their social and religious endeavours from the less penurious residents in South Coast resorts'. With insight he added 'that such a general condemnation might give offence to the people of Hoxton was either overlooked, or regarded as of little account by the writers of those begging letters'.[16] Joseph Stamper made a similar point from a working-class perspective. He grew up in St Helens in the 1880s. When he became older he read everything he could get his hands on, 'from Penny Dreadfuls to the Holy Scriptures'. He came across phrases that puzzled him, such as 'sans-culotte', 'shiftless rabble', 'dregs of humanity', 'ignorant masses'. Stamper wondered where all these worthless people lived. He 'could only think that it must be in London or some such place out of my ken'. Then 'it dawned on me, these scornful and superior writers were writing about me, and the people who lived in our street'.[17]

Neighbourhoods

In 1864, Hugh Shimmin entered an insanitary and tumbledown court in Oriel Street, Liverpool. He asked some of the inhabitants 'why they remained in such wretched places, as, for a few pence more each week, which might be saved from the grog-shop, they could get much better residences, and in a more healthy situation'. One old woman 'stepped forward to reply'. She had lived in the court for a long time and she had found friends and neighbours there. As she put it, 'a neighbour was not easy to be met with in any place or everyday, and it was not easy to leave a spot which she had known so long, and where, in sorrow or in joy, she had met with sympathetic hearts'.[18] The development of close-knit communities such as this has been outlined by Michael Anderson. He examined the censuses for the mid-nineteenth century in Preston. Out of his sample of people from 1851, seventy per cent were born outside the town. But Anderson concluded that these newcomers relied greatly for help on kin who were established in Preston already.[19] This meant that relatives settled near to each other.

Such a support system was enhanced by local migration. With the exception of Liverpool and London, English cities were filled mostly with people from surrounding villages. As a result, many newcomers had similar backgrounds and they spoke the same accent and dialect. Derek Beattie has highlighted the manner in which Blackburn was entrenched in its wider hinterland. He cited a study which showed that between 1850 and 1870 'it was mainly whole families that moved into town not just the young men and women, and that the average distance travelled was five miles per generation'.[20] A comparable situation was obvious in the poor district of Summer Lane, Birmingham. In 1881 in the back-to-back courtyards which lay off the road, seventy-five per cent of the population was born in the city. The great majority of the rest came from the encircling counties of Warwickshire, Worcestershire and Staffordshire.[21]

The movement of people from certain areas to one place in particular was as noticeable amongst ethnic minorities. Jenifer Davis has shown that in the 1860s in Jennings' Buildings, Kensington, many of the Irish inhabitants were linked 'by ties of kinship and other connections which had their roots in Cork'.[22] Similarly, most of the Italians in Birmingham came from villages by the town of Sora, lying between Rome and Naples. Through intermarriage, many of them were related. These ties became more pronounced after their emigration, and they led to the formation of large kinship networks like that of the Tavoliers, Boves, Gregos and Sartoris.[23]

Migration and immigration to the big cities declined in the second half of the nineteenth century. As Ellen Ross has noted for London, by the 1870s 'a relatively stable urban culture' was obvious in working-class areas like Bethnal Green, Bermondsey and Poplar. In these circumstances new arrivals to a district 'encountered families who had lived in the nearby streets for a generation or more'.[24] The same phenomenon was evident in other major cities. Robert Roberts grew up in the Hope Street district of Salford, where the population was generally immobile by the early 1900s.[25] He observed that 'fifty years before, our area had horrified even Friedrich Engels, and Engels knew a slum when he saw one'. Since then 'many of the vilest hovels had been swept away', but 'here, if anywhere on earth, when darkness fell, lay the "city of the dreadful night"'.[26] But Hope Street was not the city of the dreadful night. Nor was it an abyss. It was a thriving locality with its own facilities. Roberts underlined these features in *The Classic Slum*, probably the most perceptive working-class autobiography. He discerned that his own district was not unusual, arguing that every industrial city 'folds within itself a clutter of loosely-defined overlapping "villages"'. His own had about 3,000 inhabitants living in 'some thirty streets and alleys'. It was marked off to the north and south by railway lines. To the west, beyond the tram lines, 'lay the middle classes', and to the east was 'another slum' (Document 19).

The Nichol in London was another clearly defined urban village. Its boundaries were High Street Shoreditch and Hackney Road on the north, and Spitalfields to the south. Unlike Hope Street, the Nichol had its own major shopping thoroughfare. Harding proclaimed that Church Street was 'the high heaven' of everything in the district. It had pubs like the Crown, where the bird fanciers met, 'a big men's and boy's tailor's shop called Lynn's', a fish and chip shop, a timber yard, a coffee house, a wet-fish shop, a Salvation Army chapel, several wardrobe dealers', a chemist 'who sold every kind of medicines and cures for every kind of illness', a pork butcher's shop, which was 'the best in the locality', a doctor's shop, a barber, a baker, a corner shop, which was 'a God-send to the hungry children of the district' because it sold large bags of broken biscuits for a ½d or 1d, an undertaker, numerous food shops, a soup kitchen, a rag-and-bone shop, a grocer's 'selling very cheap tea, sugar, etc.', and a pudding shop which charged a penny for hot pies and a portion of jam roly-poly.

It is significant that Church Street ran into Shoreditch High Street.[27] In this way the Nichol was connected to a wider area. For all its evil reputation, it was not shut off and isolated. It was embedded within Bethnal Green and Shoreditch. Both these places were the size of towns. So were Portsea in Portsmouth, Ancoats in Manchester, and Duddeston and Nechells in Birmingham.[28] By 1871 Nechells had a population of about 46,000. It was separated from adjoining townships in the city by clear boundaries: from Aston Cross by the Birmingham to Fazeley Canal; from Saltley and Bordesley by railway lines; and from Digbeth by two main roads, Dartmouth and Lawley Streets. Duddeston occupied the southern part of the town. Within this area, two villages stood out. Vauxhall was cut off by railway lines and was home to many regularly employed railwaymen and their families. To its west, Ashted was characterised by back-to-back housing and a mainly poorer population. But both villages were brought together by the major shopping centre of Great Lister Street. This was also 'the monkey run', the road along which boys and girls walked with their 'pals' on a Saturday or Sunday night. Their hope was 'to click' with someone of the opposite sex.[29]

Shoreditch High Street had the same functions. Harding called it the local Champs Elyseés. It was 'a prosperous market place with stalls and shops on both sides of the street', and it boasted the 'London' music hall as well as many pubs.[30] Elsewhere in the East End, 'the Lane' in Whitechapel was another focal point. For Elizabeth Flint a trip there was 'one of the peaks of our existence'. Along Whitechapel Road there were hawkers selling oranges, 'Fatty White' calling out 'whelks and cockles and winkles', and a 'hot chestnut barrow on the roadway that led into the Lane' itself. This was full of stalls 'side by side, and noise and light were tossed together, a noise that had a quality of heaviness all made up of talking and screaming and laughing, yet with no part of it separate and on its own'. In the winter the Lane was lit by naphtha flares, which were 'for ever leaping and hissing like chained dogs that cannot escape the kennel to which they are tied'. Nothing was still. People were moving all the time, and it seemed there was such a friendliness and 'such a happiness that no one could ever find today'.[31]

South of the Thames in Peckham, Rye Lane was also a 'monkey parade', a shopping centre, and a place of entertainment. Alice Cordelia Davis recollected that on Saturday nights it was very busy and 'it was a common sight to see auction sales of meat and fish'. Butchers had no refrigerators and so had to resort to this tactic to off-load their goods. The meat was sold cheaply, 'not only the joint but a bundle of sausages and a knob of suet would be included in the deal'. Between 7.30 and 8.30 p.m. the local members of the Salvation Army collected outside the White Horse pub to 'hold a very large meeting with a very good brass band'. A few yards further on there was a horse and cart on which a pianist and singer performed the latest songs. Most of them were tear-jerkers because people 'who were so very poor loved sad songs'. Elsewhere there was a man selling lino, a fortune teller and a 'doctor' with a top hat and rattle.[32]

Many urban villages were not as distinct as the Nichol or Hope Street. Lying off the main shopping thoroughfares, they faded imperceptibly into one another. Still, working-class people were acutely aware of their own patch. The size of this space was flexible. It was affected by a number of factors such as age, gender, work and leisure interests. But it was clear that the lives of poorer people revolved round a smaller area than did those of the better off. This interpretation is indicated by the research of Hugh McLeod. Concentrating on the later 1800s he examined the marriage patterns in four London parishes: St John's, Paddington, was a wealthy locality; St Mary's, Lewisham, was a middle-class district; St Andrew's, Bethnal Green, was made up mostly of skilled workers and their families; and in St Clement's, Notting Hill, the unskilled were in the majority. Within these parishes McLeod identified neighbourhoods. These were less than half a mile square, they were not crossed by railways, waterways or main roads, and they were not broken up by parks or a belt of factories. In the poorest parish, eighty-two per cent of men married someone from their own neighbourhood. This compared with sixty-five per cent in the upper-working class district, twenty-five per cent in the middle-class locality and just twenty per cent in the rich area.[33]

McLeod's work is important because it gives a shape to the space underlying the urban village. A similar impression can be gained by an examination of the moves of poorer families. David R. Green and Alan G. Parton studied slum areas in London and Birmingham during the mid-1800s. In all of them 'there existed a shiftless substrata of tramps and vagrants who moved from place to place and lodging-house to lodging-house'. These people passed through the community but were not part of it. But for the rest of the inhabitants, 'residential mobility took place often within tightly circumscribed spatial limits'.[34] This contention is supported by other research. Anderson noticed that in one area of Preston in 1861 almost forty per cent of men 'were found in the same house or within 200 yards of the house that they had occupied ten years earlier'. It was probable that 'another 10–20% were living within less than half a mile'.[35] Lynn Lees discovered similar instances amongst Irish families in London in the 1850s. Some of these moved several times between Bermondsey and Southwark. On all occasions, however, their residences were within 'one half-mile at most' of their previous home.[36]

David Englander corroborated these findings, arguing that 'the migrations of the casual poor were circular and confined to a narrow radius'.[37] His point was as relevant to street traders and those in low-paid regular jobs, like my great-grandfather. My great-uncle Bill recalled that in the 1890s and early 1900s his family rented various houses in Sparkbrook, Birmingham.

> We left out of White Street to go to Studley Street. We knocked on the landlord there. Studley Street we went to Moseley Road. When we got to Moseley Road Mom had bought me a long pair of trousers. I was only twelve and her said, 'Goo and gerra job. Tell 'em y're fourteen'. I went out and got a job in no time. Got a job in Conybere Street. Eight bob a week. Then we come from Moseley Road back into Brunswick Road, worn it? Then Stoney Lane where you get on the bus and then into Queen Street . . . Alfred Street. Back to Studley Street back of Duggin's, Greenway's. Then from Greenway's we went back into Alfred Street.[38]

Over about a fifteen-year period, my great-uncle lived in nine houses. Seven of them were within one hundred yards of his first home in White Street. A. S. Jasper had a comparable experience in London. He thought that he had never heard of a family 'who moved more than we did'. Like the Chinns, they 'flitted' regularly when they fell into arrears with their rent. But until 1919 their changes of address were within a small area between Essex Road and Hackney Road. Significantly, all were within half a mile of Hoxton Street, where the Jaspers sometimes had a market stall.[39] Alice Linton also grew up in Hoxton, and she too recollected that 'we seemed to move around quite a lot but mostly in the same area'.[40]

Outsiders found it difficult to recognise these amorphous neighbourhoods. But insiders were acutely aware of them, and there were facilities which acted as linchpins. Chief of these were small corner shops. Here the poor could buy the tiniest portions of food. Fred Davies recalled that his mother would send him with a penny and a saucer to buy jam from their local store in Mount Street, Manchester. The woman 'would weigh the saucer first on the scales, then scoop the jam out of a big stone jar onto' it.[41] Lilian Slater's mother ran the same kind of shop in another district of the city. Customers 'brought empty Tiger sauce and Yorkshire Relish bottles for vinegar, jugs for their milk, and basins or cups without handles for their pickles, jam and treacle'.[42] As Alexander Paterson pointed out in 1911, such purchasing was made 'at a ruinous rate'.[43] It was impossible for those in poverty to do otherwise.

Yet these shopkeepers did not become rich on the penny economy of the poor. According to Robert Roberts, bankruptcy was always close. His mother operated their premises in Salford 'with a mixture of shrewdness and sardonic compassion'. These features were most obvious when she had to react to appeals for credit. On these occasions 'a shopkeeper's generosity fought with his fears for self-preservation – to trust or not to trust'. Many times she did trust, and throughout urban England women such as her allowed numerous poor families to eat. But the Roberts' corner shop was more than an essential economic facility. It played a vital role as a meeting place.[44] And like all corner shops, it connected one street to another. In this way, individual streets coalesced to become part of a neighbourhood.

Corner and back-street pubs performed the same function. Thomas Morgan recalled that before 1904 children could go into them. He and his friends played on the floor, amidst 'the sawdust, spit and all that', whilst their mothers sat 'peeling the 'tatoes and shelling the peas'.[45] My great-uncle Wal Chinn had similar memories, and he emphasised that it was unusual to find strangers in 'the local'. They were used by regulars 'who remained loyal to their chosen meeting place'. His dad's pub was in Studley Street, yet it was more than a drinking establishment.[46] The Gate Inn had a football team in the local league and it was the focus for the celebration of major events in the life of the street and the nation. This is shown by a photograph which was taken probably in 1900, when there was great enthusiasm upon the relief of Mafeking in the Boer War (Document 20). The pub is decorated with Union flags and bunting, and outside it are collected the people of Studley Street. Such images are vital in showing the humanity of those who were demeaned as the 'residuum'. Pubs played a significant role in small communities, as was stressed by Richard Heaton. In the Hope Street village the landlord of the Kings Arms would 'put up prizes on Saturday nights – legs of mutton, beef or rabbits – and for a copper anybody could compete for them'. The winner was 'the highest scorer with three darts'. As the captain of the darts team, Heaton's dad brought home 'more than one prize'.[47]

There was drunkenness in back-street pubs, and often there were fights outside them. But these places were not dens of iniquity. Nor were those poor areas which had infamous reputations. Amongst them was the Nichol in London, Angel Meadow in Manchester, Scotland Road in Liverpool, Johnson Street in Sunderland and Summer Lane in Birmingham.[48] This long road stretched from the city centre to Aston, giving its name to a populous district made up of the streets which ran off it. The township was split by Tower Street into two distinct villages, within which there were a number of less clearly identified neighbourhoods. All of them were dominated by back-to-back housing, and the quarter as a whole was notorious as one of the 'worst parts of the city'. It was declaimed as 'a thieves' resort', as a place which had a pub on every corner, and as the hardest district in Birmingham, through which the police had to walk in threes.[49] But Summer Lane was not the abyss it was made out to be. It was the scene of strong communal loyalties and its people were diverse in their backgrounds.[50]

Cécile Simon has examined the 1881 and 1891 censuses for information about the occupations of the people who lived on 'the Lane' itself. She split them into six categories. School children made up twenty-two per cent of the total. Industrial workers comprised eighteen per cent, as did 'those involved in crafts'. These people included saddlers, brewers, carpenters, hairdressers, shoemakers, corset makers, blacksmiths, printers, jewellers, violin makers, bricklayers, badge makers, milliners, painters, plumbers, policemen, tailors and tanners. Those in the service sector were seventeen per cent of the total. This section embraced laundresses, actors, pub managers, hauliers, surgeon-opticians, clerks, caretakers, writers who hired themselves out, housekeepers, pharmacists, photographers, teachers, servants, pawnbrokers and bar staff. Next came retailers, making up thirteen per cent of the overall figure. Amongst them were butchers, bakers, booksellers, off-licensees, drapers, grocers, fruiterers, milk sellers, fishmongers, furniture dealers, ironmongers and tobacconists. The last group was made up of those at home. It had twelve per cent of the total.[51]

Graham Davies' penetrating analysis showed that the Avon Street area of Bath was also 'a patchwork quilt of humanity'. Stereotyped images 'ignored the diversity' within the community.[52] Jenifer Davis made a similar searching examination of a London rookery, Jennings' Buildings in Kensington. Before it was demolished in 1873 this place was home to about 1,000 people –

most of whom were Irish. It was 'the focus of local anxieties about the dangerous classes'. A disproportionate number of the tenants were 'frequently in trouble with the law' and many of them were dependent on poor relief. On first sight they appeared to typify the 'residuum'. Davis dispelled this impression. The people of the buildings, 'far from constituting a homogeneous group, were divided by both material circumstances and social attitudes'. They were differentiated by their relative skills, job security and affluence. They were distinguished by their relationship to the police and Poor Law authorities. And they were marked out by varying attitudes to work, leisure, home, family and religion. Many of the criminal charges which arose from the buildings were the result of offences committed on the street – to which the inhabitants were pushed by their dreadful housing. Others 'were initiated not by the police but by residents, often against neighbours or family members'. Much of this friction resulted from a struggle for dominance within the buildings between John Simpson and Edmund Green. They acted as middlemen for the owners of the property, they let rooms, loaned money, recruited labour, and ran beer and grocery shops. The two men were linked to five extended families, who were prominent in the clashes between them.[53]

David Vincent was justified in stating that 'poor families did not all live next door to each other in permanently established enclaves of deprivation'.[54] Occasional poverty affected many members of the working class, including those who lived in more prosperous districts. But those who were poor regularly and continually did live in clearly identified areas. These had the worst housing, the most polluted environments, the highest death rates and the greatest number of residents packed into a small space. Yet even here there was an organic form of society. Not all the people of a poor neighbourhood were in poverty. Stratification was as evident amongst them as much as it was amongst the working class in general. Robert Roberts made this point about his village in Salford. His father was a skilled man and his mother was a shopkeeper. This meant that his family 'was in the slum, but not, they felt, of it'. In his community, division 'ranged from an élite at the peak' to a social base 'whose members one damned as the "lowest of the low", or simply "no class"'. The premier positions were occupied by shopkeepers, publicans and 'skilled tradesmen'.

Then came semiskilled workers, followed by those who were unskilled. Below this diverse group were 'street sellers of coal, lamp oil, tripe, crumpets, muffins and pikelets, fruit, vegetables and small-ware'. Ranked 'rock-bottom among the genuine workers' were 'the firewood choppers, bundlers and sellers and the rag and boners'. Workhouse paupers 'hardly registered as human beings at all', whilst at 'the base of the social pyramid' were bookies' runners, idlers, part-time beggars, petty thieves, 'those known to have been in prison', and 'any harlots, odd homosexuals, kept men and brothel keepers'.[55]

In East Jarrow, the New Buildings also 'held a very mixed assortment'. Catherine Cookson recalled that the residents included 'the once rich Larkins' and the 'destitute' Kanes. As well as them there were the 'social climbers' who managed to employ a daily or send their washing out, and 'the strivers' who 'neither drank nor smoked, and whose one aim was to keep their heads above water; water in this case being debt'. Then 'last and by no means least came the hard cases', amongst whom were families dominated by drink.[56]

Allen made similar observations in his autobiographical novel set in Birmingham. His family lived in a yard of back-to-backs and suffered hardships 'just because there were so many of us young and helpless at the same time'. But 'though we were poor and knew it in a theoretical way, so far as our immediate social environment was concerned, we stood high in the social scale'. Allen's father was a craftsman in regular work. He voted Liberal, unlike labourers who supported the Tories. His family had 'best' clothes to wear on Sundays, and their status was reflected in their diet. Allen remembered that another boy had boasted once that his family had eaten 'a green-bummed' goose for Christmas dinner. This was a bird that 'could be bought very cheaply towards midnight on Christmas Eve because putrefaction had begun to set in'. When, 'in all innocence,' Allen asked his mother 'whether our goose had been of such a kind she was aghast with horror and shame that I could think such a thing. Tears came into her eyes, and "Pray God we never sink so low as green-bummed 'uns" she said.'[57]

Garrison Lane in Birmingham was another place with a bad reputation. It 'wasn't quite so bad as Summer Lane' but 'it was a bit of a rough area'. Yet Alice Smith dismissed thoughts that everyone in the village was violent, shiftless and drunken. Her father 'was in charge of all the railway horses' and his family lived in one of the few large houses in Garrison Street, which ran off the lane itself. Alice went to the local council school in 1912, 'and it was a good school and all the kids was good, the families was good, but Garrison Lane had got a name for these "H" brothers'. These men were known as burglars. They 'wouldn't hurt the public but they had got their own little gang,' and they would 'get drunk' and used to gamble in the street.[58] Beattie Hamill lived by this notorious family. She was 'terrified of 'em, you'd run a mile if you seen 'em'. But she pointed out that it was 'just Dick, Dick "H"' and his three sons who were the trouble-makers. And of them 'Billy was the one in jail the most, he was the biggest terror of them all'. They were part of a large kinship network, 'but the rest of the "H" family was respectable'.[59]

As with Avon Street in Bath, there were distinctions within Garrison Lane and even within the shorter Garrison Street.[60] Here the middle section 'was a bit better quality than on the end,' where they were 'all really poor'. This part of the street was known as the Rookery. Alice Smith's family was of a higher status to the people who lived there, but she felt part of the same neighbourhood.[61] McLeod's research indicated the same phenomenon in London. He discerned that 'an occupational breakdown shows parallels between different groups in the same parish'. In the wealthy St John's, Paddington, a manual worker 'was more likely to marry outside London than a member of the professional/managerial group elsewhere, and retailers in Bethnal Green were more likely to marry within the "neighbourhood" than were manual workers in Paddington or Lewisham'. Mcleod felt that this pattern might have reflected 'deliberate choice, as with the "respectable" working man who moved to the suburbs because the prevailing lifestyle coincided with his own'. But it also suggested that in each parish 'the dominant group may have placed its own limitations on the life of the area'.[62]

Standish Meacham proposed that 'neighbourhood meant more than houses and streets. It meant the mutually beneficial relationship one formed with others; a sort of social symbiosis.'[63] Elizabeth Roberts agreed with this general statement, but she qualified her support. She argued that urban villages lacked 'a structure through which communal action could be channelled,' and that they were too large for people to feel they knew everyone. Her research focused on Barrow, Lancaster and Preston. In these places 'what seems to have been of considerably greater importance to working-class people was the street, or possibly the small group of streets, in which they lived'.[64]

There is not any tension between this assertion and my argument that the lives of the poor overlapped into spatial communities of different sizes. This contention is supported by the example of 'the Lane' area of Sparkbrook, a generally upper-working-class town in Birmingham. It was marked out by a railway line to the west, by main roads to the north and east, and by two smaller roads to the south. Internally, it was united by the Ladypool Road, described by Leslie Mayell as a 'vital and pulsating' artery. It had 'everything' – 'a rich variety of shops', pubs, a picture house, a chapel, a church, a park, a school and 'probably other things that do not immediately come to my mind'.[65] The township of 'The Lane' was split into two villages by Highgate Road. In turn these manifested a number of neighbourhoods. One of them was made up of Alfred, Queen and Studley Streets. This was seen as a poor quarter and it had a population of about 1,000. Within it, Studley Street was regarded as the poorest part. This was just 200 yards in length and in 1891 it had a population of 408 living in eighty-one houses. The street was infamous as 'the worst' in the area, and it was feared as a place where 'no copper would go down on his own'.[66] But Studley Street was not a ghetto. One end ran onto the Ladypool Road, and the other was connected to Queen Street by a 'huckster's shop' – a corner shop which was open all hours and sold everything. Nor were its people an undifferentiated mass of the poor. They formed a heterogeneous community. Most of the men 'were ordinary factory chaps, builders, labourers' and anybody 'as had rough and ready jobs', but they lived alongside a publican, a coalyard owner, a baker, and two small shopkeepers.[67]

Many of the street's people were related to each other. Between 1908 and 1910 it had five families called Warwick, three each named Jones and Stokes, and two each with the surnames of Moore, Reeves, Chambers, Harris, Hyde, Beedon, Bashford, Parton and Fawkes. The connections between the local families were enhanced by intermarriage. In the eight years from 1906, fourteen people from the street were married at the local Church of England.

In ten cases their partners were also from Studley Street; in three others, the partner was from an adjoining street; and in the last instance, the partner was from the next district.[68] The ties of blood meant that Studley Street and its people became one and the same thing. This led to a staunch loyalty, which was evident in many poor streets throughout urban England. Such an attachment was strengthened because the street was 'the great recreation room' of the slums.[69] Children played on it, mothers met there as they went to shop, young men gathered on its corners, bookies stood on it taking bets, and women sat on their steps watching the comings and goings. As Andrew Davies has shown, the activities of the street were crucial for socialising and they were 'an important feature in communal life'. Significantly, they were free.[70]

To some outsiders the gathering of the poor on the street was intimidating. To others it symbolised the new race of 'pavement folk'. But for the poor the street was a vital place. Compared with their decayed and overcrowded homes, it was spacious, lively and exhilarating. More than this, in a country which denied them so much, it belonged to them. But the street was not the smallest spatial community amongst the poor. Over one hundred people could live in a terrace of back-to-backs. Their immediate world was that of the yard and its facilities, which they all shared. In particular, this space was important for young children, the old and women who worked at home. This is shown clearly by a photograph of a yard in Cromwell Street, Nechells, Birmingham. It was taken about 1905, at a time when cameras operated too slowly to capture movement. For this reason the photographer has ensured that the people of the yard are standing still – all except the girl who is skipping and who becomes a blurred figure (Document 21).

In Studley Street one yard was known as 'Carey's', because so many members of that family lived in the same terrace.[71] Elsewhere, there were similar instances of relatives gathering especially close to each other. Basil and Ellen Sanders lived in 'the badly overcrowded' Princes Court, Bethnal Green. Ellen's mother lived next door and probably she 'had recommended or "spoken for them" to the rent collector'. The other families in the court did the same. This meant that Mrs Field and Mrs Ricketts were sisters. So too were Mrs Sullivan and Mrs Barney, Mrs Mabley and Mrs Collins, Mrs Gray and Mrs Shepherd, and Mrs Cook, Mrs Main and Mrs Newman'.[72] As this example highlighted, the English poor were distinguished not only by their endogamy but also by their matrilocality.[73] This meant that a married couple was more likely to live near the family of the wife. There was a good reason for this. Wives and mothers were in the forefront of the daily battle against poverty. They needed each other's help – and family and kin were more likely to give assistance than were strangers.

Anderson contended that his evidence from mid-nineteenth-century Preston showed that working-class people had a 'calculative' attitude towards kin.[74] This opinion cannot be discounted completely. But it is too sweeping and too scathing. Those in poverty had to live in the present. It was useless for them to store up favours, because they might never be repaid. In these circumstances, most of the poor helped their relatives because they cared and because it was the right thing to do. The thorough research of Elizabeth Roberts made this plain. Amongst other instances, she cited the case of a Lancaster woman who died at the age of thirty-two. Her husband was a drunkard 'and considered by his mother-in-law to be totally unfit' to look after his five children. Rather than see them sent into the workhouse, 'that old woman kept us all the time until she died and she must have been about seventy. Grandfather had to go on working when he might have considered retirement, and grandmother took in washing and lodgers to try and balance the budget.'[75]

The importance of kin was as marked in the rookery of St Giles in London. Green and Parton examined the Settlement and Examination Books of the local Poor Law Union for the thirty years from 1832. They extrapolated information about applicants for relief. Over half of them maintained 'some form of kinship links, the majority of which were either within St Giles or elsewhere within London'. More than one in five of them 'were either living with kin or had lived with them at a previous address in the district'. Green and Parton stressed that these relationships were 'not the only form of local contact'. The applicants called upon employers, landlords and other persons to supply them with references. Again, the majority of these referees were located either at the same address or elsewhere in the district.[76]

Elizabeth Roberts also noted the significance of neighbours.[77] There is a great amount of evidence to support her opinion. Alice Foley's parents moved from Bolton to Dukinfield because of 'poverty and chronic unemployment'. But her father lost his job and this left his family in dire distress. Poor relief was denied them and 'cautious shopkeepers' were reluctant 'to extend credit to strangers'. Her mother's plea 'was to get back to the home town, Bolton, where they might find temporary aid from friends or neighbours'.[78] In these situations, the help given was wide ranging. In East Jarrow, Cookson recalled that the Kanes were 'so destitute that the daughter not only borrowed our Kate's boots, but the mother used to borrow the gully – the bread knife'. In turn, 'Mrs Flanagan was a good friend to Kate' and used to lend her 'Mr Flanagan's suit to pawn'. Cookson also remembered that when Mrs Regan died, 'the children were distributed amongst the neighbours'.[79] Further south, in Peckham, Lilian Blore recollected that 'a neighbour would always come in to help deliver the baby', whilst Mary Chamberlain's great-grandmother was known as the 'angel of Alsace Street' because of her attendance at so many births.[80] And in Studley Street 'the call was often heard for the need of "Mother Minton"'. My great-uncle Wal explained that whatever the hour 'a quick response found her at the bedside in illness, accident, confinement, or even at death, to render aid'. Some of her remedies 'could seem old-fashioned today, but her treatment was usually effective until further help could be obtained, holding in check many a case of pleurisy, congestion and pneumonia'.[81]

Mothers were vital to the survival of poor families. It was they who found the weekly sums which paid for each member of a family to be insured for burial.[82] It was they who put precious pennies into informal 'didlum clubs' so that they could draw out their savings at Christmas.[83] It was they who went to the pawnshop to raise money by pledging clothes, ornaments and even wedding rings.[84] It was they who sought credit at corner shops to take them through hungry periods.[85] It was they who dealt with landlords and boards of guardians.[86] And it was they who contrived to feed a family. Heaton brought to mind how his mother heard of a place called Markendales, 'where all the skins were taken' from the abattoir. There 'you could get two pounds of bits of meat for three pence, if you arrived before eight o'clock in the morning'. This flesh 'was the ears and lips from the skins' and 'hundreds of families from Hulme and Salford were partly reared on stew made from them'.[87] In Birmingham, cheap meat was known as 'cag-mag', and it was also made into a stew with flour, water and 'odd vegetables'.[88]

Often mothers 'went without' so that their families could eat, as Amy Coley noticed. She grew up in Great Arthur Street, Smethwick. Her father died in 1902, when she was six and her brother was four. They survived because their mother worked at Nettlefolds, where 'it was usual for them to stop between 8 and 9 o'clock in the morning' and have breakfast. When there was no bread left 'for Mother to take out with her, she'd stuff paper into her bag to look as if she'd brought something'. At dinner time she would go to her own mother's, 'who used to make sure that she got something to eat'. The grandmother kept pigs, 'and when one of them was killed, she would let Mother have plenty of the freshly-made lard'. Help was also given by a kindly butcher. Sometimes Amy would be sent to buy '3*d* worth of plate steak, which was about half a pound in weight. The butcher knew we had no father, and I'm sure he used to give me more than 3*d* worth of meat.' Her mother was as generous to those who were even worse off than herself. On one occasion she bought five pikelets for tea. She gave them to 'a poor old man and woman, their clothes in tatters', who had come to the door 'begging for a bit of something to eat'.[89]

The significance of mothers extended into every aspect of family life. In Birmingham the home was always 'our Mom's', and as Allen made plain, 'it was mother, of course, who kept us respectable'.[90] This feat was achieved mainly through cleanliness. Foley recalled that each morning 'the "ash-hole" and grate were thoroughly raked, the hearthstone re-eidelbacked, and the floor freshly sanded'. Friday morning was given over 'to the ritual of scouring and polishing the numerous fire irons; they were then placed on the sofa, carefully covered up, and only replaced on Saturday afternoon when the house was really spic and span'.[91] The cleanliness of such houses was attained in the face of adversity. Potts emphasised that his home in Pendleton was infested by fleas, cockroaches, crickets and bugs,[92] and Dayus noted the same problems in Birmingham. Her mother ensured that their shared lavatory was also kept clean, and 'many times we had to stay in bed while she took the clothes from us to wash and dry in front of the fire so that we could go to school the next day looking clean'.[93] The washing of clothes was an arduous task. In a yard of back-to-backs water was taken in buckets from a communal tap to the 'brew'us'. It was used to fill a copper, beneath which a fire was lit and in which the clothes were boiled. These were then put into a 'maiding tub', where they were pounded clean with a thick wooden stick. After this the clothes were scrubbed in another tub, swilled, put through a mangle to make them dry, and pegged out. Finally came the tiresome job of ironing. Cookson's mother took in washing for those who were better off. For days on end, the kitchen of their home was hung with damp washing, 'week in, week out, year in, year out, it was the same. Even to this day I hate the sight of lines full of washing.'[94]

Slums were dirty places because of the pollution from industry and the inadequate sanitation. But great numbers of people in the slums were clean, and lines of washing proclaimed decency and respectability (Document 21). In the same way, many of the poor strove to maintain high moral standards. This is made clear by numerous correspondents quoted in *Maternity Letters from Working Women* (Document 9). Contrary to the excited imagination of numerous middle-class men, those in poverty were not prone to sexual licence and adventure. According to Robert Roberts, the lower working-class woman 'was in fact no subject at all for orgiastic pleasures, nor were men much freer'.[95] As Foley explained, the poor held to a fairly conventional if unexplored moral code.[96]

Poor neighbourhoods were not nether worlds. But neither were they cosy and quaint. Cookson explained that 'the lavatory was the only place in our environment where you could lock yourself in and be alone. That is, if there was no one next door, and you were not made hot and blushing by the sounds, to which you would add your imagination'.[97] Robert Roberts made the same point, stressing that 'close propinquity, together with cultural poverty, led as much to enmity as it did to friendship'. The lack of private space was a potent force, which engendered rows and violence. This absence of seclusion could excerbate tensions between the various communities which shared the same street or neighbourhood: the aged and the young, men and women, drinkers and non-drinkers, gamblers and non-gamblers, the religious and the irreligious, English and Irish, Gentiles and Jews, English and Italians, the sensitive and the coarse, and the rough and the respectable.

In every poor street there were families who could make other people unhappy and scared. There were men who abused their wives and children. There was cruelty. But there was also compassion. There was conflict. But there was also communality. There was indifference. But there was also caring. There was degredation. But there was also dignity. As Robert Roberts put it, most people were not slumped in despair. Parents brought up their children to be decent, kindly and honourable, and 'very many families even in our "low" district remained awesomely respectable over a lifetime'.[98] No greater tribute could be made to the majority of the urban poor who fought to live with pride. They bonded together to form neighbourhoods. They clung to each other against an inhospitable environment. They supported one another when the state and the wealthy ignored them. They asserted values when the upper and middle classes deemed them valueless. And in their everyday lives they adhered to the principles of duty, loyalty and comradeship.

Notes

1   H. Mayhew, 'Letter XIX', *Morning Chronicle*, 21 December 1849.

2   P. J. Keating (ed.), *Into Unkown England 1866–1913. Selections from the Social Observers*, Glasgow, 1976, p. 13.

3   G. R. Sims, *My Life. Sixty Years' Recollections of Bohemian London*, London, 1917, pp. 136–7.

4   W. Booth, *In Darkest England and the Way Out*, first published 1890, in P. J. Keating, *Into Unkown England 1866–1913*, pp. 141–51.

5   J. London, *The People of the Abyss*, first published 1903, London, 1977 edn, p. 1.

6   J. Hollingshead, *Ragged in London in 1861*, first published 1861, New York, 1985 edn, pp. 39–40 and 165–8; W. Besant, *East London*, first published 1899, New York, 1980 edn, pp. 14–17; London, *The People of the Abyss*, p. 88.

7   William J. Fishman, *East End 1888. A Year in a London Borough among the Labouring Poor*, London, 1888, p. 1.

8   J. D. Beasley, *The Bitter Cry Heard and Heeded. The Story of the South London Mission, 1889–1989*, London, 1990, p. 218.

9   B. B. Gilbert, *The Evolution of National Insurance in Great Britain – The Origins of the Welfare State*, London, 1973, p. 28.

10   D. Read, *England 1868–1914. The Age of Urban Democracy*, Harlow, 1979 end, p. 253.

11   A. Mearns, *The Bitter Cry of Outcast London. An Inquiry into the Condition of the Abject Poor*, first published 1883, London 1980 edn, pp. 9–10, 17 and 22–3.

12 G. Gissing, *The Nether World*, first published 1889, London 1973 edn, introduced by W. Allen, pp. x and 129–30.

13 T. Wright, *Our New Masters*, first published 1873, New York, 1984 edn, pp. 48–53 and 367–78.

14 C. Shaw, *When I Was A Child*, first published 1903, London, 1980 edn, pp. 121–2.

15 R. Samuel, *East End Underworld. Chapters in the Life of Arthur Harding*, London, 1981, p. 1.

16 Robert R. Hyde, *Industry was my Parish*, London, 1968, p. 29.

17 J. Stamper, *So Long Ago . . .*, London, 1960, pp. 29–30.

18 H. Shimmin, *The Courts and Alleys of Liverpool*, first published 1864, New York, 1985 edn, p. 39.

19 M. Anderson, *Family Structure in Nineteenth Century Lancashire*, Cambridge, 1971, pp. 40 and 154.

20 J. C. Doherty, *Short-Distance Migration in Mid-Victorian Lancashire: Blackburn and Bolton 1851–1871*, unpublished Ph.D. thesis, University of Lancaster, 1985, cited in D. Beattie, *Blackburn. The Development of a Lancashire Cotton Town*, Halifax, 1992, p. 55.

21 C. Simon, *La vie dans les taudis de Summer Lane: 1881–1891*, unpublished mémoire de maîtrise, Université de Franche-Comté, 1993, p. 41.

22 J. Davis, 'Jennings' Buildings and the Royal Borough. The construction of the underclass in mid-Victorian England', in D. Feldman and G. Stedman Jones (eds) *Metropolis. London. Histories and Representations Since 1800*, London, 1989, p. 22.

23 C. Chinn, *Birmingham. The Great Working City*, Birmingham, 1994, pp. 76–80.

24 E. Ross, '"Fierce questions and taunts": married life in working-class London, 1870–1914', *Feminist Studies*, 8:3, 1982, p. 577.

25 Robert Roberts, *The Classic Slum. Salford Life in the First Quarter of the Century*, first published 1971, Harmondsworth, 1973 edn, p. 29.

26 Robert Roberts, *A Ragged Schooling. Growing up in the Classic Slum*, first published 1976, Manchester, 1987 edn, p. 2.

27 Samuel, *East End Underworld*, pp. 5–8.

28 K. Haines and C. Shilton, *Hard Times Good Times. Tales of Portsea People*, Portsea, 1987, pp. 48–9 and 78–8; Anonymous, '"More than an example": Ancoats in historical perspective', *Manchester Region History Review*, VII, 1993, p. 4.

29 C. Chinn, *The Heartlands Collection at Bloomsbury Library. Finding Your Way into Your Past*, Birmingham 1993, pp. 1–5.

30 Samuel, *East End Underworld*, p. 8.

31 E. Flint, *Hot Bread and Chips*, London, 1963, pp. 41–2.

32 Peckham People's History, *The Time of Our Lives. Growing up in the Southwark Area, 1900–1945*, London, 1983, pp. 7 and 14–16.

33 H. McLeod, *Class and Religion in the Late Victorian City*, London, 1974, pp. 7–9.

34 D. R. Green and A. G. Parton, 'Slums and slum life in Victorian England: London and Birmingham at mid-century', in M. Gaskell (ed.), *Slums*, Leicester, 1990, p. 31.

35 M. Anderson, *Family Structure in Nineteenth Century Lancashire*, Cambridge, 1971, pp. 41–2.

36 L. Lees, *Social Change and Social Stability among the London Irish, 1830–70*, unpublished Ph.D. thesis, Harvard University, 1969, p. 36.

37 D. Englander, *Landlord and Tenant in Urban Britain 1838–1918*, Oxford, 1983, p. 8.

38 C. Chinn Interviews, William and Walter Chinn, 1979, pp. 16–17 and 39.

39 A. S. Jasper, *A Hoxton Childhood*, London, 1969.

40 A. Linton, *Not Expecting Miracles*, London, 1982, p. 2.

41 F. Davies, *My Father's Eyes. Episodes in the Life of a Hulme Man*, Manchester, 1985, p. 7.

42 L. Slater, *'Think On!' Said Mam. A Childhood in Bradford, Manchester 1911–1919*, Manchester, 1984, p. 17.

43 A. Paterson, *Across the Bridges or Life by the South London River-Side*, first published 1911, New York, 1980 edn, p. 36.

44 Roberts, *The Classic Slum*, pp. 42–3 and 81.

45 'Thomas Morgan', in T. Thompson, *Edwardian Childhoods*, London, 1981, p. 17.

46 W. Chinn, *From Victoria's Image*, unpublished ms, no date, pp. 16 and 62.

47 R. Heaton, *Salford. My Home Town*, Manchester, 1982, p. 7.

48 P. McLoughlin, *The Johnson Street Bullies*, Bognor Regis, 1980.

49 J. Douglas, *A Walk Down Summer Lane*, Warwick, 1977; J. G. Mantle, Weslyan Minister, 66, Trinity Road, Aston, 'Letter', *Birmingham Daily Post*, 7 January 1891.

50 P. Mannion and B. Mannion, *The Summer Lane and Newtown of the Years Between the Wars, 1918–1939*, Birmingham, 1985.

51 Simon, *La vie dans les taudis de Summer Lane*, pp. 46–8.

52 G. Davies, 'Beyond the Georgian façade: the Avon Street District of Bath', in M. Gaskell (ed.), *Slums*, Leicester, 1990, p. 175.

53 J. Davis, 'Jennings' Buildings', in Feldman and Jones (eds) *Metropolis*, pp. 13 and 20–3.

54 D. Vincent, *Poor Citizens. The State and the Poor in Twentieth-Century Britain*, London, 1991, pp. 14–15.

55 Roberts, *The Classic Slum*, pp. 14 and 17–23.

56 C. Cookson, *Our Kate*, first published 1969, 1974 edn, p. 22.

57 W. Allen, *All in a Lifetime*, first published 1959, London, 1986 edn, pp. 47 and 49.

58 C. Chinn Interviews, Alice Smith, 1987, p. 1.

59 C. Chinn Interviews, Beattie Hamill, 1987, pp. 1–3.

60 Davies, 'Beyond the Georgian façade', in Gaskell (ed.), *Slums*, p. 179.

61 C. Chinn Interviews, Alice Smith, 1987, p. 4.

62 McLeod, *Class and Religion in the Late Victorian City*, p. 8.

63 S. Meacham, *A Life Apart. The English Working Class 1890–1914*, London, 1977, p. 45.

64 E. Roberts, *A Woman's Place. An Oral History of Working-Class Women 1840–1940*, Oxford, 1985 edn, p. 184.

65 L. Mayell, *The Birmingham I Remember*, Padstow, 1980, p. 12.

66 C. Chinn Interviews, Mr N., 1979, p. 1.

67 C. Chinn Interviews, Walter and William Chinn, 1979, p. 14

68 Chinn, *They Worked All Their Lives*, pp. 27–8.

69 Roberts, *The Classic Slum*, p. 124.

70 A. Davies, *Leisure, Gender and Poverty. Working-Class Culture in Salford and Manchester 1900–1939*, Themes in the Twentieth Century, Buckingham, 1992, p. 109.

71 C. Chinn Interviews, Sam Froggat, 1981, p. 1.

72 P. Sanders, *The Simple Annals. The History of an Essex and East End Family*, Gloucester, 1989, pp. 107–8.

73 C. Chinn, *They Worked All Their Lives: Women of the Urban Poor in England, 1880–1939*, Manchester, 1988, pp. 24–7.

74 Anderson, *Family Structure*, p. 178.

75 Roberts, *A Woman's Place*, p. 171.

76 Green and Parton, 'Slums and slum life in Victorian England', in Gaskell (ed.), *Slums*, p. 82.

77 Roberts, *A Woman's Place*, pp. 183–7.

78 A. Foley, 'A Bolton childhood', in J. Burnett (ed.), *Destiny Obscure. Autobiographies of Childhood, Education and Family from the 1820s to the 1920s*, Harmondsworth, 1984 edn, pp. 100–1.

79 Cookson, *Our Kate*, pp. 22, 83 and 95.

80 Peckham People's History, *The Time of Our Lives*, p. 35; M. Chamberlain, *Old Wives' Tales, Their History, Remedies and Spells*, London, 1981, p. 76.

81 Chinn, *From Victoria's Image*, p. 45.

82 M. P. Reeves, *Round About a Pound a Week*, first published 1913, London, 1979 edn, pp. 66–74.

83 Chinn, *They Worked All Their Lives*, pp. 79–80.

84 M. Tebbutt, *Making Ends Meet. Pawnbroking and Working-Class Credit*, Leicester, 1983.

85 Roberts, *The Classic Slum*, p. 81.

86 G. Haw, *The Life Story of Will Crooks MP*, London, 1917, pp. 8–9; K. Woodward, *Jipping Street*, first published 1928, London, 1983 edn, p. 16.

87 Heaton, *Salford*, p. 1.

88 Chinn, *From Victoria's Image*, p. 27.

89 A. Coley, *Memories of Great Arthur Street*, unpublished ms, 1985, pp. 2 and 6 (thanks to Smethwick Local History Society, Mary Bodfish and Dorothy Williams).

90 Allen, *All in a Lifetime*, p. 50.

91 Foley, 'A Bolton childhood', in Burnett (ed.), *Destiny Obscure*, p. 103.

92 A. Potts, *Whitsters Lane. Recollections of Pendleton and the Manchester Cotton Trade*, Manchester 1985, p. 23.

93 Kathleen Dayus, *Her People*, London, 1982, pp. 5 and 7.

94 Cookson, *Our Kate*, p. 85.

95 Roberts, *The Classic Slum*, p. 55.

96 Cited in Chinn, *They Worked All Their Lives*, p. 146.

97 Cookson, *Our Kate*, pp. 31 and 40.

98 Roberts, *The Classic Slum*, pp. 24 and 47.

Conclusion

Victorian England was the wealthiest country in the world. Its affluence induced many upper- and middle-class people to feel superior, smug and self-assured. Such sentiments could not hide the inequalities and divisions within England. In the midst of great prosperity there persisted widespread and severe poverty. Commentators with a social conscience recognised this awful paradox. They proclaimed the unfairness of a society which did not allow millions of citizens a share in the national bounty. In the later nineteenth century, their arguments were bolstered by the results of statistical enquiries. These showed that about thirty per cent of English people were poor at any one time. This proportion was startling to all but the working class.

Social scientific investigations stressed not only the extent of poverty but also its causes. For generations the poor had been castigated as lazy, reckless and improvident. They had been told that they could escape their poverty easily. Their destiny was in their own hands. They needed to work hard, save and be cautious. Such contentions were insensitive and ignorant. In most cases poverty was the fault of adverse economic conditions. People were poor because they could not earn sufficient money to improve their situation. Their meagre incomes were the result of low pay, irregular work, unemployment, seasonality, illness, injury and other negative external factors. Many craftsmen and their families were affected by these phenomena, but the majority of the poor were characterised by their lack of skill. Prominent amongst them were women, children, the elderly, people with a physical disability or mental illness and those who belonged to ethnic minorities.

These people were driven into slums because they had no bargaining power. They could afford to rent only the worst-built dwellings in the most overcrowded and insanitary districts. Here were the small factories and workshops which gave jobs to unskilled men and women and to the sweated of the skilled. And here were the large populations which allowed street traders to scratch a living. Lacking drains, sewers, clean air and fresh water, the slums bred diseases and fostered illnesses. Public health reforms did bring improvements in sanitation, but overcrowding was made worse by clearances for railways and public buildings. By 1914, millions of English people were still living in small, dilapidated dwellings which did not have their own lavatories or supplies of water.

To many outsiders, a slum was an abyss – a bleak, depressing and dismal place. It was felt that the urban poor matched their depressing environment. They were debased as the 'residuum', they were degraded as the 'ragged', they were demeaned as un-English. Small, dark haired, sallow skinned and noisy, they were the 'pavement folk' who could not work or fight successfully for the nation. This concern about physical efficiency became prominent at the turn of the twentieth century, at a time when investigations showed that most of the poor were not at fault for their condition. Consequently there was a shift of attitude towards government intervention. In particular, it was felt that the State had a responsibility to raise a more healthy race. This could be achieved by giving help to mothers and the young.

The poor were talked about, written about, worried about and feared about. Dedicated clergymen and female charity workers pleaded on their behalf, thoughtful commentators discussed their plight, and knowledgeable witnesses proclaimed initiatives to help them. No one sought the view of those who were most expert about poverty. No one asked the opinion of the urban poor themselves. They were disfranchised in the most effective and damning way. They were excluded from the debate about their lives. But they were not inactive. Nor were they incapable. Jeered at as workshy, the men, women and children of the urban poor toiled to earn money to survive. Accused of thriftlessness, mothers developed strategies to buy food cheaply and to make appetising and nourishing meals. Calumnied as unfeeling, older women provided vital services at births and in death. Slandered as the people of hell, neighbours and kin bonded together to support each other, to help each other and to care for each other. Daily the urban poor fought their poverty. For the most part, they did so with dignity and respect for others.

Selected documents

Document 1

L. G. Chiozza Money, *Riches and Poverty*, first published 1905, New York, 1980 edn, pp. 310–11.

In 1868, Dudley Baxter, in his classical paper on the National Income read to the Royal Statistical Society, estimated that in 1867, the population being 30,000,000, the manual workers, then estimated to number 10,960,000, took £325,000,000 out of the total national income of £814,000,000. Thus the average wage of the manual workers (men, women and children) was estimated at nearly £30 per head per annum . . . . If, then, we adopt the estimate of Baxter we shall probably be as near the truth as is now possible. Accepting it, we find that the manual workers in 1867 took about 40 per cent. of the national income.

The manual workers in our present population of 43,000,000 may be estimated at 15,000,000 and they take, as we have seen, about £655,000,000 out of a total estimated income of £1,710,000,000, or less than 40 per cent. of the whole.

Thus the position of the manual workers, in relation to the general wealth of the country, has not improved. They formed, with those dependent upon them, the greater part of the nation in 1867, – thirty-eight years ago, – and they enjoyed but about 40 per cent. of the national income according to the careful estimate of Dudley Baxter. Today, with their army of dependants, they still form the greater part of the nation, although not quite so great a part, and, according to the best information available, they still take about 40 per cent. of the entire income of the nation.

Document 2

Thomas Carlyle, *Past and Present*, 1843, in A. Shelston (ed.), *Thomas Carlyle: Selected Writings*, Harmondsworth, 1971 p. 259.

The condition of England, on which many pamphlets are now in the course of publication, and many thoughts unpublished are going on in every reflective head, is justly regarded as one of the most ominous, and withal one of the strangest, ever seen in this world. England is full of wealth, of multifarious produce, supply for human want in every kind; yet England is dying of inanition. With unabated bounty the land of England blooms and grows; waving with yellow harvests; thick-studded with workshops, industrial implements, with fifteen millions of workers, understood to be the strongest, cunningest and the willingest our Earth ever had; these men are here; the work they have done, the fruit they have realised is here, abundant, exuberant on every hand of us: and behold, some baleful fiat as of Enchantment has gone forth, saying, 'Touch it not, ye workers, ye master-workers, ye master-idlers; none of you can touch it, no man of you shall be the better for it; this is enchanted fruit!' On the poor workers such fiat falls first, in its rudest shape; but on the rich master-workers too it falls; neither can the master-idlers, nor any richest or highest man escape, but all are like to be brought low with it, and made 'poor' enough in the money sense or a fataler one.

Document 3

Charles E. B. Russell, *Social Problems of the North*, first published 1913, New York, 1980 edn, p. 2.

The truth is that the magnitude and importance to the whole country of the social problems of the North have never been sufficiently grasped because people have not realised the vastness of the population concerned. London with its five million inhabitants has made effective appeal to the imagination of the philanthropic, but it has never been brought home to them that an even larger and in parts more crowded population may be found elsewhere. Within the districts covered by Manchester and Liverpool with the contiguous towns there teems a population of over seven millions, and however great the destitution and misery which certain parts of London may present, it is doubtful whether the degradation in its meanest streets in any way equals the degradation of the lowest classes in Liverpool.

Document 4

B. Seebohm Rowntree, *Poverty. A Study of Town Life*, first published 1901, New York, 1980 edn, pp. 133–5.

And let us clearly understand what 'merely physical efficiency' means. A family living upon the scale allowed for in this estimate must never spend a penny on railway fare or omnibus. They must never go into the country unless they walk. They must never purchase a halfpenny newspaper or spend a penny to buy a ticket for a popular concert. They must write no letters to absent children, for they cannot afford to pay the postage. They must never contribute anything to their church or chapel, or give any help to a neighbour which costs them money. They cannot save, nor can they join sick club or Trade Union, because they cannot pay the necessary subscriptions. The children must have no pocket money for dolls, marbles, or sweets. The father must smoke no tobacco, and must drink no beer. The mother must never buy any pretty clothes for herself or for her children, the character of the family wardrobe as for the family diet being governed by the regulation, 'Nothing must be bought but that which is absolutely necessary for the maintenance of physical health and what is bought must be of the plainest and most economical disposition.' Should a child fall ill, it must be attended by the parish doctor; should it die, it must be buried by the parish. Finally, the wage earner must never be absent from his work for a single day.

If any of these conditions are broken, the extra expenditure involved is met, *and can only be met*, by limiting the diet; or, in other words, by sacrificing physical efficiency.

That few York labourers receiving 20s. or 21s. per week submit to these iron conditions in order to maintain physical efficiency is obvious. And even if they were to submit, physical efficiency would be unattainable for those who had three or more children dependent upon them. It cannot be too clearly understood, not too emphatically repeated, *that whenever a worker having three children dependent on him, and receiving not more than 21s. 8d. per week, indulges in any expenditure beyond that required for the barest physical needs, he can do so only at the cost of his own physical efficiency, or that of some members of his family.*

Document 5

Edward G. Howarth and Mona Wilson (eds), *West Ham. A Study in Social and Industrial Problems*, first published 1907, New York, 1980 edn, pp. 400–1.

The effect of the predominance of casual labour in West Ham is that a large proportion of the population depends upon irregular earnings and is in a state of chronic under-employment. In many cases the sum earned, if evenly distributed throughout the year, would undoubtedly be insufficient for a decent livelihood; and the uncertainty of the earnings adds to the difficulty of living. These being the normal conditions, it is obvious that depression of trade or unusually severe weather may suddenly produce considerable distress. The existence of chronic poverty, and the periods of exceptional distress, must, therefore, be accepted as incident to the present industrial conditions of the district.

Document 6

Henry Mayhew, *London Labour and the London Poor, Volume I,* London, 1861–62, pp. 11–12.

'After I put my hip out, I couldn't get my living as I'd been used to do. I couldn't stand a day if I had five hundred pounds for it. I must sit down. So I got a little stall, and sat at the end of the alley here with a few laces and tapes and things. I've done so for this last nine year past, and seen many a landlord come in and go out of the house I sat at. My husband used to sell small articles in the streets – black lead and furniture paste, and blacking. We got a sort of living like this, the two of us together. It's very seldom though we had a bit of meat. We had 1s 9d rent to pay – Come, my poor fellow, will you have another little drop to wet your mouth?' said the woman, breaking off. 'Come, my dearest, let me give you this,' she added, as the man let his jaw fall, and she poured some warm sugar and water flavoured with cinnamon – all she had to give him – into his mouth. 'He's been an ailing man this many a year. He used to go on errands and buy my little things for me, on account of my being lame. We assisted one another, you see. He wasn't able to work for his living, and I wasn't able to go about, so he used to go about and buy for me what I sold. I am sure he never earned above 1s 6d in the week. He used to attend me, and many a time I've sat in the cold and the wet and didn't take a sixpence. Some days I'd make a shilling, and some days less; but whatever I got I used to have to put a good part into the basket to keep my little stock.' [A knock here came to the door; it was for a halfpenny worth of darning cotton.] 'You know a shilling goes further with a poor couple that's sober than two shillings does with a drunkard. We lived poor, you see, never had nothing but tea, or we couldn't have done anyhow. If I'd take 18d. in the day I'd think I was grandly off, and then if there was 6d. profit got out of that it would be almost as much as it would. You see these cotton braces here' (said the old woman going to her tray). 'Well, I gives 2s 9d a dozen for them here, and I sells 'em for 4½d., and sometimes 4d. a pair. Now, this piece of tape would cost me seven farthings in the shop, and I sells it at six yards a penny. It has the *name* of being eighteen yards. The profit out of it is five farthings. It's beyond the power of man to wonder how there's a bit of bread got out of such a small way. And the times is so bad, too.'

Document 7

Charles Kingsley, *Alton Locke, Tailor and Poet. An Autobiography*, first published 1850, Oxford edn, 1983, pp. 103–4.

The employer of Alton Locke has decided to move away from the honourable trade and to give out work in the homes of his men. When the announcement is made, John Crossthwaite sets out the grim future which faces him and his fellow workers:

We were all bound to expect this. Every working tailor must come to this at last, on the present system; and we are only lucky in having being spared so long. You all know where this will end – in the same misery as fifteen thousand out of twenty thousand of our class are enduring now. We shall become the slaves, often the bodily prisoners of Jews, middlemen, and sweaters, who draw their livelihood out of starvation. We shall have to face, as the rest have, ever decreasing prices of labour, ever increasing profits made out of that labour by the contractors who will employ us – arbitrary fines, inflicted at the caprice of hirelings – the competition of women, and children and starving Irish – our hours of work will increase one-third, our actual pay decrease to less than one-half; and in all this we shall have no hope, no chance of improvement in wages, but even more penury, slavery, misery, as we are pressed on by those who are sucked by fifties – almost by hundreds – yearly, out of the honourable trade in which we were brought up, into the infernal system of contract work, which is devouring our trade and many others, body and soul. Our wives will be forced to sit up night and day to help us – our children must labour from the cradle without chance of going to school, hardly breathing the fresh air of heaven – our boys as they grow up must turn beggars or paupers – our daughters, as thousands do, must eke out their miserable earnings by prostitution. And after all, a whole family will not gain what one of us had been doing, as yet, single-handed. You know there will be no hope for us.

Document 8

City of Birmingham Health Department, *Report on the Industrial Employment of Married Women and Infantile Mortality*, Birmingham, 1910, pp. 17–19.

At the end of twelve months the weight of 816 babies was accurately obtained. Of these, 260 were the infants of mothers industrially employed after confinement, 157 were infants of women employed before but not after confinement, and 399 were those of mothers not industrially employed either before or after confinement. The average weights of these children was as follows:–

		Average Weight of Babies
260	Industrially employed mothers after confinement	17.3 lbs
157	Industrially employed mothers before but not after confinement	18.0 lbs
399	Mothers not industrially employed	18.0 lbs

The value of breast-feeding has so often been referred to that it is not surprising to find that the babies so fed were heavier and better nourished children. The weight of the baby in relation to its feeding up to six months of age is shown in the following table:–

	No. of Babies weighed	Average Weight of Babies at 12 months
All infants breast-fed for 6 months	466	18.0 lbs
All infants partially breast-fed for 6 months	177	17.2 lbs
All infants bottle-fed for 6 months	173	17.2 lbs

In the course of the weighings it was found that the question of the degree of poverty had a very considerable influence on the infant, whether breast-fed or not. This is shown in the following figures:–

Income of family, excluding mothers, at time of birth	No. of babies weighed	Average Weight of Baby at 12 months
Father out of Work	107	17.6 lbs
Total Income under 10s. per week	52	16.8 "
" " 10s.–20s. " "	303	17.5 "
" " 20s.-30s. " "	300	18.3 "
" " over 30s. " "	39	18.8 "
Illegitimate Children, no income at first visit	15	18.0 "

These figures very clearly show the powerful effect of poverty on the infant. It does not very much matter whether the mother is industrially employed or not, or whether the infant is breast-fed or not, if great poverty exists the infant suffers want of nutrition, as evidenced in these average weights.

Document 9

Margaret Llewellyn Davies, *Maternity Letters from Working Women*, first published 1915, London, 1978 edn, pp. 30–1.

11. 'I Was Awfully Poor'

My first girl was born before I attained my twentieth year, and I had a stepmother who had no children of her own, so I was not able to get any knowledge from her; and even had she known anything I don't suppose she would have dreamt of telling me about these things which were supposed to exist, but must not be talked about. About a month before the baby was born I remember asking my aunt where the baby would come from. She was astounded, and did not make me much wiser. I don't know whether my ignorance had anything to do with the struggle I had to bring the baby into the world, but the doctor said my youth had, for I was not properly developed. Instruments had to be used, and I heard the doctor say he could not tell whether my life could be saved or not, for he said there is not room here for a bird to pass. All the time I thought that this was the way all babies were born.

At the commencement of all my pregnancies I suffered terribly from toothache, and for this reason I think all married child-bearing women should have their teeth attended to, for days and nights of suffering of this kind must have a bad effect on both the mother and the child. I also at times suffered torments from cramp in the legs and vomiting, particularly during the first three months. I hardly think the cramp can be avoided, but if prospective mothers would consult their doctors about the inability to retain food, I fancy that might be remedied. At the commencement of my second pregnancy I was very ill indeed. I could retain no food, not even water, and I was constipated for thirteen days, and I suffered from jaundice. This had its effect on the baby, for he was quite yellow at birth, and the midwife having lodgers to attend to, left him unwashed for an hour after birth. She never troubled to get his lungs inflated, and he was two days without crying. I had no doctor. I was awfully poor, so that I had to wash the baby's clothes in my bedroom at the fortnight's end; but had I had the knowledge like I possess now, I should have insisted at the very least on the woman seeing my child's lungs were properly filled. When we are poor, though, we cannot say what must be done; we have to suffer and keep quiet. The boy was always weakly, and could not walk when my third baby was born. He had fits from twelve to fourteen, but except for a rather 'loose' frame, seems otherwise quite healthy now.

My third child, a girl, was born in a two-roomed 'nearly under-ground' dwelling. We had two beds in the living-room, and the little scullery was very damp. Had it not been for my neighbours, I should have had no attendance after the confinement, and no fire often, for it was during one of the coal strikes. My fourth child, a boy, was born under better housing conditions, but not much better as regards money; and during the carrying of all my children, except the first, I have had insufficient food and too much work. This is just an outline. Did I give it all, it would fill a book, as the saying goes . . . . Cleanliness has made rapid strides since my confinements; for never once can I

162

remember having anything but face, neck, and hands washed until I could do things myself, and it was thought certain death to change the underclothes under a week.

For a whole week we were obliged to lie on clothes stiff and stained, and the stench under the clothes was abominable, and added to this we were commanded to keep the babies under the clothes.

I often wondered how the poor little mites managed to live, and perhaps they never would have done but for our adoration, because this constant admiration of our treasures did give them whiffs of fresh air very often.

My husband's lowest wage was 10s., the highest about £1 only, which was reached by overtime. His mother and my own parents generally provided me with clothing, most of which was cast-offs.

Document 10

Friedrich Engels, *The Condition of the Working Class in England*, first published 1845, Harmondsworth, 1987 edn, pp. 85–6.

The whole assemblage of buildings is commonly called Manchester, and contains about 400,000 inhabitants, rather more than less. The town itself is peculiarly built, so that a person may live in it for years, and go in and out of it daily without coming into contact with a working people's quarter or even with workers, that is, so long as he confines himself to his business or pleasure walks. This arises chiefly from the fact, that by unconscious tacit agreement, as well as with outspoken conscious determination, the working people's quarters are sharply separated from the sections of the city reserved for the middle class; or, if this does not succeed, they are concealed with a cloak of charity. Manchester contains, at its heart, a rather extended commercial district, perhaps half a mile long and about as broad, and consisting almost wholly of offices and warehouses. Nearly the whole district is abandoned by dwellers, and is lonely and deserted by night . . . . This district is cut through by certain main thoroughfares upon which the vast traffic concentrates, and in which the ground level is occupied by brilliant shops . . . . With the exception of this commercial district, all Manchester proper, all Salford and Hulme, a great part of Pendleton and Chorlton, two-thirds of Ardwick, and single stretches of Cheetham Hill and Broughton are all unmixed working people's quarters, stretching like a girdle, averaging about a mile and a half in breadth, around the commercial district. Outside, beyond this girdle, lives the upper and middle bourgeoisie, the middle bourgeoisie in regularly laid

out streets in the vicinity of the working quarters, especially in
Chorlton and the lower lying portions of Cheetham Hill; the upper
bourgeoisie in remoter villas with gardens in Chorlton or Ardwick, or
on the breezy heights of Cheetham Hill, Broughton and Pendleton, in
free, wholesome country air, in fine, comfortable homes.

Document 11

Royal Commission on the Housing of the Working Classes, *First
Report*, London, 1884–85, p.18.

Causes of High Rents	High rents are due to the competition for houses and the scarcity of accommodation in proportion to the population. It might be asked why cannot the pressure be relieved by a distribution of the now crowded
Compulsion to Live Near Work	masses over the area of the metropolis, inasmuch as it is a well known fact that for various causes certain districts contain a large number of uninhabited houses, many of which are suitable for the working classes. The answer to this query, which will have to be referred to again when the question of suburban residence is dealt with, is that an enormous proportion of the dwellers in overcrowded quarters are necessarily compelled to
Brighty 3498, 3534, 3548. Cobden, 4797.	live close to their work, no matter what the price charged or what the condition of the property they inhabit. It has been seen how crowded the poor central districts of London are, and one reason is that for a large class of labourers it is necessary to live as nearly as possible in the middle of the town because they then command the labour market of the whole metropolis from a convenient centre. Sometimes they hear of casual work to be had at a certain place provided they are there by 6 o'clock the next morning, so they must choose a central position from which no part of the town is inaccessible.

Document 12

Kathleen Dayus, *Her People*, London, 1982, pp. 3–5.

Our street was called Camden Street. Along one side of this street
facing the high school wall ran ten terraces called 'groves'. Ours was

called Camden Drive. There were five houses or hovels with five more back-to-backs to each terrace. They were all built the same; one large living room, one bedroom, and an attic. There were also cellars that ran under each house, damp, dark and cold. Here was where they kept their coal, 'slack', or wood when they had any, which was never very often. For this reason there was always some rubbish tipped in the cellar ready to be put on the fire for warmth or for cooking. I don't suppose this habit would be regarded as altogether healthy today but then it was essential . . . . At the end of the yard stood three ashcans and five lavatories, or closets as we called them. These each consisted of a square box with [a] large round hole in the middle. Us children had to hold the sides of the seat otherwise we could have fallen in. These were dry closets. You can imagine the stench in the summer! Next to the closets were two wash-houses where every washday everybody did their weekly wash. Like all the outhouses they were shared between the five houses in our yard and the five that backed on to us. There were always rows over whose turn it was to clean the closets so to save further quarrels Dad put a big padlock on one and gave Mrs Buckley next door a key to share. We kept our key on a cotton-reel tied with string behind our living-room door. The other closets were left open for anyone to use and they were filthy. We had to hold our noses as we passed by, but Mom and Mrs Buckley always saw to it that ours was kept clean; her girls and Liza and I had to do it in turns while the women looked. Finally there was a gas lamp in the centre of the yard and also a tap where everybody got their weather for all household uses.

Document 13

Photograph overleaf: Interior of back-to-back in Birmingham about 1905, Edward Cadbury, M. Cécile Matheson and George Shann, *Women's Work and Wages. A Phase of Life in an Industrial City,* London, 1906.

Document 14

Hector Gavin, MD, FRCSE, *Unhealthiness of London, and the Necessity of Remedial Measures,* first published 1847, New York, 1985 edn, pp. 11–12.

Thus, if we compare the average age at death of the gentry, the tradesmen, and the artisans in London, we find that while the gentry live to 44 years of age, the tradesmen live only to 23, and the artisans to 22 years of age.* But if we except the deaths of those below 21, we find that while the gentry die at 61, the tradesman dies at 50, and the artisans at 49 years of age . . . .

This frightful decrement in the scale of existence of the operatives, labourers, and tradesmen of the Metropolis and our large towns, is further established by the fact, that if a comparison be instituted between the inhabitants of St. Giles's and St. George's, Bloomsbury, it is found that those who reside in the squares and open streets of the comparatively healthy district of St. George's, live, on average, at least 40 years; while the average duration of life among the labouring classes, who chiefly reside in St. Giles's is 17 years! being 23 years less than the average of the gentry and their families, and 9 years less than among tradesmen and their families. In Shoreditch, again, the average age at death is 19 years; and the loss of life, as compared with the gentry, amounts to 28 years. The difference in favour of tradesmen is 4 years. In Bethnal Green, as has just been shown, the difference between the average age at death of the gentry at 45, and of the labourer at 16, is 29 years.

*Calculated from the deaths in 1839.

Document 15

Mrs Caswell, *Sparkhill and Greet Maternity and Infant Welfare Centre, 1920,* unpublished manuscript supplied by Ivy Caswell.

I have been asked many times how I came to be interested in the Social Problems in Duddeston Area, Floodgate Street., River Street., Milk Street., Little Ann Street. etc. and so I begin at the very beginning. I was elected on the Executive Committee of Women's Adult School . . . . We were offered a bright room at Medical Mission and our first meeting about a dozen women came 15 mins to eight. They enjoyed coming and its numbers went up then. One of the women was sick. I went to visit her in one of the worst possible slums. After coming away, I noticed a very poor looking young woman sitting at an old table with glue pot and making paper boxes. At her side was an old Pram with a tin of condensed milk beside. The young mother was dipping a teat in it putting it into the child's mouth to keep it from crying.

It was a hot day. The Courtyard smelled awful. No lavatory doors and in those days just pans to be emptied, down the child's front where the milk dribbled was covered with Blow flies, it turned me sick. I spoke to the husband inside who was just smoking feet on an old fashioned guard. His language to me to mind my own business, I was hindering his wife, he wanted the boxes done to get the money, said 'if not quick he would not be in time to put the money from the boxes on his horse', I was shocked at the conditions. I had seen before children sitting on steps with chunks of bread and pieces of haddock (uncooked) for their dinners just pulling pieces off. Father's barrow men, mothers rag market women. Neighbours I learned, just keeping an eye on them.

I went to see Miss J. Lloyd and she helped me get in touch with Health Dept. The young woman and baby were immediately taken to Hospital, both passed away in a few days. So this is just what inspired us, to Visit to see the conditions round that district and do something to help the mothers. We started a small class Miss Lloyd having been Matron of a large Hospital and so she was able to give advice on many complaints.

Document 16

Arthur Morrison, *A Child of the Jago*, first published 1896, London, 1946 edn, pp. 19–22.

The triumphs of the East End Elevation Mission and Pansophical Institute were known and appreciated far from East London, by people who knew less of that part than of Asia Minor. Indeed, they were chiefly appreciated by these. There were kept, perpetually on tap for the aspiring East Ender, the Higher Life, the Greater Thought, and the Wider Humanity: with other radiant abstractions, mostly in the comparative degree, specifics all for the manufacture of the Superior Person. There were many Lectures given on still more subjects. Pictures were borrowed and shown, with revelations to the Uninformed of the morals ingeniously concealed by the painters. The Uninformed were also encouraged to debate and produce papers on literary and political matters, while still unencumbered with the smallest knowledge thereof: for the Enlargement of the Understanding and the Embellishment of the Intellect. And there were classes, and clubs, and newspapers, and games of draughts, and musical evenings, and a brass band, whereby the life of the Hopeless Poor might be coloured, and the Misery of the Submerged alleviated. The wretches who crowded to these benefits were tradesmen's sons, small shopkeepers and their families, and neat clerks, with here and there a smart young artisan of one of the especially respectable trades. They freely patronised the clubs, the musical evenings, the brass band, and the bagatelle board; and those who took themselves seriously debated and Mutually-Improved with pomp. Others, subject to savage fits of wanting-to-know, made short rushes at random evening classes, with intervals of disgusted apathy. Altogether, a number of decently-dressed and mannerly young men passed many evenings at the Pansophical Institute in harmless pleasures, and often with an agreeable illusion of intellectual advance.

Other young men, more fortunately circumstanced, with the educational varnish fresh and raw upon them, came from afar, equiped with a foreign mode of thought and a proper ignorance of the world and the proportion of things, as Missionaries. Not without some anxiety to their parents, they plunged into the perilous deeps of the East End, to struggle – for a fortnight – with its sufferings and brutishness. So they went amongst tradesmen's sons and the shopmen, who endured them as they endured the nominal subscription; and they came away with a certain relief, and with some misgiving as to what impression they had made, and what they had done to make it. But it was with knowledge and authority that they went back among those who had doubted their safety in the dark region. The East End, they reported, was nothing like it was said to be. You could see much worse places up West. The people were quite a decent sort, in their way: shocking Bounders, of course; but quite clean and quiet, and very comfortably dressed, with ties and collars and watches.

Document 17

Jack London, *The People of the Abyss*, first published 1903, London, 1977 edn, pp. 91–2.

Class supremacy can rest only on class degradation; and when the workers are segregated in the Ghetto, they cannot escape the consequent degradation. A short and stunted people is created—a breed strikingly differentiated from their master's breed, a pavement folk, as it were, lacking stamina and strength. The men become caricatures of what physical men ought to be, and their women and children are pale and anaemic, with eyes ringed darkly, who stoop and slouch, and are early twisted out of all shapeliness and beauty.

To make matters worse, the men of the Ghetto are the men who are left – a deteriorated stock, left to undergo still further deterioration. For a hundred and fifty years at least, they have been drained of their best. The strong men, the men of pluck and initiative, and ambition have been faring forth to the fresher and freer portions of the globe, to make new lands and new nations. Those who are lacking, the weak of heart, of head and hand, as well as the rotten and hopeless, have remained to carry on and breed. And year by year, in turn, the best they breed are taken from them. Wherever a man of vigour and stature manages to grow up, he is haled forthwith into the army. A soldier, as Bernard Shaw has said, 'ostensibly a heroic and patriotic defender of his country, is really an unfortunate man driven by destitution to offer himself as food for powder for the sake of regular rations, shelter, and clothing'.

The constant selection of the best from the workers has impoverished those who are left, a sadly degraded remainder, for the great part, which, in the Ghetto, sinks to the deepest depths. The wine of life has been drawn off to spill itself in blood and progeny over the rest of the earth. Those that remain are the lees, and they are segregated and steeped in themselves. They become indecent and bestial.

Document 18

George R. Sims, *How the Poor Live and Horrible London*, articles first published 1883, 2nd edn 1889, in Peter Keating (ed.), *Into Unknown England 1866–1913. Selections from the Social Explorers*, Glasgow, 1976, pp. 65–7.

I commence, with the first of these chapters, a book of travel. An author and an artist have gone hand-in-hand into many a far-off region of the earth, and the result has been a volume eagerly studied by the stay-at-home public, anxious to know something of the world in which they live. In these pages I propose to record the result of a journey into a region which lies at our own doors – into a dark continent that is within easy walking distance of the General Post Office. This continent will, I hope, be found as interesting as any of those newly-explored lands which engage the attention of the Royal Geographical Society – the wild races who inhabit it will, I trust, gain public sympathy as easily as those savage tribes for whose benefit the Missionary Societies never cease to appeal for funds.

I have no shipwrecks, no battles, no moving adventures by flood and field, to record. Such perils as I and my fellow-traveller have encountered on our journey are not of the order which lend themselves to stirring narrative. It is unpleasant to be mistaken, in underground cellars where the vilest outcasts hide from the light of day, for detectives in search of their prey – it is dangerous to breathe for some hours at a stretch an atmosphere charged with infection and poisoned with indescribable effluvia – it is hazardous to be hemmed in down a blind alley by a crowd of roughs who have had hereditarily transmitted the maxim of John Leech, that half-bricks were specially designed for the benefit of 'strangers'; but these are not adventures of the heroic order, and they will not be dwelt upon lovingly after the manner of travellers who go further afield.

Document 19

Robert Roberts, *The Classic Slum. Salford Life in the First Quarter of the Century*, first published 1971, Harmondsworth, 1973 edn, pp.16–17.

Every industrial city, of course, enfolds within itself a cluster of loosely defined overlapping 'villages'. Those in the Great Britain of seventy years ago were almost self-contained communities. Our own consisted of some thirty streets and alleys locked along the north and south by two railway systems a furlong apart. About twice that distance to the east lay another slum which turned on its farthest side into a land of bonded warehouses and the city proper. West of us, well beyond the tramlines, lay the middle classes, bay-windowed and begardened. We knew them not.

In the city as a whole our village rated indubitably low. 'The children of this school', wrote one of King Edward VII's inspectors, commenting on our only seat of learning, are of the poorest class; so, too, is the teaching.' With cash or on tick, our villagers, about three thousand in all, patronised fifteen beer-houses, a hotel, and two off-licences, nine grocery and general shops, three greengrocers (for ever struggling to survive against the street hawker), two tripe shops, three barbers, three cloggers, two cook shops, one fish and chip shop (*declassé*), an old clothes store, a couple of pawnbrokers and two loan offices.

Religion was served by two chapels (Primitive Methodist and Congregationalist), one 'tin' mission (Church of England) and one sinister character who held spiritualist séances in his parlour and claimed from the window to cure 'Female Bad Legs'. (Through overwork numerous women suffered from burst varicose veins.) Culture, pleasure and need found outlet through one theatre (and, later, three cinemas), a dancing room ('low'), two coy brothels, eight bookmakers, and a private moneylender.

The first of our public buildings reared its dark bulk near the railway wall. Hyndman Hall, home of the Social Democratic Federation (SDF), remained for us mysteriously aloof and through the years had, in fact, about as much political impact as the near-by gasworks. The second establishment, our Conservative Club, except for a few days at election times, didn't appear to meddle with politics at all. It was noticeable usually for a union jack in the window and a brewer's dray at the door.

Over one quarter of a mile industry stood represented by a dying brickworks and an iron foundry. Several gasholders on the south side polluted the air, sometimes for days together. Little would grow; even the valiant aspidistra pined. We possessed besides two coal yards, a corn store, a cattle wharf and perhaps as closed an urban society as any in Europe.

Document 20

Photograph opposite: Celebrations outside the Gate Inn, Studley Street, possibly on the occasion of the Relief of Mafeking during the Boer War, 1900. Collection of Mike Tunnicliffe.

Document 21

Photograph page 174: Cromwell Street, Nechells, Birmingham about 1905, 'The Slum Collection', Birmingham Library Services.

Bibliographical essay

Research into the urban poor needs to be embedded within the framework of English society as a whole. There are a number of general studies which are important in this regard. One of the most thought provoking of them is F. Bédarida, *A Social History of England 1851–1990*, London, 1990 edn. Prominent amongst the other significant overviews are: J. Harris, *Private Lives, Public Spirit: Britain 1870–1914*, London, 1993, in the Penguin Social History of Britain series; and D. Read, *England 1868–1914. The Age of Urban Democracy*, London, 1979.

Several important books on the working class in general have taken fresh approaches. These include two studies in the Themes in British Social History series: J. Rule, *The Labouring Class in Early Industrial England 1750–1850*, London, 1986; and J. Benson, *The Working Class in Britain 1850–1939*, London, 1989. Other stimulating works are J. Belchem, *Industrialization and the Working Class. The English Experience, 1750–1900*, Aldershot, 1991; J. Bourke, *Working-Class Cultures in Britain. Gender, Class and Ethnicity, 1890–1960*, London, 1994; and S. Meacham, *A Life Apart. The English Working Class, 1890–1914*, London, 1977. The best book on the lives of working-class women is E. Roberts, *A Woman's Place. An Oral History of Working-Class Women 1890–1914*, Oxford, 1984.

For an excellent, short overview of the debate about poverty see M. E. Rose, 'Poverty and self-help: Britain in the nineteenth and twentieth centuries', in A. Digby, C. Feinstein and D. Jenkins (eds), *New Directions in Economic and Social History, Volume II*, Basingstoke, 1992. Another useful long-term perspective is provided in E. Royle, *Modern Britain. A Social History 1750–1985*, London, 1987.

There are few works on the poor specifically. Two which are essential are J. Treble, *Urban Poverty in Britain 1830–1914*, London, 1983 edn; and M. E. Rose, *The Relief of Poverty*, Basingstoke, 1986 edn, in the series Studies in Economic and Social History. A study which focuses on the importance of women is C. Chinn, *They Worked All Their Lives: Women of the Urban Poor in England, 1880–1939*, Manchester, 1988. A controversial and important work which attends to the poor, casual employment and ideas about poverty in London is G. S. Jones, *Outcast London. A Study in the Relationship between Classes in Victorian Society*, Harmondsworth, 1984 edn. The lives of the poor in the East End of the capital are recorded with compassion in W. J. Fishman, *East End 1888. A Year in a London Borough Among the Labouring Poor*, London, 1988. A first-rate collection of articles into one poor district is 'Ancoats: the first industrial suburb', *Manchester Region History Review*, 7, 1993.

Ethnic minorities are examined in a number of works. For the Irish there is a short but comprehensive pamphlet by R. Swift, *The Irish in Britain, 1815–1914*, London, 1990 – one of the Helps for Students of History Series; for the Jews there is V. D. Lipman, *A History of the Jews in Britain since 1858*, Leicester, 1990; and for the Italians, L. Sponza, *Italian Immigrants in Nineteenth-Century Britain: Realities and Images*, Leicester, 1988.

On urbanisation there is a wide-ranging and impressive collection of articles in the Readers in Urban History series by R. J. Morris and R. Rodger (eds), *The Victorian City. A Reader in British Urban History 1820–1914*, London, 1993. Housing in particular is examined in R. Rodger, *Housing in Urban Britain, 1780–1914*, Basingstoke, 1989, one of the Studies in Economic and Social History; and J. Burnett, *A Social History of Housing 1815–1970*, Newton Abbot, 1978. An excellent work on residential segregation and the environment of the poor is M. Gaskell (ed.), *Slums*, Leicester, 1990.

Public health is covered comprehensively and vividly in A. S. Wohl, *Endangered Lives. Public Health in Victorian Britain*, London, 1984 edn. Health and health care are the subject of H. Jones, *Health and Society in Twentieth-Century Britain*, London, 1994, in the Themes in British Social History series.

Poor Law is discussed by E. C. Midwinter, *Victorian Social Reform*, London, 1968, one of the Seminar Studies in History. The standard study on workhouses is by M. A. Crowther, *The Workhouse System 1834–1929. The History of an English Institution*, London, 1983 edn. The emergence of the Welfare State is described in D. Fraser, *The Evolution of the British Welfare State*, Basingstoke, 1984 edn, whilst the social reforms of the early twentieth century are the subject of J. R. Hay, *The Origins of the Liberal Welfare Reforms, 1906–1914*, Basingstoke, 1983 edn, one of the Studies in Economic and Social History,

Poverty as a concept is examined by G. Himmelfarb, *The Idea of Poverty. England in the Early Industrial Age*, London, 1985 edn. A revisionist work on the Poor Law and social investigators is by K. Williams, *From Pauperism to Poverty*, London, 1981.

For a detailed study on poverty in the twentieth century see D. Vincent, *Poor Citizens. The State and the Poor in Twentieth-Century Britain*, London, 1991.

Index

absolute poverty, 1–2, 23–6, 31–2,
34, 50; *see also* relative poverty
abyss, the, 114, 126–30, 169–70
Adshead, J., 26, 49
age, 25, 39, 44, 56–9, 82, 158–9; *see
also* children; old age
Allen, W., 12, 128, 138
Ancoats, 46, 65, 132
Anderson, M., 130, 134, 143
Archer, T., 103, 118
Avon Street, 78, 137, 140

Barker, P., 27
Barnett, Rev. S., 109, 110
Bass, Rev. T. J., 16, 21, 76
Bath, 78, 137, 140
Baxter, D., 14, 155
Beames, T., 87–8
Beattie, D., 131
Bédarida, F., 2–3, 10
Bell, Lady F., 31, 56
Bermondsey, 84, 105, 128, 131,
134
Besant, W., 111, 127
Bethnal Green, 42, 60, 84, 86, 93,
109, 129, 131, 132, 134, 140, 142,
167
Beveridge, W. H., 49, 110
Birmingham, 3–4, 8, 9, 11, 12, 17,
18, 19, 21, 22–3, 24–5, 26, 32–3,
44, 46 48–9, 53, 55, 60–1, 63,
66–7, 76, 77, 78, 79, 81, 82–3, 85,
86, 88–9, 90, 96, 103, 107, 108,
131, 132, 134, 139, 141, 142,
144, 145, 160–1, 164–6, 167–8
Blackburn, 131
black people, 68
Bolton, 21, 41, 83, 143–4
Booth, C., 27–8, 30, 31, 33, 60, 69,
120–1
Booth, W., 20, 127, 129
Bosanquet, H., 39–40, 60
Bowley, A., 31–2, 43, 57
Bradford, 8, 55, 78
Briggs, A., 17, 109
Brighton, 46, 55
Bristol, 78, 86
Burnett, J., 22, 82
Burnett-Hurst, J., 31–2, 43, 57

Carlyle, T., 15, 156
Caswell, Mrs, 167–8
Chadwick, E., 92
Charity Organisation Society,
39–40, 105–7
Chartism, 15, 18, 40, 51, 66
children, 25, 39, 41, 45, 48, 52, 53,
54, 57–9, 60–1, 68, 90–1, 140,
142, 160–1, 162–3, 165
Chinese, 68
cholera, 18, 91, 93
Christian socialists, 51, 109
class, 8–9, 11–13, 15, 21–6, 38–9
cleanliness, 41, 145–6, 162–3, 165

177

Cole, G. D. H. and M. I., 3
condition of England
 eighteen hundreds, 13–16, 21,
  156
 nineteen thirties, 3
Cook, C., 3
Cookson, C., 139, 144, 145, 146
corner shops, 135–6
cotton district, 17–18, 30, 62, 65,
 94–5
courtyards, 142, 167, 172, 174
Coventry, 50–1
Crooks, W., 55, 57, 102
Crowther, M. A., 104
culture of poverty, 4–5, 118–21

Daunton, M. J., 9
Davies, F., 54, 135
Davies, G., 78, 137
Davies, M. Llewellyn, 63–4, 161
Davis, J., 64–5, 87, 137–8
Dayus, K., 83, 96, 145, 164–5
death of chief wage earner, 43, 62
death rates, 60–1, 96; *see also* life
 expectancy
Denison, E., 109–110
deserted wives, 62–3
Dickens, C., 12–13, 21, 66, 84
Digby, A., 103, 105
disabilities, 39, 43, 53–6, 82, 102,
 158–9
Disraeli, B., 15, 109
dockers, *see* labourers
drink, *see* personal failings; public
 houses
Duncan, Dr W. H., 81, 93
Dyos, H. J., 87

east ends, 21, 77–8; *see also*
 London, East End
East Jarrow, 139, 144
eighteen eighties, 19–20, 27, 120
eighteen sixties, 19, 94–5, 105
endogomy, 134, 140, 141–2
Engels, F., 15, 17, 21, 65–6, 77,
 114–15, 13ı 163–4
 methodology, 17, 65–6, 77
Englander, D., 134–5

ethnicity, 20, 39, 51–55, 64–9, 82;
 see also Irish; Italians; Jews
expenditure, *see* incomes

fathers, *see* husbands
Finnegan, F., 59–60
Fishman, W., 20, 128
Floodgate Street, 44, 48, 96, 108,
 167–8
Floud, R., 97
Foley, A., 41, 57, 143–4, 146
food, 32–3, 25, 55, 60–2, 144–5,
 160–1, 167–8
Foster, J., 49
Fraser, D., 106, 115, 116
Freeman, A., 58, 63

Garrison Lane, 139–40
Gaskell, E., 17–8, 107, 111–12
Gaskell, M., 89
Gavin, Dr H., 17, 85, 89–90, 93,
 102, 165, 167
gender, 39, 41, 43, 59–64, 107–9,
 159–60, 167–8; *see also* husbands;
 wives; work, men; work, women
George, H., 14, 15
Gissing, G., 128–9
Godwin, G., 80, 87
Green, D. R., 134, 143
Gregory, I., 54–5

Harding, A., 41–2, 60, 84–5, 129,
 132, 133
Hardy, A., 94–5
Harris, J., 18, 22, 108, 115
Harrison, J. F. C., 16
Hay, J. R., 115, 118
health, 53–6, 60–1, 89–98, 160–3,
 166–8; *see also* illnesses; sanit-
 ation
Hennock, E. P., 20, 27, 28, 110, 121
Himmelfarb, G., 18, 118
Hockley, 24, 83
Hole, J., 19, 82, 86–7
Hollingshead, J., 19, 54, 118–9, 127
Holmes, C., 66–7
Holyoake, G. J., 2203
Hope Street, 131–2, 133, 136, 171–2

Horrocks, B., 83
housing
  back-to-backs, 82–4, 85, 96,
    164–6, 174
  cellars, 81–2
  government inaction, 86–7
  jerry-built, 78–9
  lodging, 66, 79–81
  rentals, 79, 82, 89
  tenements, 84–6
  'two-up two-downs', 83–4, 85
  see also municipal action;
    overcrowding; Royal Commis-
    sion on the Housing of the
    Working Classes
Howarth, E. G., 45, 62, 110
Hoxton, 110, 129–30, 135
Huddersfield, 80, 82
Hughes, M., 24–5
Hume, C., 92
husbands, 22, 33, 38–9, 40–2,
  44–5, 48, 54–5, 56, 63, 65, 82,
  102, 105, 136, 138, 143, 162, 168
Hyde, R. R., 45, 110, 129

illnesses, 43, 48, 55–6, 158–9; *see
  also* health
immorality, fear of, 79–81,
  118–21; *see also* morality;
  neighbourhoods; 'residuum'
incomes, 24–5, 28–9, 33, 43–4, 46,
  48, 49, 52–3, 61–2, 66, 157, 159,
  161, 163
industrialisation, 8–10
inequalities, economic, 2–4, 6,
  13–16, 155–6; *see also* prosperity
infant mortality, 60–1
Irish, 55, 64–6, 82, 95, 118, 131,
  134, 159
irregular work, *see* underemployment
Italians, 66–8, 131

Jago, *see* Nichol, the
Jennings' Buildings, 19, 64–5, 87,
  131, 137–8
Jerrold, B., 54, 106, 107
Jews, 20, 51, 68–9, 118, 159

John, A., 31
Jones, G. Stedman, 19, 45–6, 53,
  94, 106, 109, 110, 113, 120,
  121
Jones, H., 114, 117–18

Kellett, J. R., 88
Kensington, 19, 87, 131, 137
Kidd, A. J., 46, 106–7
Kiernan, V., 77
Kingsley, C., 16, 51, 59, 109, 159–60
kinship, 130–1, 141–3

Labour, 115–17
labourers, 43–6, 64–5, 67; *see also*
  unskilled
Lambeth, 48, 63, 79
Lancashire, *see* cotton district
Lancaster, 141, 143
Lanigan, J., 40–1, 57
large families, 43
Leeds, 8, 9, 55, 63, 68, 78, 80, 82,
  89, 93–94
Lees, L., 134
Leigh, Dr J., 78, 82
Liberal reforms, 115–16
life expectancy, 58, 93, 96, 167
Liverpool, 9, 18, 19, 22, 27, 46, 51,
  64, 68, 78, 81–2, 91, 93, 94, 95,
  130, 137, 157
London, 8, 9, 11, 17, 18–21, 23, 24,
  26–8, 41–2, 45–6, 50, 51–3, 54,
  59, 60, 66, 68, 77, 80, 84, 85, 89,
  91, 93, 94, 105, 106, 109, 112,
  113, 126, 129, 131, 134, 135, 137,
  140, 156, 165, 166
London, East End, 19–21, 27, 68–9,
  86, 109–10, 126, 168–70
London, Jack, 114–15, 127, 129,
  169–70
London, south, 21, 41, 85–6, 106,
  133
London, West End, 19, 21, 126
lower middle class, 11–12, 21–2,
  38–9

Mackay, C., 18, 51, 90
McIlhiney, D. B., 111

McLeod, H., 134, 140
Malpass, P., 108
Manchester, 8, 9, 17–18, 19, 20, 26, 30–1, 41, 46, 49, 54, 61, 65, 68, 76, 77, 78, 81–2, 83, 85, 87, 89, 95, 106–7, 112, 132, 135, 137, 157, 163–4
Manchester Statistical Society, 17, 46
Mann, K., 5
Mantle, Rev. J. G., 53, 103, 107
Marcus, S., 77
Marr, T. H., 31–1, 85, 96
Marx, K., 103, 118
Masterman, C. F. G., 30, 129
matrilocality, 142–3
Mayhew, H., 16, 18–19, 38, 45, 46–8, 51, 58, 59, 68, 84, 118, 126, 158–9
methodology, 47–8, 51–2
Mearns A., 20, 21, 128
Middlesborough, 31
Midwinter, E. C., 93
migration, 8, 64–9, 130–1
Money, Sir L. G. Chiozza, 14, 155–6
morality, 146–7, 153–4; *see also* immorality, fear of
Morgan, T., 41, 136
Morning Chronicle, 18, 26, 48, 51, 65
Morrison, A., 16, 111, 120, 168–9
mothers, *see* wives
municipal action, 80, 82, 87–9, 95–6
Murray, C., 5

Nechells, 132–3, 142, 172, 174
neighbourhoods, 130–45
neighbours, 144–5, 168
Newcastle, 9, 48, 54–5, 84, 86
Nichol, F., 48, 57, 81, 119, 168–9
Nichol, the, 16, 84, 119–20, 129, 132, 133, 137
Northampton, 31–2, 57, 83
Nottingham, 22, 65, 82
nutritional status, 97

O'Day, R., 27–8

old age, 39, 43, 58–9, 82, 104, 142, 158–9
Oldham, 49, 65
outdoor relief, *see* Poor Law
overcrowding, 78, 80, 84–6, 87–9, 164

Parton, A. G., 134, 143
Peckham, 133, 144
Pendleton, 98, 145, 164
People's Palace, 111, 168–9; *see also* settlements
personal failings, 4–5, 13, 29–30, 39–42, 49
philanthropy, 41, 42, 106–8, 114
and gender, 107–9, 167–8
reasons for, 107–8
physical efficiency, 29, 157–8
physical inefficiency, 20–1, 111–15, 169–70
'Pictures of the People', 23, 32–4
Pooley, C. G., 64
Poor Law, 25, 102–5
population, 9
Porter, G. R., 11, 15
Portsmouth, 44, 46, 132
Potteries, the, 11
Potts, A., 98, 145
poverty
causes, 4, 29–30, 38–69
extent, 13–15, 26–34, 49
punishment of, 102–5
reactions, 102–22
poverty cycle, 44, 63
poverty lines, 3–4, 26–34, 63–4, 157–8
Preston, 12, 130, 134, 141, 143
primary poverty, 29–20, 42–3, 57
prosperity
aristocratic, 11
middle class, 11–12, 24–5
national, 10–11, 14–15, 155–6
working class, 22–3, 52
see also inequalities, economic
prostitution, 59–60
public health, 89–98
public houses, 136–7, 172
Public Health Acts, 93, 95

public health movement, 91–3
Pugh, M., 2

racism, 51, 65–6, 119, 126, 159
ragged, *see* residuum
Ransome, A., 19, 77, 95
Reach, A., 18, 63, 65
Read, D., 109, 116
Reading, 31–2, 57
redevelopment, 87–9
Reeder, D. A., 87
Reeves, M. Pember, 63, 79
relative poverty, 3–4, 6, 24–6, 32–4
residential mobility (local moves),
    134–5
residential segregation, 17–20,
    77–8, 96, 163–4
'residuum', 117–22, 136, 138
respectability, 52, 147
Roberts, E., 140–1, 143, 147
Roberts, J., 81–2
Roberts, R., 43, 45, 54, 65, 104,
    131, 136, 138, 146, 171–2
Robertson, Dr J., 17, 44, 61, 86,
    160–1
Rodgers, R., 78
rookeries, 84, 119–20; *see also*
    slums
Rose, M. E., 6, 28, 105, 107
Ross, E., 131
Rowntree, B. S., 17, 28–30, 33, 34,
    42–3, 44, 45, 56, 58, 62, 63,
    156–8
Royal Commission on the Housing
    of the Working Classes, 79, 88,
    164
Royston, W., 19, 77, 95
Russell, C. E. B., 21, 156–7

Saffron Hill, 66, 84
St Giles, 80, 84, 88, 119, 143, 167
Salford, 8, 19, 30–1, 43, 46, 54, 65,
    77, 78, 83, 95, 96–8, 104, 112,
    131, 136, 138, 144, 163, 171–2
Samuel, Raphael, 80
Sanders family, 84, 142
sanitation, 76, 82–3, 89–96, 98, 165,
    167–8; *see also* health

seasonality, 39, 53
secondary poverty, 29–30; *see also*
    personal failings
Select Committee on the Health of
    Towns, 17, 81, 86, 87, 92
settlements, 108–11
Shaftesbury, Lord, 85, 93
Sheffield, 8, 78
Sherard, R., 59, 60
Shimmin, H., 19, 82, 87, 94, 130
shopping thoroughfares, 132–3, 141
Shoreditch, 132, 133
Simmons, J., 88
Simon, C., 137
Sims, G., 20, 119, 127, 170–1
skilled, 22–3, 40–1, 49–53, 59–61,
    59–60, 67–9, 159–60
Slaney, R., 13, 93
slums
    economic basis, 87; *see also*
        overcrowding
    environment, 76–8, 89–90,
        91–2, 94, 167–8; *see also*
        housing; public health;
        sanitation
    heterogeneity, 137–40
    location, 76–8
    see also rookeries
Smith, H. Llewellyn, 27, 113
social exploration, 126–9, 169–71
social investigation
    impressionistic, 16–21, 26–7,
        46–8, 49–52, 54–6, 58–60, 63,
        65–6, 76–81, 84–5, 87–8, 89–90,
        93–4, 111–14, 118–121, 126–30,
        156–7, 158–60, 163–4, 167–71
    national foci, 16–21, 156–7
    statistical, 16–17, 26–31, 42–6,
        49, 56–7, 91, 61–2, 79, 81,
        85–7, 91–3, 96–8, 112–14,
        120–1, 155–6, 157–8, 160–1,
        167
social mobility, 12–13, 21–3
social novels, 17–18
social reform, 115–17
South Asians, 68
South Shields, 48, 81
Southwood Smith, Dr, 91, 93

Sparkbrook, 135, 141
Sponza, L., 66
standard of living
    debate, 13–14
    mid-Victorian years, 95
Stanley, 31–2, 43, 57
Stevenson, J., 3
stratification, 22–3, 28, 96–7,
    138–40
streets, importance of, 142
street traders, 43–4, 46–8, 54, 65,
    67–8
Studley Street, 134, 136, 141–2,
    144, 172–3
Summer Lane, 53, 59, 103, 107,
    131, 137
Sunderland, 77, 137
sweating, 51–3, 60, 68, 159–60
Swift, R., 64

tailors, 51–3, 59–60, 68, 159–60
Thompson, E. P., 18
Thorne, W., 24–5, 57
Townsend, P., 2–3, 39
Toynbee, A., 109
Treble, J., 40, 49, 52
two nations, 8–16, 21
typhus, 94–5

'underclass', 5
underemployment, 39, 43, 44, 53,
    158
unemployment, 39, 43, 49
unskilled, 22, 24–5, 39, 43–8, 54–8,
    94, 60–2, 64–8, 128, 139, 141,
    158–9
urban degeneration, *see* physical
    inefficiency
urban villages, 134–42, 171–2
    boundaries, 132–4, 141
urbanisation, 8–11, 16, 79

Veit-Wilson, J. H., 29, 34

wages, *see* incomes
Walkowitz, J., 60
Waller, P. J., 9
Walters, J. Cuming, 76, 81
Warrington, 31–2, 57
weavers, 49–51
Webb, B., 27, 69, 108
Welfare State, 2
West Ham, 45, 62, 158
West Yorkshire, 19, 40
White, A., 51, 113–14, 121
Whitechapel, 68, 91, 118, 133
widows, *see* wives
Williams, B., 68–9
Williams, K., 30, 52, 66
Williamson, J., 64, 6 6
Wilson, M., 45, 62, 158
wives, 22, 25, 33, 38–9, 40–3, 45,
    48, 55, 60–3, 65, 81–2, 83, 102–5,
    136–9, 142, 143–6, 160–2
Wohl, A. S., 56, 92
work
    children, 25, 41, 48, 52, 53, 54,
        57–9, 68, 165
    men, 22, 41–53, 43, 55–6, 61–2,
        64–5, 67–9
    women, 22, 25, 41, 43, 52, 53,
        55, 59–63, 64–5, 103, 160–1,
        165
workhouses, *see* Poor Law
working-class evidence, 14–15,
    22–3, 24–5, 32–3, 38–9, 40–2,
    43–5, 48, 50–1, 53, 54, 56, 61–3,
    65, 67–9, 81, 82–5, 96, 98,
    102–5, 129–30, 131–3, 135–7,
    138–40, 141, 142–7, 164–5, 171–2
Wright, T, 14–15

Yelling, J. A., 88
York, 9, 28–9, 57, 58, 62, 157